CHERITON 1644

Sir William Waller   Robert Walker

Cheriton 1644
The Campaign and the Battle

JOHN ADAIR
MA, B Litt, Ph D, FR Hist S

Kineton: The Roundwood Press
1973

John Adair has also written

HASTINGS TO CULLODEN, with Peter Young

TRAINING FOR LEADERSHIP

ROUNDHEAD GENERAL: A Military Biography of Sir William Waller

TRAINING FOR DECISIONS

ACTION-CENTRED LEADERSHIP

TRAINING FOR COMMUNICATION

First Impression June 1973
Copyright © John Adair 1973
Published in 1973 by The Roundwood Press (Publishers) Limited, Kineton, Warwick
SBN 900093 19 6

Set in 'Monotype' Caslon series 128 and printed by Gordon Norwood
at The Roundwood Press, Kineton, in the County of Warwick
Plates made by The Process Engraving Company Limited, Coventry
Made and printed in Great Britain

To

Peter Young

That great God which is the searcher of my heart, knows with what a sad sence I goe upon this service, and with what a perfect hatred I detest this warr without an enemie, but I looke upon it as opus domini, which is enough to silence all passion in mee. The God of peace in his good time send us peace, and in the meane time fitt us to receive it: Wee are both upon the stage and must act those parts that are assigned us in this Tragedy: Lett us do it in a way of honor, and without personall animosities . . .

From a letter written by Waller to Hopton on 16 June 1643

Contents

		Page
List of Illustrations	... ...	ix
List of Maps and Diagrams	... ...	x
Acknowledgements	... ...	xi
Abbreviations	... ...	xii
Preface	... ...	xiii

PART ONE: THE CAMPAIGN

Chapter I:	Waller and Hopton...	1
Chapter II:	Strategic Situation on 29 September 1643	12
Chapter III:	New Armies and Old Soldiers ...	18
Chapter IV:	Basing House Besieged	32
Chapter V:	Farnham Delivered	50
Chapter VI:	Alton Stormed	61
Chapter VII:	Arundel Taken	72

PART TWO: THE BATTLE

Chapter VIII:	The Strategic and Political Backcloth	93
Chapter IX:	The Royalist Army	101
Chapter X:	The Parliamentarian Army	110
Chapter XI:	Cheriton	116
Chapter XII:	The Aftermath	142
Chapter XIII:	Conclusion	148

PART THREE: BACKGROUND NOTES AND DOCUMENTS

| Section I: | Further Contemporary Accounts ... | 155 |
| Section II: | The Regiments of Waller's Army ... | 171 |

Section III :	Casualties at Cheriton	... ...	192
Section IV :	Site of the Battlefield	... ...	195
Section V :	The Court Martial Papers of Sir William Waller's Army, 1644	...	198
Select Bibliography	... ...		222
Index	... ...		227

Illustrations

	Plate	Facing page
Sir William Waller	frontispiece	
Sir Nicholas Crisp	1	xiv
Pikeman	3	14
Musketeer	4	15
Sir Edward Dering	5	30
Wenceslaus Hollar's Map	6	31
The Siege of Basing House	7	46
Sir Marmaduke Rawdon	8	47
Alton Church and Churchyard	9	62
Alton Church: Pulpit and Door	10	63
Arundel Town and Castle	11	78
Sir William Waller	12	79
Lord Ralph Hopton	13	94
Patrick Ruthven, Earl of Forth	14	95
Sir Michael Livesey	15	110
Aerial View of the Battlefield	17	126
Colonel Alexander Popham	19	142
Colonel John Birch	20	143
Sir Richard Browne	21	158
A Medallion of Sir William Waller	22	159
Sir Edward Bishop	23	174
Sir Arthur Heselrige	24	175
Lord John and Lord Bernard Stuart	25	
Contemporary tracts relating to the Campaign	26	Between pages 190 and 191
Aerial View of Basing House Ruins	27	
The Grange Barn at Basing	28	

Aerial View of Arundel Castle 29 206
William Lenthall, Speaker of the
    House of Commons 30 207

Maps and Diagrams

Cheriton—The Campaign Area   2   *Facing page* xv
Cheriton—The Approach Marches 16   *Facing page* 111
The Battle of Cheriton   18   *Facing page* 127

The Author and Publishers acknowledge with gratitude the assistance which they have received from the following bodies, institutions and individuals.

For the frontispiece: Viscount Harcourt, K.C.M.G.
For plates 1, 5 and 23: Mrs P. A. Tritton, Parham Park, Sussex.
For plates 3, 4, 11, 21, 22, 26, The Trustees of the British Museum.
For plates 6, 14: Bodleian Library.
For plates 7 and 12: Robin Adair.
For plate 8: G. Marmaduke Alington Esq.
For plates 9, 10 and 28: Nigel Bradley and Bryan Boyd.
For plate 13: H.M. Treasury and the National Trust—Egremont Collection.
For plate 15: Ashmolean Museum.
For plates 17 and 29: John Wright.
For plate 19: David Seton Wills Esq.
For plate 20: The Vicar of Weobley and Sarnesfield
For plate 24: Lord Hazlerigg
For plate 25: Earl Mountbatten.
For plate 27: Department of Aerial Photography, Cambridge University.
For plate 30: National Portrait Gallery.

The maps were drawn by R. G. Sharp of Leamington Spa.

Acknowledgements

It would not be possible to list all those friends, colleagues, and former students who have contributed in some way or other to the contents of this book, but I should like to express my deep gratitude to the following, who have given me direct help:

To Brigadier Peter Young and Dr Ian Roy for their notes and references upon the Royalist army at Cheriton, and for our discussions upon visits to the battlefield.

To Dr Margaret Toynbee for both reading the manuscript and making many suggestions for improving it.

To Mr Richard Sawyer of Winchester for allowing me to reproduce his transcript of Yonge's notes on Heselrige's account of the battle.

To the Kent County Council and Lord Brabourne, my renewed thanks for permission to publish the unique set of Waller's Court Martial Papers.

To R. E. Hutchinson, Keeper of the Scottish National Portrait Gallery, for advice and assistance.

To Stephen Beck for his delightful pen-and-ink drawings in this book, which so ably evoke the atmosphere of the period.

To Mr Nigel Bradley for much help with illustrations, and for some useful contemporary references as well.

To Mr Gordon Norwood of the Roundwood Press, to whose enthusiasm and professional skill this book owes both its existence and appearance.

Lastly, to the staffs of the British Museum, Public Record Office and the Hampshire Record Office, who have extended to me their customary unfailing courtesy and assistance.

Abbreviations

Add. MSS.	Additional Manuscripts, British Museum.
Bellum Civile	*Bellum Civile. Hopton's Narrative of his Campaign in the West (1642–1644)*, ed. C. E. H. Chadwyck-Healey, Somerset Record Society, Vol. 18 (1902).
B.M.	British Museum.
Bodl.	Bodleian Library, Oxford.
C.J.	*Journals of the House of Commons*.
Clarendon	E. Hyde, Earl of Clarendon, *History of the Rebellion and Civil Wars in England*, ed. W. D. Macray, 6 vols. (1888).
C.S.P.D.	*Calendar of the State Papers, Domestic Series*.
D'Ewes	Sir Simonds D'Ewes, 'A Journall of the Parliament begunne Nov. 3. Tuesday Anno Domini 1640, 3 Nov.' British Museum, Harleian MSS. 162–166.
D.N.B.	Dictionary of National Biography.
'*Experiences*'	Waller's 'Experiences' printed in *The Poetry of Anna Matilda* (1788).
Experiences	MS. of Waller's 'Experiences' in Wadham College Library, Oxford.
Harl. MS.	Harleian Manuscript.
H.M.C.	Historical Manuscripts Commission.
L.J.	*Journals of the House of Lords*.
Luke	*Journal of Sir Samuel Luke*, ed. I. G. Philip, 3 vols., Oxfordshire Record Society (1950–53).
P.R.O.	Public Record Office, London.
Peacock	*The Army Lists of the Roundheads and Cavaliers*, ed. E. Peacock, 2nd edn. (1874).
Slingsby	'Relation of Colonel Walter Slingsby,' printed in *Bellum Civile* (see above).
S.P.	State Papers
T.T.	Thomason Tracts, King's Library, British Museum.
Whitaker	L. Whitaker, 'Diary of proceedings in the House of Commons, 8 October 1642–8 July 1647'. British Museum Additional MS. 31116

Preface

EDGEHILL, MARSTON MOOR, NASEBY: the battle honours of the English Civil War have a familiar ring to all who have read our island history. The battle of Cheriton is not among this list of Civil War encounters which springs so readily to mind. Yet in retrospect the Cheriton campaign in the Autumn of 1643 and early months of 1644 could be described as the turning-point of the whole war.

What makes such a 'turning-point' in the course of a war? In many wars one side starts off by taking the initiative and carrying the struggle into the enemy's territory. Sometimes for years, in spite of local set-backs, the war seems to be going in its favour, until a single reverse — perhaps only marginally larger than several others — marks the high tide, and thenceforth the drift of the war moves towards the other's advantage. Gettysburg and Stalingrad are two later examples of such turning-points.

Certainly in the Autumn of 1643 King Charles could look back upon a slow but rising tide of successes, notably the capture of Bristol in the late Summer. He had not been dislodged from Oxford, the centre of the chessboard, and he could therefore regard himself as still holding the military initiative. His despatch of Hopton with a Royalist army towards Kent in October 1643 underlined the fact that Charles could still threaten London, still call a tune to which his opponents must dance. After Hopton's defeat at Cheriton, however, all was different. No less a person than Sir Edward Walker, the King's Secretary at War, would later declare that the disaster 'necessitated His Majesty to alter the scheme of his affairs, and *in the place of the offensive to make a defensive war*'.

In the light of such an opinion readers may wonder at the

comparative neglect of this campaign and battle. Certainly it suffers from several disadvantages as far as 'making the history books' is concerned. Cheriton stood neither at the beginning nor the end of the Civil War; none of the more famous participants—King Charles, Prince Rupert, the Earl of Essex or Oliver Cromwell — graced it with their presence; and, thirdly, the numbers engaged were by no means the largest in the war (although about the same as at Naseby in 1645).

Yet, as I hope the reader will agree, the generals who opposed each other at Cheriton — Sir William Waller and Ralph, Lord Hopton — were certainly interesting men, both as individuals and as a pair of friends whose present enmity highlighted the eternal tragedy of internecine civil war. Moreover, their campaign and battle aptly illustrate the nature and tenor of the English Civil War.

To restore the battle and campaign of Cheriton to its rightful place in English history, to commemorate the generals and soldiers who fought in it, and to introduce the reader to one of the most fascinating episodes of the Civil War: such are the aims of this book.

In order to let the struggle come alive I have, as far as possible, allowed the soldiers tell their own stories, supplementing their eyewitness accounts with other contemporary documents at the end of the book. We are unusually fortunate in possessing so much from the pens of the participants: perhaps no other Civil War campaign is so well served by such a variety of writers, ranging from generals to a common soldier's wife. The sources of these extracts will be found in the Notes and References under the chapter heading in which they first appear.

The book is so arranged that the reader may enjoy the contemporary eyewitness accounts, with only a brief glance at the Notes and References should he wish. In order to help him do so I have included some short chapters on the strategic situation, the generals and the composition of the armies. These are not meant to be comprehensive, for it is obviously not possible here to re-tell the history of the English Civil War. Should the reader wish to know more about the political background to the war, or the fighting in other regions, he would do well to consult the

PLATE I
Sir Nicholas Crisp
Parham Park

Cornelius Jansen

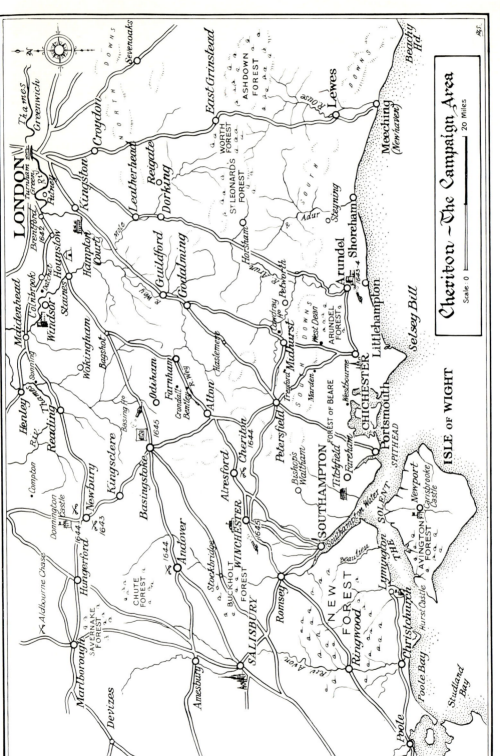

PLATE 2

standard general works, such as C. V. Wedgwood's *The King's War*: a select list of these books is included in the General Bibliography. Nor can I do more than summarize the lives of Waller and Hopton, both of whom have been the subjects of full-length biographies in the last few years.

The diligent reader, or even one who gets no further than the List of Contents, may note that I seem to have paid more attention to the forces of Sir William Waller than to those of Hopton. This emphasis results partly from the sources, but partly from the fact that I first saw the campaign and battle through the eyes of Sir William (as his biographer), and inevitably I have accumulated more notes on his army. In this book, however, I have given Lord Hopton every opportunity to tell his side of the story. Although yielding to none in my admiration for Ralph Hopton and some of his brave regiments, I must not disguise the fact that had I the choice I should have fought beside Sir William Waller at Cheriton Field on that Spring day in 1644.

For King and Parliament!

PART ONE
The Campaign

Chapter One

WALLER AND HOPTON

IN NOVEMBER 1620 Queen Elizabeth of Bohemia fled from Prague towards Frankfurt-on-the-Oder through the winter snows, leaving behind her scenes of confusion and defeat as the Imperial army under Tilly closed in upon the city. Escorting the coach of the 'Winter Queen' rode a troop of sixty young English volunteers, among them 22 year-old William Waller from Kent, and 25 year-old Ralph Hopton from Somerset. Waller had already risked his life in a skirmish with the Cossacks in Bohemia: his horse was shot under him, and with his foot hanging in a stirrup he was dragged through them, a pistol bullet grazing his head. When deep snows halted the coaches, Ralph Hopton carried the Queen behind him for forty miles. It is just possible that her infant son, Prince Rupert, was mounted behind William Waller. Be that as it may, the party arrived safely at their destination on 5 December. Not long afterwards Waller and Hopton, now firm friends, returned to England.

The two young men shared much the same social background. Waller was the son of Sir Thomas Waller, Lieutenant of Dover Castle, who died in 1613. As hereditary Chief Butler of England Sir Thomas inherited a sizeable income from a tax on wine imports. William spent a year or two at Oxford University, and then travelled on the Continent before his twenty-first birthday. In Paris he learnt to manage a military charger, the 'great horse,' and then moved on to Italy, where he completed a 'Giro d'Italia' fraught with minor dangers: over-turning boats, epidemics of sickness and the unwelcome attentions of the Inquisition. He served for some months in the mercenary forces of the Republic of Venice, then at war on its northern borders with the Holy Roman Empire. 'Att the leaguer before Rubia,' he wrote, 'I escaped severall very neere shott; one grazing att my foot, another lighting between Sir John Vere and me, as we sate close together by the battery . . .'[1] In 1620 he volunteered for service with Sir Horace Vere, who had been commissioned by King James to secure the possessions of his son-in-law, Frederick, Elector Palatine, and the life of his daughter, the young and beautiful Elizabeth, that 'queen of women, the Queen of Bohemia,' as Waller called her, who had accompanied her husband when he accepted the Bohemian crown.

Ralph Hopton, born at Witham Friary in Somerset in 1596, came from a family which had made its fortune in that county through the dissolution of the monasteries. He was admitted to the Middle Temple in 1614, and then studied at Lincoln College, Oxford, but like Waller he does not seem to have graduated, an omission not uncommon in those days.

After his service with Elizabeth of Bohemia, who was exactly his own age, Hopton spent a further five years on the Continent, becoming a lieutenant-colonel in Sir Charles Rich's Regiment of foot by 1624 under the command of the celebrated mercenary Count Mansfeldt. For some reason, now obscure, Hopton did not take part in the Cadiz expedition of 1625, despite the fact that he had been brought to the notice of the Duke of Buckingham and the new monarch, King Charles I. Instead he returned to Somerset, and settled down to a country life. The following year he received a Knighthood of the Bath, and with his wife Elizabeth, the widowed daughter of Sir Arthur Capel, whom he had married in 1623, he set up house at Evercreech Park, not far from the family home, Witham Friary.

Hopton served as M.P. for Shaftesbury in 1621, Bath in 1625 and Wells in 1628. From 1629 to 1639 he was both a J.P. and Deputy Lieutenant in Somerset, offices which he fulfilled with diligence. In the abortive Scots War of 1639 he commanded a troop of horse in the regiment of the Earl of Pembroke. In the Long Parliament he followed the lead of Hyde and Falkland in opposing the unconstitutional aspects of the King's 'personal rule.' For example, he voted for the attainder of the Earl of Strafford in May 1641. But he was essentially a reformer of the old order, not a harbinger of a new one. In particular he wished to see episcopacy reformed but not abolished: he was no Root and Brancher.

In December 1641 Hopton led the delegation that presented the Grand Remonstrance to the King, the most important single act in his career as a Member of Parliament, but events soon exposed his fundamental adherence to the Crown. He even defended the King's attempted arrest of the Five Members in January 1642, and went on to 'contradict everything without scruple' that the majority of the House of Commons resolved thereafter, so much so that the House imprisoned him for two weeks in the Tower of London. As soon as Hopton was released in March he returned to Somerset, where he was the first to implement the King's Commissions of Array, designed to secure the royal control of the militia.

F. T. R. Edgar, the biographer of Hopton, concluded: 'His royalism, always latent, was bound to emerge when the crunch came. It had three roots: first, his non-Laudian high Anglicanism, akin to Falkland's, manifest in Hopton's alignment with the 'Episcopal Party' and his defence of the bishops; second (in common with his colleague Culpeper), a concern for the militia and a recognition of the need on the King's side for a show of strength; and third, it would be hard to deny, a sense of personal loyalty to the throne itself.'[2]

At the time of Hopton's imprisonment in the Tower, Waller had not even entered the House of Commons as a member, although he did so the following month, April 1642, sitting for Andover. Nor had he been nearly as active as Hopton in national or local government, preferring the quiet life of a country gentleman at Forde House in Devon, which he eventually inherited from his wife's father, Sir Thomas Reynell. Jane, the bride he had married in 1623, died in 1637 and William brought his only surviving child, Margaret, to London in order to find a step-mother for her. After a time his choice fell upon Lady Anne Finch, daughter of the Lord Keeper, who had come under attack by the reforming party in 1641, including Hopton.

Lady Anne, a forceful Puritan lady, and her husband received the grant of Winchester Castle, and set about renovating this imposing residence in 1639 and 1640. Possibly through Lady Anne's influence, Waller came into Pym's circle in 1641, but failed in a disputed election to win a seat in the Commons that year.

Once in the House he threw himself into the struggle against the King with vigour. Although Clarendon insinuated that Waller's opposition to the Court sprang from a personal grudge, incurred when he struck a relation of his wife in Westminster Hall and received a heavy fine for his pains, there is no evidence for this story, and it is likely that more general reasons lay behind Waller's decision to draw his sword for Parliament. As a Puritan, Waller seems to have wanted only good church government; he was indifferent as to whether bishops or presbyters should supply it. He was certainly not a 'high churchman.' His constitutional views, however, were moderate and reforming in nature, and the political points which divided him from such old friends as Hopton and Sir Bevil Grenvile were fine ones indeed. Waller's experience of the House of Commons was much more limited than Hopton's. He appears to have committed himself to the cause mainly out of religious fervour. He certainly did not entertain extreme political, social or religious opinions.

In the late Summer and Autumn of 1642, Waller distinguished himself by capturing Portsmouth, Farnham, Winchester, Arundel and Chichester. At Edgehill, although his regiment was scattered by Prince Rupert's charge, Waller escaped in the confusion. Some senior officers who served with him at this time would do so again in the Cheriton campaign of 1643/4: Sir Arthur Heselrige, Colonels John Middleton and Richard Browne, both the latter then commanding regiments of dragoons. Some Royalist foes would also turn up again: Sir Edward Ford, Sir William Ogle and the jocular Earl of Crawford.

Parliament hoped to associate together for mutual defence Surrey, Sussex, Kent and Hampshire, but the committees of gentry who ran the counties opposed the move, cherishing their independence and preserving their pockets as much as they could. Waller, who would have received command of their forces, instead became Major-General of five western counties (11 February 1643).

In a series of swift marches Waller secured the lower Severn Valley for Parliament that Spring. Whilst laying siege to Worcester in May, he learnt that two Royalist armies had marched to meet each other in Somerset so that they could take him in the rear: one, under the Marquess of Hertford, had come from Oxford, the other had moved up from Cornwall and Devon, commanded by Waller's old friend Sir Ralph Hopton. In Cornwall Hopton had raised a fine army for the King, based on five stout Cornish regiments of foot. At Braddock Down (19 January 1643) he defeated the Devonshire Roundheads. The Earl of Stamford, Waller's predecessor in the Severn Valley, marched south to deal with Hopton, but was thoroughly beaten by him at Stratton (16 May). On 4 June Hopton joined Hertford and Prince Maurice at Chard, and turned towards Waller.

While the two armies lay some miles apart, Waller at Bath and Hopton at Wells, the latter either suggested a meeting or wrote urging his old friend to change sides, possibly mentioning Waller's former major, Colonel Horatio Carey, who deserted sometime during that June. Waller replied with a letter[3] that reveals not only his deep affection for Hopton but also the spirit with which he had espoused the cause of Parliament:

To my Noble frend Sr Ralphe Hopton at Wells
S^r
   The experience I have had of your worth, and the happinesse I have enjoyed in your frendship are woundinge considerations when I look upon this present distance betweene us. Certainely my affections to you are so unchangeable, that hostility itselfe cannot violate my friendship to your person, but I must be true to the cause wherein I serve: The ould limitation usque ad aras holds still, and where my conscience is interested, all other obligations are swallowed up. I should most gladly waite on you according to your desire, but that I looke upon you as you are ingaged in that partie, beyond a possibility of retraite and consequentlie uncapable of being wrought upon by any persuasion. And I know the conference could never be so close betweene us, but that it would take wind and receive a construction to my dishonour; That great God which is the searcher of my heart, knows

with what a sad sence I goe upon this service, and with what a perfect hatred I detest this warr without an enemie, but I looke upon it as opus domini, which is enough to silence all passion in mee. The God of peace in his good time send us peace, and in the meane time fitt us to receive it: Wee are both upon the stage and must act those parts that are assigned us in this Tragedy: Lett us do it in a way of honor and without personall animosities, whatsoever the issue be, I shall never willingly relinquish the dear title of
your most affectionated friend
and faithfull servant
W^m. Waller.

Bath, 16 June 1643.

At the battle of Lansdown (5 July) Waller occupied the brow of a long down above Bath, and unleashed his cavalry and dragoons to skirmish with the combined Royalist armies as they approached him from the north. Having cleared the field Hopton's Cornish foot stormed the heights, the pikemen marching up the steep incline in the centre, and two bodies of musketeers moving round on the wings to occupy the woods at each end of Waller's ridge, a tactic the Roundhead general would himself employ at Cheriton. At nightfall the Cornish had lodged themselves on Lansdown, but at the cost of Sir Bevil Grenvile's life. This Puritan Cornish gentleman, a natural leader in his county, fell not many yards from Sir William Waller, who had been one of his closest friends. In happier days Sir Bevil had once procured a fine horse for Waller, 'the best I can get in all this County,' but would receive no payment: 'I beseech you name not money between you and me, it is a thing so much beneath my thoughts, and under the respect I owe you, my noblest friend...'[4] That night he was carried down from Lansdown dying of his wounds.

Soon after midnight the Roundheads, who had retired to a stone wall that stands to this day some 200 yards from the edge of the hill, lit fires, draped lengths of spluttering musketeers' match on the wall and left pikes standing upright in the ground to simulate an army while they slipped back into Bath, leaving the Royalists with the field and a hollow victory.

Next morning Hopton, already wounded in the arm, rode

over with Major Thomas Sheldon to talk to some Parliamentarian prisoners who were sitting on precious barrels of gunpowder in a waggon, smoking pipes. Captain Richard Atkyns spoke to Sheldon and then moved off:

> I had no sooner turned my horse, and was gone 3 horses lengths from him, but the ammunition was blown up, and the prisoners in the cart with it; together with the Lord Hopton, Major Sheldon, and Cornet Washnage, who was near the cart on horseback, and several others: it made a very great noise, and darkened the air for a time, and the hurt men made lamentable screeches. As soon as the air was clear, I went to see what the matter was; there I found his Lordship miserably burnt, his horse sing'd like parched leather, and Thomas Sheldon (that was a horse lengths further from the blast) complaining that the fire was got within his breeches, which I tore off as soon as I could, and from as long a flaxen head of hair as ever I saw, in the twinkling of an eye, his head was like a blackamore; his horse was hurt, and run away like mad...[5]

The Royalists conveyed Hopton away in the Marquess of Hertford's coach to lodgings in Devizes, and he had recovered sufficiently to take command of that town while the Cavalier horse rode off to Oxford to get reinforcements. On 13 July Waller faced these returning forces on Roundway Down, and suffered a humiliating defeat at their hands. Hopton, still in Devizes, took no active part in the battle.

After Roundway Down, Waller returned to London where the most militant wing of the House of Commons, the 'vehements' who were fed up with the dilatory Earl of Essex and suspicious of the peace negotiations with which the Lord General and the 'moderates' were flirting, voted him to command a 'New Army.' The 'vehements,' who included many nascent later Independents and some of that ilk who had already hatched out, such as Sir Arthur Heselrige, favoured Waller, not only because of his military reputation, albeit dimmed by 'Runaway Down,' but also on account of his personal piety.

Essex, jealous of his position and scornful of Waller's failure in the West, opposed the granting of a commission which would make him virtually an equal and delayed giving it for as long as he could. At the end of August, when at last he signed the document, the Lord General was about to leave for the relief of Gloucester, a campaign which re-established his authority and enabled him to withdraw Waller's commission in September. The 'New Army,' an abortive attempt to create a New Model, began to wither away.

Waller accepted the verdict for mixed reasons. He did not want to heighten the political tensions which existed between the House of Lords and the Commons, or between the 'moderates' and 'vehements,' at a time when the strategic situation looked dark, if not black. His services as a reconciling bridge between the factions in the Commons at this critical juncture in the war have not hitherto been fully recognized by historians.

Secondly, he received an assurance from Pym that Essex would grant him a commission to lead an army into the West 'in as ample manner as ever any commission was granted to a commander by any Generall.'[6] The promise would not be fulfilled, for Pym died on 9 December 1643, in the middle of the Cheriton campaign, and Essex proved faithless to the promise in the Summer of 1644, if indeed he had ever been party to it.

Thirdly, Waller had fallen out with his political sponsors. According to him they wanted 'their' general to employ only 'godly' officers, that is, those who were known to be Puritans. Waller did not want to have his hands tied in this way, because he knew that professional ability, as well as religious convictions, were necessary in a Parliamentarian officer. Waller placated them by appointing a committee under none other than Sir Arthur Heselrige as president with power to veto officers who were not sufficiently 'refined.' 'But this did not satisfy,' wrote Waller in 1649 or 1650, 'and I then found they had it in their designe to modell and form an army, that should be all of their owne party, and devoted to their own ends. Upon this we differed. I trusted not them, nor they me, and so we agreed. From that time forwarde I may date the expiration of their friendship.' Still, these sponsors continued to support Waller as a lesser evil than Essex whom they abhorred.[7]

While Waller oscillated between hopeful opportunism and wary caution in the politics of London that Summer Hopton received a commission as Prince Rupert's lieutenant-governor in

Bristol, which had fallen to the King in July. On the 4th of September the King made him Baron Hopton of Stratton, a fitting reward for his services that year. Whether or not Hopton had quite regained his health by the end of the month is a doubtful point — his signature looks very shaky.

After the first battle of Newbury, he went to Oxford, the King's headquarters. After some days, as Hopton writes of himself:

> His Majestie commanded him to attend a Committee of the Lords at the Lord Threasurer's lodging in Oriell-Colledge, where was imparted to him His Majestie's resolution, that being reasonably well recovered of his hurts, he should draw into the feild for the cleering of Dorsettshire, Wiltshire and Hamshire, and so point forward as farr as he could go towards London.[8]

What particular talents as a general did Hopton bring to the coming campaign? As an administrator — recruiting, quartering, and supplying his regiments — he was exceptionally good within the limitations imposed by the times, and his personal courage is beyond question. As a general, however, he had not yet showed much strategic judgement and imagination, but it could be argued that he had not occasion to do so. On the other hand, he had proved himself as a tactician of solid ability; calm and competent in crises, he had also shown more than once that he could conduct an orderly retreat in the face of the enemy.

As a general he had not yet carried full responsibility for an army, although in the Cornish campaign and at Stratton he had certainly been leader in the field, whatever his rank. At Lansdown, against Waller, the Marquess of Hertford and Prince Maurice shouldered the psychological burden of command. The Cheriton campaign would test Hopton's ability to stand on his own feet, think for himself and bear the responsibility for his decisions. No longer would he be acting in the obscurity of remote Cornwall, upheld by the natural courage of the Cornish and the leadership of such men as Sir Bevil Grenvile, but upon the open stage of the South, the area watched closely by the King at Oxford and Parliament in London.

Sir William Waller had earned an early reputation in the war for speedy night marches, a difficult feat with half-trained soldiers, as he had discovered on one occasion in March that year. When attempting to break through a cordon of Prince Maurice's men in the Forest of Dean, the Roundhead column lost order through the sleepiness of an officer, and Waller arrived at the enemy's quarters in the dawn light almost on his own. But his practice of swift marches and night operations had earned him the nick-name 'The Night Owl' from the Royalists.

On the whole he had shown good strategic sense, both in the South during Autumn 1642 and in the West in 1643, but his attempt at taking Worcester in May instead of adopting the classic strategy of defeating the two Royalist armies in detail before they could join in Somerset, deserved the contemporary criticism it received. Yet by the moves around Bath in late June, when Waller consistently seized the high ground and used the reverse slopes and night marches to disguise from the Cavaliers his lack of infantry, he richly deserved the Royalist eyewitness Lieutenant-Colonel Walter Slingsby's generous compliment: 'Indeed that Generall of the Rebells was the best shifter and chooser of the ground when he was not master of the field that I ever saw, which are great abilityes in a Souldier.'[9]

The defeat of Roundway Down had thrown a shadow over this bright reputation: some critics even impugned Waller's own valour by spreading rumours that he left the field while his foot still fought, mutterings that died after his return to London. Why did he lose? Those who disliked Sir Arthur Heselrige claimed that he disobeyed orders. If so, Waller never accused him: he bore the responsibility of the defeat on his own shoulders, a sign of one pre-eminently fitted for independent command. In the Lansdown and Roundway campaign Waller's strategy and tactics could hardly be faulted. He was not surprised at Devizes, but his army panicked and broke. Call it ill luck or providence, the seed for his later and fatal reputation as an 'unfortunate' general had been truly sown. Steadied by his wife's confidence in him and encouraged by the support he had received in London, Waller had survived the shock of defeat as tolerably well as Hopton had recovered from being blown sky-high: outwardly confident, both were still more than a little shaken. Both knew that their reputations rested upon their next campaign, but in late September neither knew for certain who their opponent would be.

For the early life of Waller and Hopton, see:
   John Adair, *Roundhead General: A Military Biography of Sir William Waller* (Macdonald, London, 1969)
   F. T. R. Edgar, *Sir Ralph Hopton: The King's Man in the West (1642–1652): A Study in Character and Command* (Clarendon Press, Oxford, 1968).

[1] 'Experiences', f. 13.
[2] F. T. R. Edgar, *op. cit*, pp. 22–3.
[3] M. Coate, *Cornwall in the Great Civil War*, 2nd edn. (1963), p. 77. The facsimile of the letter on the facing page (from the MSS. of Colonel Prideaux-Brune of Prideaux Place, Padstow) is not the original as Miss Coate believed. Neither the handwriting nor the signature are Waller's, but it differs only in detail from his own draft (Clarendon MS. 22, f. 113), and it is clearly a copy of the final version. The gist of Hopton's letter and Waller's reply were noted in *A Weekly Account*, 3–10 July, TT:E 249 (25). It is possible that Waller spread copies of the letter abroad as a personal manifesto. Another exists, for example, among the MSS. of the Duke of Somerset, H.M.C., *15th Report*, App. VII.
[4] R. Granville, *History of the Granville Family* (1895), pp. 235–6.
[5] 'The Vindication of Richard Atkyns,' in *Richard Atkyns and John Gwyn*, ed. Peter Young and Norman Tucker (1967).
[6] Whitaker, f. 82.
[7] Sir William Waller's *Vindication* (1793), p. 132.
[8] *Bellum Civile*, p. 61.
[9] Slingsby, p. 91.

Chapter Two

STRATEGIC SITUATION ON 29 SEPTEMBER 1643

BY 29 SEPTEMBER 1643, when Lord Hopton received the royal orders to command a new army in the South, the English Civil War had lasted for over thirteen months. During this period no decisive event had occurred: fortunes had indeed changed, but not in such a way as to alter radically the balance of military power. If anything the King stood in a slightly better position than his adversary.

After the first main encounter at Edgehill (23 October 1642) the King had marched south and established his headquarters at Oxford, not 60 miles from Parliament's own chief base at London. Parliament allowed its Captain-General, Robert Devereux, Earl of Essex, to deploy the main Roundhead field army in the Chiltern counties to shield the capital from any repetition of the Royalist onslaught of November, which had been turned back at Brentford. The Autumn of 1643 found the army of the Earl of Essex once more encamped in and around northern Buckinghamshire.

By this date, however, Essex had achieved one signal feat of arms. After Sir William Waller's defeat in the West at Roundway Down (13 July 1643), the King took Bristol and besieged Gloucester. With a reinforcement of London trained bands, Essex marched across England, relieved Gloucester and returned to London, having avoided defeat on the homeward journey at the first battle of Newbury (20 September).

Almost all the West except Gloucester, and some other beleaguered towns and ports, notably Plymouth, lay in Royalist hands. In Yorkshire the Fairfaxes, father and son, had energetically defied the Earl of Newcastle's Royalist army from the North-East, only to be beaten at Adwalton Moor on 30 June 1643. Yet several military actions kept Newcastle from marching southwards, notably Cromwell's defeat of some Royalist cavalry at Gainsborough. The Earl of Newcastle then laid siege to Hull, whither the Fairfaxes had resorted. Already the Yorkshire commanders were working in close liaison with Lord Willoughby of Parham (Parliamentarian commander in Lincolnshire) and Colonel Oliver Cromwell of the Eastern Association. Indeed these two officers joined the Fairfaxes for a conference in Hull on 26 September. Further south, the Earl of Manchester had just captured Lynn, and was making ready to advance into Lincolnshire. Elsewhere the local struggles between Royalists and Roundheads continued fitfully, and without real influence on the main course of the war.

Whether or not the King intended a three-pronged attack on London (Newcastle from the North, Hopton from the West and himself at the head of the main 'Oxford' army) has been disputed by historians. It is clear, however, that in the late Summer of 1643 Parliament could be forgiven if it feared such a possibility. The Fairfaxes and the Eastern Association army would keep Newcastle in the North, but there remained two of the three prongs in the South and West. Should the military resources of Parliament be deflected into the Midlands the capital could become extremely vulnerable.

Parliament's national strategy, if such it could be called, seems to have been entirely defensive at this stage of the war. Essex, who regarded himself as the strategy-maker, does not appear to have formulated any plan, except to stand fast, defend London and do nothing elsewhere unless compelled to do so. He was a stolid, unimaginative man, who favoured a peace settlement at a table rather than a bloody decision on a field of battle, and he richly derserved the general unpopularity that his relief of Gloucester had only mitigated.

Politically the situation had deteriorated for Parliament throughout 1643. In the House of Commons splits had developed between the 'moderates,' led among others by Essex, and the 'vehements,' between those who would accept a negotiated peace generous to the King's side and those who were suspicious, for one reason or another, of anything that smacked of compromise. Yet by his march to Gloucester, the Earl of Essex had blunted those sharp criticisms of his conduct of the war levelled at him by the most extreme wing of the House of Commons. Under the ailing John Pym the House of Commons closed its ranks in late September and braced itself for a second Winter of war. No doubt Pym placed much of his hopes on the prospect of drawing the Scots into the war on Parliament's side: negotiations were already in progress. For his part the King had been unsuccessful in engaging foreign aid, but his efforts in that direction were far from over.

An introduction to the Cheriton campaign, albeit a strategic one, would not be complete for a reader unacquainted with seventeenth century warfare without a brief description of the common soldiers who made up the armies of the Civil War, and performed its strategic and tactical moves. How were they armed and dressed? What manoeuvres could they be expected to master? Let us look at each of the distinct types of soldier in turn.

THE FOOT

The infantry, or 'foot' as they were called, were divided into two types: pikemen and musketeers. Pikemen carried an 18-foot pike made of ash and steel. In theory they should have worn an iron ridged helmet or 'pot,' a corselet or back-and-breast plate over a leather coat, tassets and a gorget to cover their thighs and neck respectively. In the Civil War, however, tassets and gorgets were going out of fashion, and were probably only worn by the London trained bands. Most pikemen would have a helmet, corselet and sword, cloth breeches and square-toed shoes. In action pikes were held in two positions: level with the ground at shoulder height, gripped with both hands, or (in defence) with the base of the pike against the inside of the right foot, the other being advanced. In the latter case the pikeman steadied his main weapon with his left hand and wielded his sword with his right.

During cavalry attacks the square phalanxes of pikemen opened out to shelter in their midst the musketeers. Felt-hatted

PLATE 3
Pikeman
From Jakob de Gheqn, The Exercise of Arms for Calivres, Muskettes, and Pikes (The Hague, 1607)

PLATE 4
Musketeer

Jakob de Gheyn

and without armour, the musketeers could only defend themselves at close quarters by upturning their muskets and using them as clubs. They carried a heavy matchlock piece, fired on a rest by pulling a trigger which clamped down a smouldering length of 'match' into the flashpan. On a cross-belt bandolier dangled charges of powder ready made up in small metal containers. Bullets were carried in a bag over the left shoulder, or in the mouth ready for use. Only the musketeers guarding the train of artillery shouldered firelocks or snaphance muskets (the flint-locks of a later age), which were ignited by a clamped flint striking against the steel pan cover. Spluttering match cord could not be safely handled near barrels of gunpowder, hence this precaution.

The proportion of musketeers to pikemen in a foot company tended to change steadily in favour of the former. In the London regiments (see pp. 188-9) it will be noted that the musketeers already out-numbered the pikemen; in many regiments the ratio was probably as much as 2 :1. The foot were organized into companies, which varied in size according to the ranks of their captains. Regiments ranged from 1,200 to 300 men or less in actual strength, and they were not dissimilar in their essential structure from the infantry-of-the-line regiments of today.

THE DRAGOONS

Dragoons were musketeers mounted on rather inferior horses or ponies, and as such they were the successors of the mounted bowmen of the late fifteenth century. They were also organized into companies, which seem to have been more independent than those of the foot. The process of grouping the companies into regiments certainly took place, but there were wide variations between dragoon regiments: some possessed a definite sense of identity, others remained little more than loose associations of companies. Generals increased their mobility occasionally by turning some of their foot soldiers into dragoons by finding nags for them.

Tactically dragoons had a special role. It was their duty on the battlefield to 'line the hedges,' i.e. to dispute with the enemy's dragoons for the possession of the available hedgerows to the front and flanks of the army, from where they could effectively fire and break up formations of enemy cavalry before they fell on the main body.

THE HORSE

Troopers were equipped with a corselet worn over a buff coat, helmet, sword and a pistol (if they were fortunate). Tactically they either charged home against the enemy using their swords (in the style popularized by Gustavus Adolphus) or halted short of the enemy, fired their pistols and wheeled off to the flanks to reload and join the back of the troop.

Troops of horse, usually between 50 and 60 strong, formed regiments of varying strengths. When his regiment of Ironsides grew too large Cromwell divided it into two, but most commanders preferred to maintain a large single unit. Just as each foot company had its own colour, carried by the ensign, so each troop of horse rode behind its captain's colour, borne aloft by the cornet. Also, as in the case of the foot, regiments were known by the name of their colonels.

Lancers made only rare appearances in the Civil War, but cuirassiers — troopers clad in complete three-quarter length armour — were more common. The most famous regiment of them on either side, Sir Arthur Heselrige's, nicknamed the 'Lobsters' by the Royalists, took part in the battle of Cheriton. Not every colonel of horse could afford the capital outlay required for cuirassier armour, and the sturdy mounts needed to bear such heavy cavalry.

THE TRAIN OF ARTILLERY

The train of artillery included various grades of gunners, craftsmen and their mates needed to maintain the guns and the numerous waggons, pioneers (or 'matrosses' as they were then called) and several companies of musketeers armed with firelocks to protect the train on the march or in camp.

The cannons were divided into different sizes, from the heaviest siege pieces to the lightest field guns. Nomenclature for these sizes still varied in the seventeenth century, as it had done for over 200 years, but a list of cannons under their commonly accepted names and their 'vital statistics' is given below:

	Calibre of piece*	Weight of piece	Length of piece	Weight of Shot
Cannon Royal	8 ins	8000 lb	8 ft	63 lb
Cannon	7	7000	10	47
Demi-Cannon	6	6000	12	27
Culverin	5	4000	11	18
Demi-Culverin	4½	3600	10	9
Saker	3½	2500	9½	5¼
Minion	3	1500	8	4
Faclon	2¾	700	6	2¼
Falconet	2	210	4	1¼
Robinet	1¼	120	3	¾

* Probably ¼" should be allowed for windage.

By great good fortune a unique collection of buff coats, helmets, pistols, muskets and swords of the English Civil War period has survived at Littlecote House in Wiltshire, which is open to parties of visitors by arrangement. This fascinating array, which now decorates the great hall, once belonged to the troopers and soldiers of Colonel Alexander Popham's troop of horse and his regiment of foot, which he had tried unsuccessfully to complete for service in the army of Sir William Waller in 1643 and 1644. As Popham was almost certainly at Cheriton it is possible that some of this equipment and these arms saw service there as well.

SUMMARY

Strategically and politically the outcome of the English Civil War was still open in the Autumn of 1643. Although in economic terms Parliament's resources were much greater than those available to the King, by their own ingenuity, some aid from overseas and the generosity of certain magnates the Royalist generals were still able to take the field on a more-or-less equal footing with their opponents. Much more than later historians have allowed, the fate of the kingdom still depended on the drift or tide of battle. Besides the exertions of the common soldiers, with their limited weapons and varying morale, the outcome would rest also on the will and experience of the opposing generals, whose careers to date we have briefly reviewed above. Now we must look in more detail at the rival armies as they began to assemble in October 1643.

Chapter Three

NEW ARMIES AND OLD SOLDIERS

BOTH THE ARMIES at the beginning of the Cheriton campaign could claim to be new ones formed around cadres of veteran regiments. Despite the shattering defeat at Roundway Down, which broke up the Western Army, and the arrival of the London Brigade, Waller's forces, in early November 1643, possessed much more homogeneity than the Royalist army. Moreover, for all its drawbacks, London was a better place than Bristol to gather and recruit an army. Some account of how and where the regiments were found or raised will reveal the difficulties under which both generals laboured, besides illuminating the histories of two armies which have been generally recognized by scholars of the period hitherto as very obscure.

THE PARLIAMENTARIAN ARMY

Waller's army in the Cheriton campaign may be divided into three distinct parts, according to their paymasters: the Western, Southern Association and London regiments. Although a resident of Winchester with a house also in London, Waller owned land in Devon and still had many ties in that county. His first service as a major-general had been in the West, and his army had been formed for that country. Therefore it would be logical to consider first the enduring core of Western regiments in his army. For detailed notes on each unit the reader is referred to Section II; here only an outline of the army's growth can be given.

THE WESTERN REGIMENTS

On 11 February 1643 Essex signed a commission appointing Waller as Major-General over the Parliamentarian forces in the associated counties of Worcestershire, Somersetshire, Gloucestershire, Wiltshire and Shropshire. This may be regarded as the foundation date of Waller's army as a separate entity.

The ordinance established the forces of the five counties at ten regiments of horse and foot. Waller planned to take with him two regiments of horse, one of dragoons, and a train of six field pieces. He expanded his own regiment to ten weak troops, no doubt to serve as cadres for new recruits. The Lord General sent him several companies of dragoons. Sir Arthur Heselrige busied himself raising the second regiment of horse in London.

On 15 March Waller entered Bristol. By this time his small forces had swollen to about 2,000 men, mostly local recruits garnered on his way, but including one or two troops of Heselrige's new Regiment of horse that had caught up with him. For the lightning raids on the Royalist forces in the Severn Valley, which Waller made that Spring, he had the assistance of Colonel Thomas Essex's Regiment of foot.[1] When the Earl of Essex laid siege to Reading in April 1643, compelling the King to withdraw his garrisons from the West to swell his relief army, Waller had leisure to enforce the collection of subsidies in the counties under his control, so that he could build up his regiments. Yet, like most Civil War generals, he could never collect enough funds for his needs.

Most of what he could gather went in wages for the troops and companies at his headquarters in Gloucester, but the account books of Captain Thomas Blayney, the treasurer of war in Gloucester, catalogue many others who clamoured for coin from Waller's thinly lined chests: tailors, haberdashers, innkeepers, and a yeoman who had lost a field of hay; sick, wounded or maimed soldiers; and officers seeking money to prevent their men from disbanding, starving or going unrewarded after some arduous service. The many petitioners who gathered at Waller's quarters ranged from some shipmen who wanted £38. 1. 8d for the transport of 144 tons of iron, to a brace of young cornets who had been discharged from the army by a court martial and wanted their arrears of pay to settle their billets, having been 'assured by old soldiers that this is according to the ancient and usuall disipline of warre.' Waller stipulated that they should be paid when the troops making ready for the field had received their wages.[2]

There are glimpses in these accounts of Waller's staff. David Craddock, his secretary, often drew money for the General's troop and became a friend of Captain Blayney. James Bucknor, 'my chirurgion,' had also accompanied Waller into the West. John Haynes served as Commissary-General in the brigade with responsibility for procuring or buying provisions. The train reproduced on a miniature scale the artillery organization in the Lord General's army. Indeed Captain Robert Bower, who was both Comptroller and a gentleman of the ordnance, had held the latter post in the main Parliamentarian army,[3] and it is therefore likely that the Lord General had supplied Waller with at least a nucleus of experienced personnel for his train.

The aim of all this administrative work was to build up the forces in the Western Association (as it may be called) by maintaining, paying and recruiting the old regiments and raising new ones to fill the military establishment laid down by the ordinance. Soon after Ripple Field (13 April 1643), Heselrige rode up to London with twenty officers in order to raise more horse for Waller, and the Royalist spies in the capital seem to have mistaken this cadre for the remnants of Sir Arthur's own troop.[4] As a result of his speech setting forth the needs of Waller's Brigade the House of Commons passed an ordinance on 25 April promising to repay all who contributed towards reinforcements for Waller.[5] Meanwhile at Gloucester Waller issued commissions to five new colonels. The foot regiments of Henry Stephens and Sir Robert Cooke were essentially Gloucester regiments, although Waller used the latter to garrison Tewkesbury. But he intended Robert Burghill's horse, Arthur Forbes' dragoons[6] and Horatio Carey's foot, when complete, to march with the field army, These officers possessed considerable experience, and Burghill in particular had distinguished himself as an independent commander against a Royalist troop in the Wiltshire village of Sherston on 19 March, and again a few days later in the Forest of Dean.

In June, in order to face the combined Royalist armies

of the Marquess of Hertford and Sir Ralph Hopton, an impressive total of 4000 foot, 2000 horse, 300 dragoons and a train of 16 field pieces, Waller concentrated his forces at Bath. Here he received that notable reinforcement, the enlarged and re-equipped regiment of cuirassiers known to the Cavaliers as Heselrige's 'Lobsters.' These brought Waller's cavalry up to a strength of about 2500, but he was short of foot. Despite a recruit of perhaps 500 foot from Bristol, Waller could muster no more than between 1200 and 1500 compared with the 4000 in the Royalist army. With this army Waller at least held the Royalist commanders to a draw at the battle of Lansdown (5 July).

After his 'dismall defeat' at Roundway Down, Waller returned to London with perhaps 60 officers and a few weak troops of horse. Somewhat to his surprise, the militant or violent party in City and Parliament, weary of Essex's dilatory strategy, or lack of it, succeeded in obtaining a commission for him to raise a new army, ten regiments each of horse and foot. As we have seen, this abortive 'New Model' fell to bits when the Captain-General, newly returned to popularity after his dramatic relief of Gloucester, revoked Waller's independent commission. Consequently this phase in the history of Waller's army lasted no more than six weeks (29 August–9 October). Chronic shortages of money, the political hostility of the 'moderates' and Waller's own quarrels with his sponsors, combined to prevent all but a few of the regiments from ever being raised.

The planned 'New Army' was to be an enlargement of the Western Brigade, with the horse of Waller and Heselrige, and the regiment of dragoons as its nucleus. Such veteran regiments as Burghill's were retained, although Burghill himself retired (presumably on account of his Lansdown wounds) and handed over command to his major, the Dutchman Jonas Vandruske. Majors Francis Dowett (a Frenchman) and William Carr, who had both served with distinction in the West, received commissions as colonels of regiments of horse. Of the foot, four new colonels — Alexander Popham, James Carr, Edward Cooke and Edward Harley — were well known in the West.

Waller gave his own regiment of foot to a Scot, Lieutenant-Colonel Ramsay, with John Hillersdon, another Western veteran, as his major. Lieutenant-Colonel John Birch of Heselrige's foot came from Bristol, but he had not taken part in the Summer campaign. Colonel Andrew Potley's new Regiment of foot alone seems to have had no links with the old Western Association brigade.

As September wore on, Waller transferred his army from the London suburbs to Staines and Windsor, whence he could march out if necessary to succour Essex on his return from Gloucester. The London Committee of Militia lent him Colonel Richard Turner's Regiment of horse, eight troops strong,[7] bringing the total of his cavalry up to perhaps 30 troops.[8] Waller's Regiment of dragoons remained in London until September, when a Royalist saw them at a muster of City trained bands and auxiliaries.[9]

Meanwhile three regiments of London foot had already been alerted to join Waller, for without a strong body of infantry he could not march. The Westminster Regiment, the Yellow Auxiliaries, and the Green Auxiliaries, selected by lot on 7 September, had all received warning orders.[10] Nor did the staff of the artillery train neglect their preparations. On 20 September Commissary John Frowke signed for a hundred barrels of powder which were ferried down the river to Windsor.[11] As far as possible Waller had made ready his incomplete army for the field.

Besides lack of funds due to a temporary waning in the influence of Waller's political sponsors, and the loss of the Western subsidy-producing counties, his insistence upon appointing many professional officers may have created further difficulties as he attempted to raise the projected regiments. The standing of a colonel counted much towards the number of recruits he could attract. Londoners certainly entertained warm feelings for Waller and looked upon him as one of themselves. Heselrige, a national figure and later a prominent Independent, possessed a popularity of his own. Both were known as men who had spent large sums out of their own pockets towards the expense of outfitting their regiments. On the other hand, the remaining colonels were either professional soldiers, including a Frenchman and a Dutchman, or West Country gentlemen whose names might have raised regiments in Gloucestershire but could hardly muster a company in London or the Home Counties.

Cavalry regiments required a considerable outlay of money and neither William Carr[12] nor Francis Dowett could complete their regiments. Towards the end of October, 14 deserters from the latter's command had reached Oxford with this encouraging news.[13] Yet the old regiments of Waller, Heselrige and Vandruske were brought more or less up to strength. Colonel Turner's London horse, however, left Windsor in October with the Lord General when he marched to take Newport Pagnell. Waller's own Regiment of 500 dragoons, commanded by Major Archibald Strachan, completed the cavalry of the Western Brigade.

The colonels of foot made slow headway with their regiments. On 29 August Waller granted at least one commission for a company in Alexander Popham's foot, but the captain discharged his 49 soldiers three months later 'for want of further employment,' having received no wages during that period.[14] Presumably the other officers in this regiment followed suit. The trials encountered by the remaining five colonels may be illustrated by the correspondence and accounts relating to Edward Harley's Regiment, which should have contained 800 musketeers and 400 pikemen. Captain Francis Hakluyt, enlisting a company in Essex, wrote to Harley on 22 October thanking him for £10 and adding simply: 'If you intend to raise any more men or to lead those I have raised to any rendezvous you must send me more money.' By 15 November the pay arrears of those men Harley had mustered amounted to £408. 6. 8d. On that day the colonel estimated that the sum necessary to complete his regiment, supply it with a month's wages, provide drums, colours, halberds and a surgeon's chest would be £1,707.[15]

The county of Essex belonged to the newly formed Eastern Association, and the Earl of Manchester multiplied Harley's problems by ordering the Deputy Lieutenants to take Hakluyt's soldiers as recruits into his own army. Nor would he allow any more men to be enlisted in regiments other than those belonging to the Association. In spite of the willingness of the Essex Committee to comply with his lordship's direction, Hakluyt kept his men together. One of the county's trained bands then stole their winter quarters ! Want of pay and privation turned them into deserters or marauders, twin scourges driving the country folk close to revolt.

Harley seems to have cared little for his regiment or the sufferings of the soldiers, but even so he was not wholly accountable for their misery.

Scots professional soldiers commanded five of the eleven known 'New Army' regiments and the train of artillery, while many of the more junior officers also came from over the Border. 'I acknowledge that I have, and ever have had, a particular respect and value for that nation,' Waller wrote after the war, 'I love their constancy to their covenant, their steadiness in their counsells, their gallantry in the field. Some of them I have had the honour to command, and braver men I am confident no man could command.'[16] It may be surmised that Waller's political sponsors disliked the employment of these Presbyterian stalwarts.

In spite of the officer selection board set up by a political group which included many later Independents, not many officers of that religion or political persuasion found their way into Waller's army. Heselrige seems to have shared Waller's principles for choosing officers. His position as a great Leicestershire landowner and the fact that he was brother-in-law to Lord Brooke,[17] killed at Lichfield earlier in the year, explains many of his appointments. At least five officers who had formerly served under Lord Brooke received commissions in Heselrige's two Regiments. Although Lord Brooke's second captain had been none other than 'Freeborne John' Lilburne there is no reason to suppose that this regiment had been a particular hotbed of Independency.

On the other hand, there is some evidence that at least some of the common soldiers in Waller's army were influenced by those opinions usually associated with Cromwell's Ironsides. In June 1644 *Mercurius Aulicus*, for example, comparing Waller's men with those of the Earl of Essex, could describe them as 'a rabble of such keene rebellious Brownists, that they usually call his Excellencies followers *Malignants* and *Cavaliers*.'[18]

Faced with the threatening possibility during October that the main Royalist army at Oxford and Hopton's forces would join together, Parliament urged Essex and Waller to take the field. On 17 October the Lower House selected Waller for a committee directed to meet the Lord General that afternoon to discuss how this would be achieved. Next day 'the Western Gentlemen,' sponsors of the regiments raised for service in the West, assembled with the same end in view at Bedford House in the Strand, a mansion which had been placed at Waller's disposal in August.[19] As a result more money from loans and sequestrations found its way to the two armies.[20] Consequently, when Waller began assembling his army in Windsor during the last weeks of October, it was composed mainly of western men paid by money found by the Western Association committee in London.

The train of artillery was probably on the Western Association payroll. General James Wemyss, a Scot and former Master Gunner of England, became its commander in September or October 1643, and at once raised some companies of blue-coated 'firelocks' to guard the guns. There were ten brass pieces of ordnance, which probably included: one twelve pounder, one demi-culverin, five sakers, some lighter minions, and six 'cases' (waggon loads) of drakes — small cannon with a calibre of less than about three inches, which were used to fire case shot at close quarters — the 'medium machine guns' of the Civil War armies. A small but useful train, exceptionally well-officered.

THE SOUTHERN ASSOCIATION FORCES

Not until later in the Autumn of 1643 did the change in Royalist strategy confirm the need for a new Parliamentarian army in the South-East. To counter this threat Waller was nominated for command of the forces of Sussex, Surrey, Hampshire and Kent — the Southern Association.

On 4 November the House of Lords approved an ordinance associating Sussex, Surrey, Hampshire and Kent, and also agreed to a motion from the Commons asking the Earl of Essex to grant a commission to Waller as commander of their forces.

These counties had already resisted association in the spring of 1643. Governed by committees of Parliamentarian gentry, they preferred to confine their military activities to self-defence (with the exception of Kent which possessed money and security enough to spare regiments for the wider service of Parliament). The four counties resisted the yoke of unity with political quibbles for as long as they could, and then bore it with obvious reluctance. Sussex proved the most unco-operative of the four. In

June 1644, Waller could bitterly write: 'I would not have anything to do with the gentlemen of Sussex, from whom I have received nothing but constant incivilities.'[21] The Lord General fell back upon the old tactic and delayed granting a commission for as long as he possibly could — until 2 January 1644. Consequently the regiments which served with Waller in the first phase of the Southern campaign that Autumn did so in the capacity of volunteers; they were not legally under his authority.

The only regiment from the four counties with Waller at the beginning of the campaign was Colonel Samuel Jones' Regiment of Greencoats. As the garrison of Farnham Castle, Waller's base, they could hardly avoid active service! Yet before Christmas some good reinforcements arrived from Kent: Colonel Sir William Springate's Whitecoats and some troops of horse under Major Anthony Weldon in November. A fine Brigade from the same county took part in the siege of Arundel Castle, where Colonel Herbert Morley's Sussex Regiment of foot and some horse from the same county joined them.

Hampshire provided only Colonel Richard Norton's horse for the attempt on Basing House: almost the only military objective capable of prodding that county committee into action. The Hampshire gentlemen never fielded a regiment of foot for Waller, presumably holding that the garrisons of Portsmouth and Southampton fulfilled their military obligations. With less good grounds Sussex would not draw Colonel Anthony Stapley's Regiment of 1000 foot out of Chichester either.

THE LONDON TRAINED BANDS

The regiments selected by lot in September to march with Waller, joined him in early November. It was the first time that Londoners had served under his command.

The Westminster Liberty Regiment, or the Red Regiment, as it was known, mustered on 26 September 1643 no less than 1084 musketeers, 854 pikemen and 80 officers. Only two captains were named in the list of that muster: Mr Fauconbridge 'older brother of ye Tally office,' and the second captain, George Warren, a tailor in Sheere Lane, who received his commission on that very day. Besides men from Sheere Lane, his company included those from 'Bell-yard; from Holborne barrs to ye Kings-gate, & all Purpoole Lane.'[22] Their colonel, Sir James Harrington, son and heir to Sir Edward Harrington of Ridlington in Rutland, and a resident of Highgate, acted also as commander of the London Brigade.

The Green Auxiliaries numbered 1200 officers and men on that day, and their colonel was named as Christopher Whichcott, a merchant who was also second captain in the White Regiment, although Waller later referred to him as a lieutenant-colonel. At that time, in 1650 as Governor of Windsor Castle, Whichcott had become Sir William Waller's jailer.[23] The Green Auxiliaries were probably recruited around Cripplegate.

The Yellow Auxiliaries of the Tower Hamlets were commanded by Colonel Robert Tichborne, a linen merchant who lived by the little Conduit in Cheapside, and also served as first captain in the Yellow Regiment. Only two companies of this regiment were observed on 26 September, both of 112 musketeers and 20 pikemen. The auxiliary regiments, each below 1000 officers and men in nominal strength, were further weakened by desertions.

The Londoners made themselves ready in the second week of October and set out on Tuesday 17 October towards Windsor. Lieutenant Elias Archer, marching in his brother's company of the Yellow Auxiliaries, noted some early desertions:

> Upon Monday *October* the 16. our yellow Regiment was rallyed in *Wel-close*, intending to march out of *London*, but being late we returned that night to our owne houses.
>
> Tuesday *October* 17. our men were rallyed there againe, and that day we marched through *London* to *Kensington*, where we quartered that night.
>
> Wednesday the eighteenth we marched thence to *Hammersmith*, where we staied two dayes.
>
> Friday the 20. we marched thence to *Brainford*, where we stayed foure dayes, for some of our Companies and Souldiers which staied at *London*; while we staid there, divers of our men who pretended fairly to march with us went back to *London*, some hiring others in their roome, others wholly disserted us.
>
> Tuesday *Octob.* 24. the other Companies which were behind came to us, this day we mustered & received our fortnight's pay.

Wednesday 25. (being Fast day) we marched from *Brainford* before day, and that night we came to *Windsor*, where we met the Trained bonds of *Westminster*, who were quartered in *Windsor*, and the Green Auxiliary Regiment, which was quartered at *Dotchet* a little mile from *Windsor*, likewise at *Windsor* and *Eaton*, our Regiment was quartered, where we continued foure dayes, in which time some more of our men returned to *London* as the others did from *Brainford*.[24]

THE ROYALIST ARMY

On 29 September, when Hopton attended the committee meeting at the Lord Treasurer's lodging in Oriel College and received the King's strategic directives, he also discussed what forces would be available to him. Not all the units on the draft list of forces drawn up at this meeting (which still exists), however, joined Hopton, and those who did proved to be below their estimated strengths.

The horse assigned to Hopton on paper[25] consisted of a mixture of old and new regiments, some being raised already and some merely proposed. With their estimated number of officers and men, the units were as follows:

Hopton's horse and dragoons	250
Earl of Crawford's horse and dragoons	250
Sir George Vaughan	60
Sir Nicholas Crisp	100
Sir Edward Dering	120
Sir Edward Ford	260
Sir James Hamilton	50
Sir Horatio Carey	100
Colonel Richard Spencer	60
Colonel John (or Thomas) Covert	80
The Marquess of Hertford	100
Sir Edward Stawell	150
Total	1580

In contrast to these twelve cavalry regiments Hopton had to find his own infantry. His own regiment in Bristol would provide 300; Prince Maurice's foot another 250, while the Marquess of Hertford's Regiment under Colonel Bernard Astley and Colonel Conyer Griffin's Welshmen might possibly make up another

400 men[26] In order to reach a total of about 2000 foot, it was thought necessary to add to them the forces of:

Sir Allen Apsley	300	
Colonel Washington	200	Neither Regiment materialised in
Sir James Hamilton	50	Hopton's Army
Dorset and Somerset Companies	300	

Hopton returned to Bristol in early October, only to find that the actual number of foot available to him fell short of 2000. His cavalry, including Hertford's, Vaughan's and Stawell's Regiments which were still in Wiltshire, came to 1600 horse. As for a train, he possessed only some small field pieces, later augmented by four iron guns from Weymouth. Then a windfall arrived at Bristol: two seasoned regiments of foot, both between four and 500 strong, fresh from Ireland where they had been helping to quell the Irish rebellion. Commanded by Sir Charles Vavasour and Sir John Paulet, they could be described by Hopton as 'bold, hardy men, and excellently well officer'd, but the common-men verie mutenous and shrewdly infected with the rebellious humour of England, being brought over meerly by the vertue, and loyalty of theire officers, and large promises, which there was then but smale meanes to performe.'[27] Money, the 'meanes' in question, was in very short supply, as Waller had also found out during his sojourn in the Severn Valley.

After marching towards Wardour Castle, held for Parliament by Edmund Ludlow, Hopton received an order from the King to move into Hampshire and support Sir William Ogle, who had seized Winchester once again. Reluctantly Hopton sent ahead Colonel Apsley with 600 foot and Major Philip Day of his own regiment with some dragoons, while he attempted to settle his military affairs in Dorset, intending to leave Astley in command with the weak foot regiments of Hertford and Griffin as stiffening for the local Royalists.

At Amesbury, eight miles north of Salisbury, on Saturday 4 November, Hopton held a muster of his 'moving' army. The horse turned up in good numbers, but there were almost no foot except the 300 he had drawn from his own regiment in Bristol. With Apsley's 600 men in Winchester this meant that he had less than 1000 foot available to him. That night Hopton marched to

Andover in Hampshire, where he received the news that Waller had left Windsor for Winchester at the head of an army.

1. Essex, a former governor of Bristol, was relieved of his command for drunkenness and incompetence.
2. P.R.O. S.P. 28/129, 299. Accounts and Receipts of Captain Thomas Blayney.
3. Peacock, p. 24.
4. *Mercurius Aulicus*, 16–22 April, TT: E. 100 (18).
5. *C.J.*, Vol. III, p. 555; *C.S.P.D.* 1644, p. 443. *A Collection of all the publicke Orders, Ordinances and Declarations of both Houses of Parliament from 9 March untill December 1646*, printed for Ed. Husband (1646), p. 45. See *Mercurius Aulicus*, 23–28 April, TT: E. 101 (10), for a report that Heselrige had moved for 2000 men to be sent to Waller.
6. P.R.O. S.P. 28/144, Pt. 10, f. 18. Forbes had received a commission from Essex on 3 March 1643 to raise 1000 dragoons. Forbes, a veteran of the Swedish service and officer in the Lord General's Army, had been employed by the Gloucestershire Committee in August 1642, with Lt. Col. James Carr and Major George Davidson (S.P. 28/14, Pt. 2., f. 67).
7. P.R.O. S.P. 28/132. According to this account Turner's Regiment of horse was raised on 23 August as part of 6500 cavalry voted to be raised by Parliament on 18 July.
8. *The True Informer*, 23–30 September, TT: E. 67 (38).
9. 'On a MS. List of Officers of the London Trained Bands in 1643', ed. H. A. Dillon. *Archaeologia*, Vol. 52 (1890). The MS. list is to be found in B. M. Harl. 986 with annotations by Richard Symonds.
10. *A Perfect Diurnall*, 4–11 September, TT: E. 250 (8).
11. P.R.O. W.O. 55/460. Ordnance entry book (not paginated).
12. William Carr subsequently quarrelled violently with Heselrige and was sent to the Compter in Southwark (*C.J.*, Vol III, pp. 455–6).
13. *Mercurius Aulicus*, 22–28 October, TT: E. 75 (13).
14. Alexander Popham served with Waller's army at the siege of Arundel (Bodl. Tanner MS. 62, f.508). On 23 May 1644 the Commons voted that he should be recommended to Waller for some employment worthy of him, and that he should have leave to go down upon that service (*C.J.*, Vol. III, p. 505). He was then sent to raise recruits in the West (see E. Ludlow, *Memoirs*, Vol. I, pp. 90–1).
15. H.M.C., *Portland MSS.*, Vol 3, pp. 116, 119–120.
16. *Vindication*, pp. 215–16. The Scots evidently reciprocated this affection, for their commissioners in London could refer to Sir William in December 1654 as 'our noble and worthy friend' (*Correspondence of the Scots Commissioners in London, 1644–1646*, ed. H. W. Meikle (1917)).

PLATE 5
Sir Edward Dering
Parham Park

Cornelius Jansen

17 Robert Greville, 2nd Baron Brooke, see *D.N.B.*
18 *Mercurius Aulicus*, 23–9 June, TT: E. 2 (6). 'Brownists', strictly speaking the name of only one religious sect, was used as a general term to describe those of sectarian religious persuasion at this time.
19 *C.J.*, Vol III, pp. 278–9.
20 *Ibid*, pp. 284, 286–7.
21 *C.S.P.D.* 1644, p. 220.
22 'On a MS. List of Officers of the London Trained Bands in 1643', ed. H. A. Dillon, *Archaeologia*, Vol. 52 (1890).
23 'Experiences', ff. 45–7.
24 E. Archer, *A True Relation of the trained-bands of Westminster, the Greene Auxiliaries of London, and the Yellow Auxiliaries of the Tower Hamlets; under the command of Sir William Waller; from Munday the 16 of Octob. to Wednesday the 20 of Decemb. 1643*, B.M. 101, f. 64.
25 B.M., Harl. MS. 6804, f. 224. item 171.
26 *Ibid*, item 137.
27 *Bellum Civile*, pp. 62–3.

PLATE 6 *(opposite)*
Wenceslaus Hollar's Map of 1644
Hollar's map, of which this is an enlarged section, may well have been used by officers in the 1644 Campaigns. It gave England and Wales in six sheets 'Portable for every Man's Pocket... Useful for all Commanders for Quarteringe of Soldiers, and all sorts of Persons, that would be informed, where the Armies be, never so Commodiously drawne before...'
Bodleian Library

Chapter Four

BASING HOUSE BESIEGED

THE AUTUMN CAMPAIGN opened in late October with both rival generals ignorant of the intentions of each other. Sir William Ogle's seizure of Winchester in mid-October dictated the early marches, for the King had finally commanded Hopton to consolidate this gain, while Waller—who had already captured Winchester once before from Ogle (14 September 1642)—could hardly let this prize fall into Royalist hands without a response. Consequently it was the Royalist *coup* at Winchester which triggered off the campaign.

The events in Winchester were watched by Parliamentarian scouts, and one of them brought this report, somewhat exaggerated, of the Royalist strengths to the Earl of Essex's Scoutmaster General on Thursday 26 October:

> 'John Lane came this (day) from Winchester and saith that there are about 2000 foote and 2000 horse of the Kings forces and hee heard there were 3 drakes, but hee sawe none, and they report that they will fortifie the towne and keepe a garrison there this winter. That there are 1000 horse alsoe quarterd at Andever and Whitchurch and 7 collours of horse at Alston, and that on Tuesday last they were to have their randevous at Wallers Ashe in Hampshire, and expect dayly the comming of the Lord Hopton and the Lord Moone [Mohun] and tis thought that they intend eyther for Chichester or Southampton, and that the hearts of the people had much hardned against them for burning of Okeingham, and hee heard that the Cavallyers threaten to burne Farneham, and on Monday last 4 troopes of their horse faced Farneham Castle which putts the contry thereabouts in great feare.

Lord Hopton, who had already reinforced Ogle with Colonel Apsley's 600 foot and some dragoons and consequently found himself extremely short of foot at the Amesbury muster of his army (4 November), resolved to advance to Andover. He later recounted his march, writing about himself in the third person:

> Depending upon his intelligence for the state of the Enemy in that Country, he came (as he had design'd it) into Andover, 3 or 4 howers within night, and there kept his men in guard, till he had consulted with Coll: Gerard, who came immediately to him at his lodgeing, and the Earle of Craford with him. The Lord Gerard presently assured him that Sir Wm. Waller was that night come into Alsford (six little miles from Winchester) with a form'd Army, reputed to be about 5000. foote, and between 2000 and 3000 horse, and a good trayne of Artillery, and that he resolved to advance to Winchester the next day. In this exigent there being little hope but in the reputation that he had there, rather then in his strength, the Lo: Hopton presently gave out his orders for all to be ready to marche, an hower or two before day, but gave secret orders to the trayne to appointe onely two field-pieces with amunition on horseback to marche with him, and the rest of the trayne and foote to turne off back to Amesbury. Himselfe with the horse and dragoones, and those 2. little pieces, advanced to Winchester.
>
> It pleased God that this resolution succeeded verie well; for Sir Wm. Waller haveing intelligence of his speedy advance, and beleving his power to be greater, retired with his Army from Alsford, and sate downe before Basing-house; Which proved very convenient for the Lo: Hopton, who thereby gayn'd 10. or 12. dayes to forme his busines at Winchester whither he with ease and safty drew his trayne, and those few foote from Amesbury.

Waller's army had left Windsor for Farnham Castle at the end of October, and set out for Winchester on 3 November. After several days of marching the rain, snow and cold began to affect the Londoners, as Lieutenant Archer noted:

> Sabbath day *October* 29. the whole Brigade was drawne out into the fields, intending to march away that day, but (being late) we returned to our quarters.
>
> Munday *October* 30. we marched to a Greene about a mile from *Windsor*, where we made Alt and Rallied our men, each Regiment drawing into a Regimentall forme, where likewise

our Traine of Artillery and Waggons of warre came to us, and so we marched towards *Farnam* through *Windsor* Forrest, where in the Afternoone we met some of Sir *William Wallers* Troopes of horse, his owne Regiment of foot, and one Company of Blew-coats with Snaphans-muskets, which guard the traine of Artillery onely: all these marched with us.

When we came within a mile of *Bagshot*, we made Alt again in the closing of the evening, and refreshed ourselves about an houre, and then marched forwards, and about one or two a clocke on Tuesday morning we came into *Farnam*, where we rested all that day and the next night.

Wednesday *November* the first, all our foot Forces (except the Greene Regiment which was quartered two miles from *Farnam*) were rallyed in *Farnam* Parke, where there was added to our former advancing Forces, foure Companies of the Souldiers belonging to *Farnam* Castle; so that then in the Parke were 29 Colours of foot Companies, besides Horse and Dragoones; this day a Clerk of a Company in Sir *Williams* owne Regiment of foot, was (by a Councell of warre) condemned to dye, for a mutiny by him and some others raised in the field, and on Thursday *November* 2. he was hanged on a Tree in the Parke to the example of the whole Army.

While we remained there, we had much provision sent to our Regiment from our neighbours where our Regiment was raised, which was very thankfully received.

Friday *November* 3. we marched out of *Farnam* towards *Alton*, where by the way at *Bently-greene* the greatest part of our Army met together, *viz.* 16 Troops of horse, eight Companies of Dragoones, and 36 foot Companies (as appeared by their Colours) our Traine of Artillery consisting of ten peeces of Ordnance, and six cases of small Drakes, where having made Alt and refreshed our selves about an houre, we marched away to *Alton*, but our Regiment was quartered two miles thence at two little Villages called East *Worldom* and West *Worldom* [Worldham].

Saturday the fourth, the whole Army intending to march was rallyed about two miles from *Alton* towards *Winchester*, but by the extremity of wet and snow, we were all forced to return to our quarters againe.

Sabbath day *November* 5. the Army was rallyed in the fields neere *Alton*, and thence marching away pretending to march to *Winchester*, and when we came within nine miles of *Winchester* (or thereabout) in the evening we turned to the right, and that night quartered in the fields neere a Village called *Chilton* (this was a very cold night and very tedious to many of our men which never were accustomed to such lodging) although for the most part they lay in Barnes and such like at *Windsor* and *Alton*.

That night Sir William Waller, who had just received news of Hopton's presence in western Hampshire, changed his mind and decided to lay siege to Basing House, the Marquis of Winchester's home which had been held for the King since the start of the war:

> When I came to the generall rendevous att Farnham, I tooke a view of the army, which consisted of 18 troopes of Horse, 7 companyes of Dragoones, three citty regiments, mine own — yet imperfect and not above three hundred strong — and four companyes of Colonell Jones his regiment. With these I marched to Alton with intention to have proceeded on to Winchester, where the body of the enemy then lay. But I there received information from good hands—some out of the citty, and some out of the country — that there were very considerable forces drawn out of (the) King's army to cutt off my retreat. Whereupon I (altere)d my resolution, and marched to Basing; up (on the gro)und, that if the intelligence were true (I should) either fight with them singly — before any (other par)ty should joyne with them — or if I found my (sel)f too weake, make a safe retreat to Farnham, but a few miles distant from thence. If it were false, I might either make an assay upon that house — which by all men was represented to me to be but a slight peece and if I could carry itt, itt would have been a great encouragement to the soldiour — or otherwise I might advance towards Winchester, which that way was but two dayes march and the most direct way from Alton thither was no less.

As the eyewitness accounts reveal, Basing House presented a formidable task to a besieger. Built near the River Loddon it consisted of a mansion standing close to an old fortified keep. Secured on the south and west sides by great earthworks in Basing Park, whose bastion shapes can still be made out in the photograph of plate 27, the inner fortifications were protected to the north by the walled vegetable garden, studded with dovecote towers, and to the east by a dry moat skirting the Tudor mansion. Besides many gentlemen volunteers and family retainers John Paulet, the 45 year-old Marquess of Winchester, had under his command his own and Colonel Marmaduke Rawdon's Regiments of foot, perhaps 500 men in all, well victualled and supplied from Oxford with military stores. Lord Winchester's devotion to the King's cause and his stubborn defence would earn for Basing the proud title 'Loyalty House,' derived in part from the family motto 'Aymez Loyaulté' which was engraved on many of its windows.

An unnamed Roundhead soldier, author of *The Souldiers Report* and present at the siege, left his readers in no doubt as to the difficulty of the task facing Waller's army:

> Concerning the place, it is to be understood that there is first a town Basing, secondly, another towne called Basingstoke, & thirdly there is Basing-house, otherwiyes called the Marquesse of *Winchesters* house, almost within some two mile each from other in *Basing*, and about some 500 men, all of them in a manner Papists, with their Wives and Children, and great store of Wealth, and Treasure, which they together with the Malignants of those parts have brought thither for safety: and it is the only Rendezvous for the Cavaliers and Papists there about.
>
> This place is very strongly fortified the walles of the houses are made thick and strong to beare out Cannon bullet, and the house built upright, so that no man can command the roofe, the windowes thereof are guarded by the outer walles, and there is no place open in the house save onely for certain Drakes which are on the top of the said house wherewith they are able to play upon our Army though we discern them not.
>
> The house is as large and as Spacious as the Towr of *London*, and strongly walled about with earth raised against the wall, of such a thicknesse, that it is able to dead the greatest Cannon bullet, besides they have great store both of ammunition and victualls, to serve for supply a long time and in the wall are divers pieces of Ordnance about the house.

Lieutenant Elias Archer described the arrival of the Roundhead Army on 6 November at Basing House, the summons and the preliminary skirmishes which lasted well into that evening:

> Munday the sixt, about an houre before day, we marched away towards *Basing*, and about noone our whole Army was drawne up about halfe a mile from *Basing-house*, then there was a Forlorne-hope of about 500 musketeers drawne out of our Army and Captain *William Archer* (my worthy Captain) appointed for our Regiment, with considerable Captaines

and Officers out of other Regiments, who upon the returne of the Trumpeter, which Sir *William* sent to summon the enemy to surrender the house to the use of the King and Parliament) led on the said Forlorn-hope and continued in fight against the said house till they had spent all the powder and shot they either had, or could at the present be procured: At length they were relieved by a Regiment of Dragoones, who maintained the fight till the edge of the evening, in the meane time the Army and Traine of Artillery marched about through *Basing-stoke*, and came upon a hill over against the house, upon the side of which hill, our Ordnance were planted, which having made some few shot the enemy sounded a parley, which was answered, and a Trumpeter sent to the house, who (by reason of an unfortunate accident of scattering powder which fired two of our Drakes) was there detained till they sent a messenger to Sir *William* to know the reason of firing those Drakes, which being answered, their messenger returned, and then they sent forth our Trumpeter by a strange way which he knew not, and being dark they pretended to direct him the best way, telling him there was no danger in it, onely one small leape for his horse over part of a little brooke; which small leape proved so dangerous, that the horse, (although a very stout one of about 20.li. valew) stucke fast in the mud and mire, but by Gods great providence the man got away, and leaving his horse there came afoot and delivered his message to Sir *William*, who presently gave order to the whole Army to prepare for another onset the next morning; in the meantime our Ordnance made about 80 shot at the house betweene midnight and foure a clocke in the morning, and then we rested till day light, onely casting up a little brest-worke before the Ordnance.

On the following morning Waller decided to mount an assault against the farm buildings and outhouses, which clustered (as they still do today) around the great brick barn just north of the outer vegetable garden wall of Basing House. The Royalists anticipated this move by firing these buildings. Lieutenant Archer, an eyewitness on Cowdrey Down, narrates the course of the attack, which was spearheaded by Sir William Waller's own Regiment of foot:

> Tuesday *November* the 7. when it was day-light, we saw divers houses set on fire, which the enemy did to destroy all helps and shelter for our men, who presently after fell on by a forlorn party so closely, that we gained all their out-houses,

wherein was much provision of bread, beere, bacon, pork, milk, creame, pease, wheat, oats, hay, and such like, besides pigs and poultery, and diverse sorts of household goods, as brasse, pewter, fether-beds, and the like, some of which things diverse of our men seized upon, some eating and drinking, others bringing away such things as they liked best, and could with most convenience carry; others continued still fighting against divers parts of the house, and when one party was weary another party relieved them, of all which parties divers were wounded and some slain, as in such cases it cannot likely be avoyded.

The enemy perceiving that our men had possession of their out-houses and provisions, sent out a party of men to salley out and fire the said houses and the barns adjoining to them, which were full of wheat and other graine; in which salley I beleeve they did fire the said houses and barnes, but they lost their Serjeant which led them, and most the men which followed him were slain in the yard betweene the house and the barne: in which conflict divers of our men were wounded but none slain out-right (that I could heare of;) by this time night began to approach, and the fire of those houses began to burne very hot and fiercely, so that being constrained by the heat and smoak of the burning houses, and night drawing on, our men were withdrawn from the house to their severall Randevous in the fields, where we quartered that night, wherein our lodging and our service did not wel agree, the one being so hot, and the other so cold.

From the Royalist point of view the day had been a considerable success, and morale must have soared. After all Hopton with a competent army stood not many miles away at Winchester. The Royalist newspaper *Mercurius Aulicus*, no doubt basing its report on first hand accounts, told the story from the besiegers' angle:

> Soone after this *Waller* sent his *forlorne hope* down the hill to surprize the Grange and other out buildings, together with the New House (for the Castle was to defend both) who came boldly on, but being to passe up a narrow lane, the Garrison soudliers through a halfe Moon, and divers holes made in the walls, gave [fire] so thicke upon them that many of them were slayne, and the rest retired to tell what was become of their fellowes. The surprizall of these buildings was so necessary for the Rebels designe, that they attempted it againe with severall bands of fresh men, and (to distract the Garrison) drew 3 peices of Ordnance to the North side of the

New buildings, whilst others fell on upon the *Grange*; Captaine *Clinson* (Captain Leiutenant to *Waller* himselfe) led those up to the *Grange*, who with small hurt possessed themselves of all the buildings on that side, whence having steddy aime at the holes, and fighting from safe places, they much annoyed the Garrison, who were strongly assaulted on the North side of the workes, but so bravely quit themselves, that they forced the Rebells back into the Houses, whence they shot thicke upon the Garrison, the great guns all the while thundring at the Castle and new buildings. The Rebels having got possession of all the adjoyning houses, necessitated the Garrifon to a speedy remedy, which was to set them all on fire, and at the same time to sally out into the Grange, & take them at their removing, whilst the Garrison from the North side plyed the Rebels in the Houses with shot of all forts. The businesse on the Grange fide was undertaken by the two Lieutenant Colonels *Peake* and *Johnson*, who bravely issuing forth with some few men, made boldly to the Barnes in despight of the enemies shot, and in two or three places fired the corne, and retreated in safety; then Lieutenant Colonell *Johnson* coragiously ventured out into the very *Grange* yard, with 25 men onely, and encountring with *Clinson*, grappled with him, and was too farre ingaged, when two or three stout fellowes of the Garrison hasted to his rescue, where Captain *Clinson* received his deaths wound, leaving intelligence what he was by his *Commission* found in his pocket; Col. *Rawdon* himselfe mean-while with exceeding diligence and courage directing all the Souldiers, & heartning them still, that *he knew Waller would not stay it out*. This bold enterprize seconding the fire, made the Rebels thinke among so many deaths at hand (as fire, sword, and water) how to save themselves by flight, which they hastily practised, leaving all their Armes, and many of their fellowes behinde them, some dead, others in the Barne wounded, shortly to end their lives by fire. Thus was the place (I cannot say the *Grange*, which now hasted to be ashes) freed from these noysome guests ...

Thus discouraged by the Royalists Waller encountered for the first time the mutinous humour of the London regiments, who had done nothing all day but act as spectators of the reversal in the farm buildings:

Att my first coming to Basing I received an assurance that there was no danger could threaten me — for the present —

from Oxford, whereupon I resolved to attempt that place. I was first guided to the north side of the house which was most commanded and fittest to batter but upon a triall I found that the enemy had fortified most strongly on that side, with diverse retrenchments one under the command of another. Wee tooke in some outhouses adjoyning to their workes, but the enemy fired them so that wee were faine to quitt them. Wee lost in that fight twelve or thirteen men, and as many more hurt. This and the coldness of the night with fowle weather was a great discouragement to the London regiments, who were not used to this hardness in so much as the officers came to me and made itt their request they might be drawn off, with an intimation that many of the souldiours were hirelings, and their monye being spent, they began to thinke of their returne. The first remonstrance in this kinde was made by the field officers, the second by the captaines and inferiour officers. This was a great surprise to me, but the weakness of my condition without them, inforced me to yeeld upon condition they would give me in their desires under their hands which they did. Upon this, I drew the army into Basing Stoke to refresh itt for two or three dayes. In the meantime I seised upon the Vine — an house so called belonging to Mr. Sands — and putt some forces into itt, intending to fortify itt, and in regard of the neerne(ss to Basing) to make itt a bridle to that place to cutt off their contributions, and [blank space] subsistence.

The morale of the garrison stood high, as Sir Edward Nicholas reported from Oxford to Prince Rupert:

'Monday last, Waller sat down before Basing-house, and Wednesday last he drew off his ordnance and forces to Basingstoke, a mile from Basing-house where he now lies with all his forces, and threatens to return thither to assault that house again; and hath sent for scaling ladders to Windsor for that purpose. The Marquis of Winchester writes cheerfully, saith he hath 400 men and three weeks' victualling, and that he hath killed divers of the rebels, and lost only one man and one hurt.'

When the army had rested for three or four days Waller decided to assault Basing House once more, this time launching simultaneous attacks from the south and east:

The army beeing sufficiently refreshed, I resolved (to have ano)ther fling att Basing, upon an information I had received of a place that might give me some advantage. I intended to have fallen on before day, but the sluggishness of the soldiours was such that itt was afternoone a good while before I could come upp. The order was to give the ennemy allarums on all sides, and to fall on, on two sides, the one thorough the Parke, the other on the side towards Basing towne. Att this last place I set upp my rest where Major Strahan, — as gallant brave gentleman as drawes a sword — fell on with his dragoones, seconded by mine own regiment, and the four companyes of Colonell Jones, and the petardier with them.

The task of storming the large earthworks facing outwards into Basing Park fell to the London regiments. One party from the Westminster Regiment suffered a grievous loss of life, as Lieutenant Archer relates:

> Sabbath day *November 12.* in the morning we were all drawn out against the house, on the other side of it Sir *William* intending desperately to storme it and scale the wals, and when we came before it we gave a very hot and desperate charge against it on every side, and (in some places) came so neere to the wals that some of our ladders were raised (which ladders were not scaling ladders, for there were then none come to us) moreover we fixed one of our Petards to a part of the wall, thinking therewith to blow up the wall and so make a breach, but the wall was so thicke and strongly lined and supported with earth and turfe within side, that the Petard did no considerable execution.
>
> While we were thus close under the wals, the women which were upon the leads of the house threw down stones and brickes, which hurt some of our men; in the meane time, the rest of our Forces continued firing against other parts of the house, and performing such other service as it was possible for men to doe in such a desperate attempt, till it was darke night that we could not see their loop-holes (although we were within Pistoll shot of the wals) then we were drawne off into severall grounds and fields neere adjoyning, where we quartered that night.
>
> I know something is expected should be spoken of the losse we their sustained, I conceive our losse of men in all the three dayes service against the house, to be about 250. or 300. at the most, in which losse Sir *Williams* owne Regiment, and the Regiment of *Westminster* Trained-bands to beare the greatest shares; for upon Munday being the first onset, I am certaine that in all we did not lose foure men slaine out-right, besides what were wounded. On Tuesday (being the

second dayes service) Sir *Williams* Captaine-Lieutenant by an unfortunate mistake in the way to the place where he was designed to goe on, went with his party which he then commanded up a lane where the enemy had planted two Drakes with case-shot, which being fired slew both him and many of his men, whose losse was very much lamented, being a man of undantable courage and resolution. And on the Sabbath day being the third and last dayes service against the house, the said Regement of Trained-bands being designed to set upon the south-west part of the house through the Parke (being upon a plaine levell ground before the wall, without any defence or shelter) whether the fault were in their chiefe Leader, at that present either throgh want of courag or discretion I know not, but their Front fired before it was possible they could doe any execution, and for want of intervals to turne away speedily the second and third wranks, fired upon them, and so consequently the Reare fired upon their owne Front, and slew and wounded many of their owne men, which the enemy perceiving fired a Drake or two among them which did them much injury, and was a lamentable spectacle; it was told me since by a Captaine in that Regement, that they had seventy or eighty men slaine and hurt in that disorder. But now to returne to my quarters where I left off, because time will not permit me to relate every scruple.

On the east side, after marching through the woods between Basing village and the Tudor house, the Roundheads attacked with courage under the eye of their general, but their petardier failed to fix his bomb to a weak section of the outer wall. The anonymous eyewitness Parliamentarian soldier tells the story of the fighting, and the depressing effects of the weather on their morale:

Sir *William Wallers* forces were billited at *Basingstoke Basing*, and divers others villages in severall places about *Basing* house, and on *Sunday* morning being the twelfth day of *November* 1643, Sir William drew his force together, and with a brave resolution, marched out of Basingstoke, and mustered his men in the field; and pitched against Basing house with about eight thousand men or as some say six thousand besides five *(sic)* Regiments of Dragoneers, both which are much upon the matter, ten pieces of Ordnance, and with scaling ladders, Petarres Granadoes, and other train of ammunition, and pitched within Musquet shot of the enemy letting fly a Cannon bullet upon the house which was answered by one of their Drakes from the top of the house, we played upon them, and they upon us very hot, and about noon some of our men got to the wall, and struck in their Petarres, and their scaling ladders, and began to climb up the wall, but the enemy beat them downe againe so fast with stones, that they were forced to retreat from the walles again, yet did our Army continue beating upon the house, in which they made some batteries. The Dragoneers, and indeed generally our Army did fight with as much vallour as Souldiers could expresse.

Sir William Waller himselfe fearing no danger by his valour to encourage the Army, and considering that our Army had no shelter, not so much as any village hovill, nay not very trees, save onely by Basing park side some few young groves which could not shelter them to any advantage they were constrained to fight in a champion place, which was a great disadvantage to Sir Williams army, yet did nothing at all discourage their resolution: towards the evening about three of the clock, the winds begin to rise, and it rained, so that it did much hinder the army, which rain increased so much that the Army sounded a retreat, and to give them content S. William Waller retreated halfa mile or thereabouts to refresh his Armie, but continued the siege, & although it grew darke and the rain fell, and the coldwinds blew, yet was Sir William Waller so resolute, and vallorous that he would not depart the field, but lay himself all night on a bundle of straw in the open meadow, resolving that if the raine ceased to make a fresh onset upon the house, but it continued al night, and ceased not, and in the morning, being Monday morning last, Sir William Waller seeing the weather crosse, tooke Counsell with his Commanders, and upon debate on the matter, it was thought best to depart for that time, whereupon he retreated and returned to Basingstoke & there received some more scaling ladders granadoes, powder, and ammunition, which was sent him from London.

Waller gave his reasons for the failure at Basing House, and recounted to the Speaker of the House of Commons why he felt compelled to march away from Basingstoke not towards the Royalist field army but into Winter quarters at Farnham. At first the onslaught from the east against Basing House had gone well:

This was performed with as much courage and resolution as could be don by men. The ennemy had quitted one of their workes, our men gained the rampart, and the petardier applied his petard, but unluckily mistooke the place; for whereas he should have applied to a place in the ould wall which was but a brick and a half thick, he sett it against a doore that was bricked upp and lined with earth, so that it tooke no effect. In the mean time that squadron of the red regiment that should have fallen on upon the Parke side on a worke that flanked us, and where there remained but six musketiers, the rest beeing runn away, could not be drawn upp, only they fired out of distance, and so fell off againe. This gave the enemy new courage, so that they fell againe into their workes and beat our men off. I lost in this service, thirty men upon the place, and neere upon one hundred hurte. That night fell out so fowle that I could not possibly keep my men upon their gards, so that I was forced to draw into Basing. The ne(xt morning) early my scowtes came in, and gave me advertisement that Sir Ralph (Hopton with his) whole strength was upon his march within six miles of me, and by a party (which I) had sent out towards Reading, I was informed that Sir Jacob Ashly had drawne a considerable body of horse and foot out of Reading and the parts thereabouts, and was not farr from me. Whereupon I speedily drew the army into the field, and sent out fresh partyes on all sides to discover what way the ennemy held, for by some prisoners which my men fetch't in I was informed that Sir Ralph struck out of the road towards me, and marched Newbery way towards Kingscleare, — which was to joyne with the Reading forces —. When the regiments were drawn out, as I was riding about to give orders, I was saluted with a mutinous cry among the citty regiments of 'Home, Home.' So that I was forced to threaten to pistoll any of them that should use that base language, and an ennemy in the field so neere. With this they were all very well accquietted. I then sent for all the field officers, to take advice with them concerning my proceeding. There were three propositions moved. The first, to march upp to the ennemy, and fight with him; the second, to march to Winchester, and seise upon that; the third to retire to Farnham and to preserve the country from thence, untill further supplyes came to strengthen us. The first was carried cleere, and the officers dismissed to their severall charges. But they were no sooner returned to their regiments, but the mutiny broke out againe, with a protestation those of the citty would not march one foot further. Upon this I was enforced to retire to Farnham where I now am. A great part of those regiments are already gon to London, and the rest threaten to follow immediately, so that I am in a deserted condition. What I can do with my horse, and an handfull (of foot) I will, God willing, perform with my uttermost endeavours. Itt (grieves m)y soule that I can do no more. I have some requests to make which w(ith reason)ableness, I shall tender to you. The first is that those regiments, which are levying for the West, may be immediately compleated, and sent upp to me with all possible speed. 2^{ly} that wee may have some monyes sent to releeve us, for wee are all in a most wretched degree of want. 3. That command may be given that what forces may be spared out of Kent, and the neighbour countyes may be dispatched away to me indelaidly. I have written to them, but I suppose some signification from the House would quicken them. 4. I desire that what I have written concerning the London regiments may not be taken in such a sence as might have a reflection of dishonour either upon the citty unto which I owe all service and respect and particular obligations, or upon all the regiments, for there be many worthy gallant men amongst them. But the truth is, amongst the hirelings which were promiscuously taken upp, I have reason to suspect there (were) Malignants, that putt themselves upon this service only to overthrow itt, and they are the men that have blown these coles. 5. (That there) may be some examplary punishment inflicted upon runnaways; And lastly, that you will vouchsafe to pardon my many f(ailings in this ser)vice which are not only my fault but my punishment.

Lieutenant Archer, not surprisingly, does not mention the mutiny and wholesale desertion of the London regiments, but rather stresses their willingness to meet Hopton in battle:

On Munday *November* 13. in the morning, in regard of the bad successe of the precedent dayes service, and the disheartning which our men susteyned by it, together with the present foulnesse of the weather (for it was a very tempestuous morning of wind, raine and snow) all our Forces were again withdrawne to *Basing-stoke*, where we refreshed our men and dried our cloaths.

Tuesday the 14. we had a generall Alarm, and it was by divers Scouts and Troopers reported, that Sir *Ralph Hopton* was within two miles of *Basingstoke* with all his Forces, intending to give us Battell, which much encouraged our men, for then they hoped they should fight with men face to face; whereas before, for the most part, they fought against stone-walls. And to that end, all our Forces in generall were drawne into the field, but no Hoptonians appeared, and newes was brought that they were retreated: whereupon Sir *William* marched presently away towards *Farnham*, but that night quartered in the field, about two miles from *Basing*, expecting (as I conceive) that *Hopton* would have come thither with some forces, and by that meanes of withdrawing we might have purchased a Skirmish; but he comming not in the morning, we marched away towards *Farnham*, and about two aclock in the afternoone we marched into *Farnham*, where Sir *William* tooke up his quarters for a time, and began to fortifie the Towne with Brest-workes, and the like.

At first Hopton had been held up by his shortage of foot and the mutinous behaviour of the two Irish regiments. As the above accounts suggest, however, he had succeeded in joining forces with Sir Jacob Astley and part of the Reading garrison at Kingsclere before marching to raise the siege of Basing House:

> But finding his great want of foote and the necessity that there would be within few dayes to advance towards the releife of Basing house, he cast every way to supply himselfe. And not haveing heard of the proceedings of the Irish Regiment at Warder, and doubting that nothing but money would make them tractable, he went himselfe thither from Winchester, and carryed 130l. with him; where comeing to Funtill he was presently entertain'd by Sir Cha: Vavaser and Lo: Arundell of Warder (who was then there) with a complaint, that the Regiment lying at Henden was in a high muteny against theire officers, insomuch as they durst not adventure to come amongst them. Whereupon the Lo: Hopton that night appointed a Rendez-vous of Sir George Vaughan's Regiment of horse, and of the two troopes of dragoones neere Henden, and with them, the next morning early fell into the Towne upon the mutineers, took some of the Principale, and commanded the rest of the regiment to drawe out. And upon that terror, and the execution of two or three of the principale offendours he drew the Regiment quietly to Winchester. And, to supply the block of Warder, he drew Coll: Barnes thither with a new Regiment of about 300 foote, (as the Coll: accompted them,) which he had some moneths before bin leavying in Dorsetshire by Commission from the Lord Hopton; Who in his returne to Winchester mett on the way Sir Thomas Biron, with the Prince's Regement of horse, which, through His Majestie's favour

A. THE OLDE HOVSE. B. THE NEW. C. THE TOWER THAT IS HALFE BATTERED DOWNE. D. THE KINGES BREAST WORKS. E. THE PARLIAMENTS BREAST WORKS.

PLATE 7

The Siege of Basing House (1645)   by Wenceslaus Hollar

Hollar was present inside Basing House during the later siege of 1645. The 'Kinges Breast Works' (marked D above) was his diagrammatic representation of the graceful earthwork bastion in Basing Park, the outline of which can still be clearly seen from the air (see Plate 28)

PLATE 8
Sir Marmaduke Rawdon

and goodness, was sent to his assistance, and, by the excellent conduct of that honest Gentleman, was afterwards of great use to him.

He had likewise about this time drawen from Bristoll Sir John Paulet (whom he made his Major Generall of foote) with his Regement: And by other fortunate recruits grew able to draw out of Winchester about 2000 foote, for any service; for which he was quickly called upon; for the Lo: Marquis of Winchester being hard prest in Basing-house by Sir Wm. Wallers forces, sent him out a letter by a woman, wherein he gave him notice of the last day that he was able to hold out, which (as the Lord Hopton remembreth) was the 12th day after Sir Wm. Wallers comeing before it and earnestly prest for reliefe. The Lo: Hopton sent back the woman with assurance of reliefe by that time, and writt to Oxford to desire what assistance might be spar'd out of Reding for that service, which was granted and very well executed by Sr. Jacob Ashley (now Lord Ashley) who, upon signification from the Lord Hopton, mett him at Kingscleere with 900. excellent foote, Lord Percyes Regiment of horse, and two field pieces. And at the same time came to him Coll. Bellasis his Regiment of horse commanded by Major Bovill. From Kingscleere they advanced very early the next morning to Basing, being now a very handsome little army of neere 3000. foote, and dragoones, about 2000. horse and a good trayne of Artillery; when they came neere Basing, they found Sir Wm. Waller risen, and retreated with his Army to Farnham. So the Lo: Hopton haveing rested, and refreshed his troopes that night at Basing, with the advice of his Councell or Warr, resolved to advance towards the Enemy, and to quarter in, and about Odiam.

How many men Waller lost dead or wounded is not known for sure, but his own estimate of 30 killed and about 100 wounded is probably near the mark. The only consolation had been the seizure at Newbury, during the interval, of Lord Saltoun, who had just landed in Sussex with money collected for the Royalist cause in France. Captain Samuel Gardiner of Heselrige's 'Lobsters' effected the arrest, and lodged his prisoner in the Bell Inn at Basingstoke before sending him up to London. On this 'high note' the anonymous author of *The Souldiers Report* ends his account of the siege:

Sir *William Wallers* vallour and courage is such in this

business as divers Souldiers who were the witnesses do testifie as deserves great honour, and respect, and his resolutions still continue to let slip no opportunity, whereby he may gain any advantage upon the enemy.

How many men Sir *William Waller* lost in his fight is not known, for in the morning we found not one dead corps, but there is some fourty men wounded and how many of the enemies are hurt we cannot tell, nor what detriment they received save only one of their Cowes which being frighted with the noise of the gunnes leaped over the wall, by which it seemes to be of a great thicknesse.

Sir *William Waller* hath sent up to *London* to the Parliament the Lord *Saltan* a Scotch Lord, Friar King his Ghostly Father, and one that is his man: This Lord *Saltan* was to raise 2 Troops of Horse in the West, and had raised six thousand pound for that purpose, and Father King was with him to counsell him in the disposing of the businesse; but Sir *William* hearing thereof sent out a party against them and took them, carrying them to *Basingstoke*, and now has sent them to the Parliament.

As a tailpiece to Waller's attempt on Basing House the very human letter of Susan Rodway to her husband in the Westminster Regiment serves to remind us that the common soldiers who fought—and died—in the campaign, were not just pawns or counters in a strategic or tactical game, but flesh-and-blood people like ourselves :

Most deare and loving husband, my king love,—I remember unto you, hoping that you are in good helth, as I ame at the writting heareof. My little Willie have bene sick this forknight. I pray you to comeiv whome, ife youe cane cum saffly. I doo marfull that I cannot heere from you ass well other naybores do. I do desiere to heere from you as soone as youe cane. I pray youe to send me word when youe doo thenke youe shalt returne. You doe not consider I ame a lone woemane; I thought you woald never leave me thuse long togeder, so I rest evere praying for your savese returne.
Your loving wife,
Susan Rodway.

Ever praying for you till deth I depart. To my very loving husbane, Robert Rodway, a traine soudare in the Red Reggiment, under the command of Captaine Warrin. Deliver this with spide, I pray youe.

Sources quoted in order of first appearance:
Journal of Sir Samuel Luke, ed. I. G. Philip, 3 vols., Oxfordshire Record Society, (1950–1953), pp. 175-6.
Hopton, *Bellum Civile.*
Archer, *A True Relation* ... B.M. 101, g. 64.
Waller to Speaker Lenthall (16 November), H.M.C., *Portland MSS*, Vol. 1, p. 154.
The Souldiers Report concerning Sir William Waller's fight against Basing House, TT: E. 76 (5).
Mercurius Aulicus, 12-19 November. E. 77 (18)
E. Warburton, *Memoirs of Prince Rupert* (1849), Vol. 2, p. 325.
Susan Rodway's letter, from G. N. Godwin, *The Civil War in Hampshire* 2nd edn. (1904), pp. 121-2. This letter, entrusted to 'Robert Lewington, the Hampshire carrier', was intercepted by a lieutenant of Hopton's army, and published in *Mercurius Aulicus.*

Chapter Five

FARNHAM DELIVERED

AFTER A FEW DAYS of skirmishes between the two armies, with their respective quarters at Odiham and Farnham only a few miles apart, Hopton marched on Farnham Castle, but weather and luck (or providence) intervened in Waller's favour. His run of ill-fortune, unchecked since Roundway Down in July, at last had turned. While Hopton settled the Royalists into Winter quarters his opponent kept the Parliamentarian army together, hoping to seize the initiative once more.

In the first week in Farnham the Londoners were much cheered by the arrival of provisions, and Sir Michael Livesey's Kentish Regiment of horse, which was to serve with Waller for the rest of the year:

> In the time that we lay there, we had sundry Alarm and other accidents, among which these were the chiefe.
>
> *Saturday Novemb. 18.* There came to us much Provision of Victuals, and strong waters to our Regiment, which was very thankefully received, although (thanks be to God) we had no great scarcity before.
>
> *Tuesday Novemb. 21.* Some of our souldiers went abroad, to a Parke called the *Holt*, about a mile and a halfe from *Farnham* to kill Deere, and (being a very thick misty day) the Enemies Scouts came upon them and tooke 9. of them prisoners, all Captaine *Levets* men.
>
> *Thursday Novemb. 23.* There came to us a very faire Regiment of Horse, and a company of Dragoones, consisting of 120. out of *Kent*, under the command of Sir *Myles* [sic] *Lewsy*.
>
> *Friday 24.* It was reported there, that the King was at

Basing-house, and intended with 2000. Horse which came thither with him, to be assistant to *Hopton*, in the taking of *Farnham-castle* : and the same day, about ten in the morning, we had an Alarm, and expected an assault with the Enemies full body ; & to that end, the Castle Colours were set upon the walls, and all our other Forces were drawne into the Parke, wher we stood upon our guard al that day, and the night following, and about eleven a clock the next day, newes was brought that the Enemies Forces were all withdrawne to *Odiam*, five miles from us, whereupon we marched into the Towne, and refreshed ourselves for that day and the night following.

While the army thus foraged Waller addressed himself in a letter to the Speaker, dated Thursday, 23 November, seeking for money and supplies, and giving an accurate description of the poor morale of his army :

> Having acknowledged the readiness of the House to take care for the preservation of this poor Brigade and protested their faithfulness I crave leave to offer to your consideration the necessitous condition under which we labour. Want of money and want of clothes have produced want of obedience and want of health, I had almost said want of heart in this army ; working like a malignant fever upon the spirits of our men, and dulling the edge of our swords, though I am confident the metal is unaltered. I cannot but take notice with humble thankfulness of 5000l. voted for our supply, but I beseech you give me leave without offence to tell you it is impossible for this sum or less than double the proportion of this sum to stop the clamorous wants of our soldiers, for the last payment was so small that it would not enable them to buy themselves so many necessaries as they wanted for this winter service and their hopes being fixed upon this supply, if this should fall short, it would instead of a satisfaction prove an irritation to them. God knows, I write this with a sad sense, but I have reason to doubt what command I shall be able to retain upon those, whom I can neither reward nor punish. I humbly desire there may be some present course taken to supply the army. I have presumed to send some parties to Godalming and Midhurst to take up some coarse cloths, linen, shoes, boots and stockings for the soldiers, and if there may be any assurance given to pay for their commodities, I am confident it would be best both for the soldiers and the country.

In the last days of November the Royalist generals decided to advance upon Farnham, and arrived with their army on high ground a mile north of the Castle, causing considerable alarm. Lieutenant Archer was among those who stood to arms in the park under the guns of Farnham Castle:

> *Sabbath day Novemb. 26.* Newes came, that a great part of the Enemies Forces were upon their march towards us, and presently there were divers parties drawne out to meet them; some of which parties marched to a Village, called *Crundle* two miles from *Farnham*, and comming thither, they were informed that the Enemy was retreated, whereupon they returned presently.
>
> *Monday 27.* In the morning there came to us 5. Companies of foot, under the command of Sir Arthur *Haselrig*, and before noone we had an Alarm, and it was reported, that the Enemy was at hand with a very great Force: Whereupon we presently stood upon our guard, and made good all the passages about the Towne, and drew the rest of our Forces into the park where we planted our Ordnance, and drew our foot Forces into a convenient form ready for Battell; by this time the Enemy appeared in a great body upon a hill, in the heath above the Parke, about a mile from us: whereupon we had divers Ambuscadoes, & a forlorn hope drawn out, expecting that they would have come on, but they never attempted any assault at all, (neither doe I think they intended any) although many of our Forces, especially of Horse and Dragoones, lay cleane out of their sight behind a hill in the Parke (hoping that seeing so small a force, they would have come on:) while the 2 bodies stood thus facing one another at that great distance, and Sir *William* seeing they had no mind to advance towards us, he sent a party of Horse which fell upon their Scouts, and other small parties of their Horse, and forced them all up to their maine body then our Ordnance made divers shot at them, both from the Castle and out of the Parke; three of which shot tooke place, and slew (as I heard it reported to Sir *William*) 17. of their Horses and 15. men. Whereupon they moved their body further off, and stood and faced us againe a little while, but soone marched away towards *Odiam*, and divers of our Horse and Dragoones followed and fell upon a party of them, and slew some, brought in 19. prisoners, and forced them to forsake their quarters at *Crundle*, and betake themselves to *Odiam* and *Basing-stoke*.

It is since credibly reported, that this day the King dyned at *Basing-house*, as soon as he had dyned, went presently away towards *Oxford*, and this party was sent onely to face us, & by that meanes keepe us from thence in the meane time.

Waller's own account reveals also his change of spirits as a result of the rebuff he had given the Royalists. In his religious 'Experiences' he could write:

'Att Farnham God appeared wonderfully for me, when the Lord Hopton drew upp his whole army within demi-culverin shott of me, being with the forces of Sir Jacob Astley (who was then joined with him) att the least eight thousand horse and foot; and (thorough the mistake or neglect of my adjutant-generall, and the slackness of my men, in drawing to the rendevous) I was not able to face him with two thousand. In that extremity the Lorde tooke opportunity to shew himself for me, by sending a mist all the morning, that by reason thereof the ennemy durst not give on'.

In his account to the Speaker, sent on Monday, 28 November, Waller wrote in more sober language:

Yesterday morning I had notice by my scouts, that the enemy showed himself in a party of about 300 horse upon the heath a mile and a half from me. Whereupon I sent out a party to visit them who entertained them with a warm skirmish for near two hours. In this time we discovered their whole body advancing. Whereupon I drew out that small stock I had into the Park under the favour of the Castle. Besides foot I had not above ten troops with me, the rest being quartered in villages more remote, where they can find provisions, came not up to me till towards evening. The enemy drew up in a full body before us upon the heath, as near as we could judge about 5,000 horse and foot, and after a while advanced into the Park to us with their foot and some horse within musket shot, but we gave them such entertainment with our pieces that they thought it their best course to retire to the heath again, where they made a stand, but were quickly driven from thence in disorder by our culverins, whereupon they all retreated. I sent some parties of horse and dragoons after them, who charged them in the rear and beat them off the down into the lane. We took some prisoners and killed some men and divers horses. If my horse had come up time enough I might have done good execution upon them. That night the enemy quitted Crundall and retired further off towards Hook. I have sent out parties after them to discover which way they move. The Kentish troops came last night hither from Guildford to quarter with me. There came with them likewise five companies of Sir Arthur Heselrig's regiment. But to allay this accession of strength I am now informed that the London Regiments resolve to be gone to-morrow or the next day at the furthest, but I hope they will not. I humbly desire there may be some course taken that they may stay, till some other strength come up to me, otherwise I am left at sixes and sevens, neither able to follow the enemy nor defend myself, and my old friend is so gallant an enemy, that he will quickly take his advantage (of) it to my destruction. I have received information that (his) Majesty is drawing this way. *Postscript.* — I am informed that Colonel Carr's soldiers, which were about 200, are turned out of their quarters and thereupon all disbanded and gone, to the great discontent of the officers who raised the men out of their means, and yet never received their full fortnight's pay. If they had received any help the Regiment might have been completed before this. I desire I may not be deprived of his service, for he is an honest man and a brave old soldier.

In his own description of the advance on Farnham Castle, Hopton first mentions a skirmish in which Colonel Jonas Vandruske, a Dutch officer in Waller's army, received a shoulder wound:

While these two Armyes lay at Odiam and Farnham, scarce a day passed without some action or other. Amongst the rest Van Drust a principale Commander of horse of Sir Wm. Waller's army, taking notice that Sir Edw. Stowell with his Regiment, and a troope, or two more, quartered at Sutton (a quarter very untenable and therefore the Lo : Hopton had given Sir Edw. Stowell an Officer of his owne with 30. dragoons, to helpe to strengthen it). The said Van Drust, with a strong party of horse and dragoones attempted that quarter about two howers before day, but he was at the entrance so well entertain'd by the dragoones, and so hansomly charg'd by Sir Edw. Stowell himselfe in the middest of that quarter, as he was broken, rowted, and chaced some miles homeward, having lefte behinde him 7. or 8. of his men dead in the quarter. Sir Edw. Stowell's major was there unfortunatly taken, els Vandrust carryed nothing away with him, but 2 pistoll-bulletts shott in his shoulder and divers of his men hurt. At Odiam Sir John Berkely came up to the Army with a reasonable good party of horse and dragoones, and about 1000 of his foote came up a day or two after him. So the Lo: Hopton being now growen to a competent strength, with the advice of his Councell of warr did resolve to draw out to Farnham to see the countenance of the Enemy;

And so . . . [on Tuesday, 28 November 1643] about an hower before day he drew out all his horse and foote, (saving reasonable guards which he left upon his quarters and upon the trayne (for he carryed but 2 smale pieces with him) and presented himselfe in battell upon the neerest part of the heath towards Farnham, and drew out 1000 Muskettiers and some partyes of horse to advance towards their quarters to draw them out. But Sir Wm. Waller, resolving not to hazard a battail, drew out his foote into the little Parke, close under the Castle, and kept his horse close, playing onely with his cannon out of the Castle, and resolving, as he did afterwards, very souldyer-like, to take his advantage upon our retreate. The Lo: Hopton, after some time perceiving that there was nothing counsellably to be done in that place retreated, advancing his foote, and his two little pieces to the ende of the Heath, there to make a stand towards Odiam upon the edge of the inclosures, and made his retreat, as orderly as he could, over the hill with his horses, his reare being all the way very smartly entertain'd by the Enemy; And so he retreated without disorder, or any considerable losse, back to his quarters.

Once back in Odiham Hopton and his chief officers reviewed their situation and decided that the time had come to break the army up into three brigades (or tertias) and quarter them in Alresford, Petersfield and Alton. He hoped also to capture Cowdray House, and thereby secure an open gateway into Sussex and Kent for the Spring campaign:

Where, upon consultation with his Officers, it appearing that those quarters grew bare, and that there was little good to be done upon the enemy, being so sheltered under the Castle of Farnham, he remov'd his own Tertio to Alsford, Sir Jo: Berkely with his horse, and foote to Petersfield, and left Sir Jacob Ashleys foote, and the Lo: Craford's horse and dragoones at Alton, intending speedely to remove them from thence to Midhurst, and Cowdrey-house, having by Sir E. Ford sent order to the Lo: Craford and Sir Jac. Ashley, and by another Officer to Sir Jo: Berkley, assoone as they should come to their quarters, to prepare eache of them a party of dragoones to meete at Cowdrey-house, and possesse themselves of it the next morning; But, by great misfortune the designe was discovered, and the Enemy putt men into Cowdrey-house that night; which fayler proved to be the beginning of the Lo: Hopton's misfortunes, for till that time, it had pleased God to blesse him from the beginning of the warr with reasonable good successe, without any considerable disaster. But, by this fayler, he was prevented in the most important part of his designe, which was, by fortifying the passe at Midhurst, to have had that winter a fayer entrance through Sussex into Kent, besides he had escaped the great misfortune that befell him afterwards at Alton.

Colonel Joseph Bamfield, a young Royalist officer who wrote his account many years later, gives us a slightly different version. Besides recording a division of the army into four (not three) parts, he mentions some doubts expressed at the council of war at the wisdom of the move:

> Towards the end of October, the King sent order to my Lord Berckely, to dispatch mee with my own Regiment, and what other troupers he could spare, with all expedition, to joyne with my Lord Hoptons Army, for the relief of Basing, then besieged by Sir William Waller. I was immediately sent away with a Brigade of Foot, consisting of his Lordships Sir William Courtenays (not he of Devonshire, but another of the same name) Sir John Acklands, Colonel Strangeways, and my own Regiment: with three troupes of Horse: I joyned my Lord Hoptons Army; Basing was relieved, Waller retired, incamped advantagiously under *Farnham* Castel; General Hopton followed him; presented him Battaile; the one would not dislodge, nor the other attacque him as he lay; the day following, a Councel of war was held, about the beginning of December, where it was resolved, that the Army should separate into four Brigades, and retire to Winter quarters, one with my Lord Hopten to Winchester, another under Sir Charles *Vavasour* to Alsford, a third commanded by Colonel Boles to Alton, the fourth with mee to Petersfield, the Horse were divided accordingly, a party with every Brigade of Foote, whereof I had with mee Sir Edward Stowels Regiment of Cavallery, Sir Edward Fords, Sir Edward Bishops, four Troupes of my Lord Bellasis his Regiment, commanded by his Major Bovel, with the three Troupes which came with mee out of Devonshire. One present at the Councel, declared his opinion, that it was dangerous to divide the Army into so many open quarters,

whilest Sir William Wallers remained in one entire Bodie, since he could in one night (as his custome was to march) force any of the neerest to him, before the others could be advertised, joine, and succour the quarter attacqued; this comming from a verry young man was neglected as of no moment, though the consequence, ten days after, made it appeare, as one of Cassandra's predictions, which though always true, were never believed, till accomplished, or past remedy.

Hopton still wanted to secure a firm foothold in Sussex if he possibly could, before settling into Winter quarters, and he sent Sir Edward Ford and Colonel Bamfield to capture Arundel Castle. According to Bamfield all went well:

> Four or five days after, my Lord Berkeley arrived at my quarter, from Oxford, bringing with him Sir William Butler his Regiment of Horse, with the Kings commands, to march incontinently towards Arundel, to take it if possible. I marched all tuesday with the Horse, and as many Musquetiers as I could mount, being favoured by a great mist, without any discovery, about four of the clock, wednesday morning, wee surprised, and forced the Towne; the greatest part of the Enemie retired into the Castel, which was rendered the Saturday following (when my foote came up) that the Souldiers should goe whither they would, leaving all Armes, and Ammunition . . .

Lord Hopton tells us that the taking of Arundel was not so easily accomplished as Colonel Bamfield would have us believe:

> His Army being thus drawen into severall quarters betweene Winchester, and the Enemy, and haveing yet, by his quarter at Petersfield, an entrance into Sussex, he consulted with Sir Jo: Berkley to send a considerable party of horse and foote to endeavour the surprize of Arundell Castle. Upon which Sir Edw. Ford, and Coll. Bampheild, were sent, and lodg'd in the Towne of Arundell. About that time Sir Jo: Berkly went himselfe to Oxford, and so returned into the West. And the party at Arundell dispayring to take the Castle, and apprehending theire owne danger in that place; writt to the Lo: Hopton to desire him to send a stronger party to fetch them off. Hee, being loath to quitt the hope of that place, took a suddaine resolution to draw a stronger party of horse and foot out of Petersfield, and marched with them himselfe by night to Arundell, where comeing in in the morning with shew of as much terror to the

Castle and new endeavours upon it as he could make, the Captaine delivered it up to him that day, and marched out with about 80 men, with reasonable conditions. So he putt Sir Edw. Ford (the then high sheriffe of that County) into the command of the Castle, and appointed Coll: Bampheild to command the whole quarter, with about 700 foote and three Regiments of horse besides some loose troopes.

The Cavaliers under Sir Edward Ford, Sir Edward Bishop and Bamfield achieved complete surprise in Arundel. Colonel Edward Apsley, a Sussex officer who lived at Warminghurst, midway between Arundel and Horsham, was awoken by the news at 5.00 a.m. on the morning of Thursday 7 December. As his foot company was garrisoning Cowdray House he resolved to flee to London or eastwards. Coming downstairs, however, he saw 'twenty or thirty men in my hall, standing with their arms as ready for service.' Stout fellows! He ordered a Captain Leighton to exercise the men. Rumours of an evening advance were contradicted, but after dinner that evening Apsley rode to Horsham and thence to Shoreham, riding all night. A rendezvous for all the local Sussex forces was arranged next day at Cobden Hill.*

Under the presidency of Colonel Herbert Morley, the officers who gathered there decided to blockade Arundel, but in the meantime Lord Hopton had come into that town with a much larger force. The Sussex Roundheads marched on Friday afternoon through the mist which eddied about the wooded hills and valleys, blown by sudden gusts of the strong wind. Lacking information, the column halted in the gathering darkness while an advance party went forward to find out if the bridge into the town still stood or if the Royalists had broken it down. As they could not return before the darkness thickened in the valley bottoms, the foot soldiers were sent to quarter for the night at Parham. Meanwhile, wrote Apsley:

> Colonel Morley and myself with some others rode out upon the hills to discover the country and to see what became of the party sent out. In our absence the horsemen unbitted their horses, and turned them into a load of hay which they had taken from the cows. In our return was one musket shot off, and some dags [wheel-lock pistols] that sparkled fire much

*Four miles east of Arundel. Known today as Harrow Hill.

like a match lighted with gun-powder. This was a party of the enemy upon our body, unsuspected by us. Colonel Morley was told it was not well to lie so openly; he said he would close them; one replied that they thought if he did but speak to them, it was enough. He rode towards them, and I rode softly upon the way, till meeting this party of the enemy coming up from our own body, out of any road, taking it to be a party of our own, for the mist fell thick that I could not discern my horse length. I rode to them; they said 'who are you?' I said, 'a friend;' they said, 'who are you for?' I replied, 'what! do you not know me?' and gave them the word, 'God with us.' They asked again, 'who are you for?' I returned the word again angrily, doubting that they might not know the word. With that, one of them caught hold of my horse, another of my sword, and asked me 'who I was for?' I said, 'for king and parliament;' and laying my hand upon my sword, they pulled and brake it. A third came up and caught hold of my rocket coat, and threw it over my head when divers with their drawn swords rode about me, pulling by my coat that was about my head. I told the properest man that I could spy (this man I understood to be called Mr. Montague) that I was his prisoner. He replied that none should wrong me, but before they would let go my horse caused me presently to alight. They took my coat and gloves, and told me they should search my pockets. I replied they should not need, for there was money for them, and so gave the silver that I had in that pocket, some to one, some to another, wherefore the one would not let the other rifle me; whereby I had the opportunity to convey away Sir William Waller's letters, and the Committee's, which I had then about me, and left a little money to myself.

Apsley soon secured his release, or escaped, because he received a commission to raise a regiment for Waller later in 1644. His interesting story, however, really conjures up the atmosphere of the English Civil War among the misty and snow-covered hills of Sussex during this phase of the campaign.

William Waller

Sources in order of first appearance:
Archer, *op.cit.*
Waller to Speaker Lenthall (23 November), H.M.C., *Portland MSS*, Vol. 1, pp. 159–60.
Waller's 'Experiences'. The 'Experiences' were compiled later in Waller's life for a religious purpose, probably for his family as meditations. Two versions of the 'Experiences' are extant. The earliest survives only in print as an appendix to *The Poems of Anna Matilda* (1788). The MS. was 'present in a family to which its editor is allied', but the name of the editor cannot be traced. The second version was an autograph fair copy in Wadham College Library, unhappily stolen in 1968. From internal evidence it was almost certainly intended for Waller's daughter, Margaret, who lived in Devon. The MS. first came to light in that county, for it is endorsed 'Rd. Warner 1726. The gift of Mr. J. Howard, who had it from Sir John Lear of Devon. R. T. Warner, 1765 of Woodford Row, Essex.' Both extracts in this chapter are from the Wadham MS., f. 28.
Bellum Civile.
Colonel Joseph Bamfield's Apologie, Written by himselfe and printed at his desire, (? The Hague 1685.)
Colonel Edward Apsley's account is quoted in C. Thomas-Stanford, *Sussex in the Great Civil War and the Interregnum, 1642–1660* (1910), pp. 76–7. The authorship of this account can be deduced from internal evidence. Edward Apsley, M.P. for Steyning, received a commission to raise a regiment of foot for Waller after Cheriton, but the Committee of Sussex objected to the financial burden.

Chapter Six

ALTON STORMED

AFTER THE CAPTURE of Arundel, Hopton also occupied Romsey, intending to use it as a base for operations against Southampton, but Colonel Richard Norton led a sally from that town and fell upon the two Royalist regiments in their new quarters. While Hopton was digesting these ill tidings, he heard news that made him fear for the safety of his men in Alton:

And so the Lo : Hopton retyr'd to Petersfield where having the dangerous quarter of Alton continnually in his care, he went thither the next day to visite it, and there to conferr with the E. of Craford, and Coll : Bolles. (Sir Jacob Ashley having some few days before desired leave to returne to Reading for awhile). There the Lo : Hopton, viewing the large extent and unsecurity of that quarter, left expresse order with the E. of Craford, and Coll : Bowles, to keepe as good guards and intelligence upon the Enemy as possibly they could, and that if ever he found that the Enemy moved out of Farnham with a body, they should presently quitt that quarter, and retreate to him. And so he returned to Alsford, and to Winchester. He had some few dayes before commanded Sir Humfry Benet with his Regiment of horse, and Sir Wm. Courtney with his Regiment of foote to possesse Rumsey, to the end they might be always in action against the garrison of Southampton ; But Sir H. Benet, being then high Sheriffe, and, by reason of his great services in that office, not able to attend his Regiment, and there falling out, in his absence, disorder and discontent, amongst his officers, which caused likewise disorder, disobedience, and carelesness in theire guards ; And Sir Wm. Courteney observing the inconvenyencies that were likely to grow by it, comeing over himselfe to Winchester to speake with Sir Humphry Benet about it, it happened, that Coll : Norton out of Hampton, fell suddenly upon that quarter in the absence of both the chiefe Officers, and beat it up, and, in effect, ruin'd both those Regiments.

The Lo : Hopton coming back from Sussex to Alsford the same night that this misfortune happened, and haveing early newes of it the next morning, went presently to Winchester to consider the best course to repayre it, and being there that night Sir Hum. Benet shewed him a letter, which he just then received from a friend, that advertized him out of the Enemye's quarters, that Sir Wm. Waller had gotten a recrewt of men from London, and some Leather-gunnes, which gave cause to suspect that he had some present designe that requir'd a nimble execution ; The Lo : Hopton presently suspected Alton, and forthwith writt, and dispatc'd a messenger on horse-back thither to the E. of Craford, with a letter wherein he sent him a transcript of that intelligence, and desir'd him instantly to send out scouts and partyes every way, and that, if he found but the least suspition, that the Enemy marched with a body, he should presently drawe off from those quarters, and retire to him, with all that he had with him. This letter the E. of Craford received before 11. of the clock, as he himself afterwards acknowlidged, and I am confident will allwaies acknowledge, and presently, as he was ordered, sent out partyes upon all the wayes towards Farnham ; But Sir Wm. Waller had verie politiquely, and souldier-like taken advantage of the woodines of that Country, and drawen his men, and his light leather-gunnes into the woods, and with pyoneers, made his way through them, without comeing into any of the high-waies ; And so, notwithstanding the advertizement and orders the Lo : Hopton had given, and all the dilligences of the officers upon those orders, Sir Wm. Waller was drawn out the next morning with his Ordinance, and all his forces into the next feild to Alton, before they had the least notice of his moveing, and at the same instant sent severall partyes of horse and dragoons to beate up theire horse quarters that were without, and fell upon theire foote with his horse and cannon.

Waller's army had remained for about a fortnight at Farnham, with the scouts out in the countryside watching the Cavaliers' movements. A lieutenant in his army, probably in the Green Auxiliaries, wrote to a friend in London :

PLATE 9
Alton Church and Churchyard

The west end of the church, showing the low wall around the churchyard used by the defenders

Photographed by Brian Boyd

PLATE 10

The pulpit in which Colonel Bolle was killed. In 1644 it stood in the centre of the church. Bullet marks, with the lead still in them, can be seen upon the inside walls of the church

The door of Alton Church. At the time of the fight it stood at the west end; the blocked-up doorway can b seen in Plate 9. A loophole for a musket and the scars pike thrusts still adorn this historic door.

Photographs by Bryan Boyd

> We are at Farnham, and look every day to give Battell to the Cavalliers, under Lord Hopton, the Lord Crafferd, and Sir Edward Dearing. As for Bazing House, it is absolutely the strongest place in England, and requires a Summers siege by report of some prisoners, we have taken a great number of their men, and divers gentlemen, and Ladies of great quality . . .
>
> The Green Regiment of Auxiliaries did so good service in the execution at Bazing house, though some others failed, that Sir William Waller hath since advanced Captaine Web to be a Sergeant Major, and his Lieutenant Master Everet who was valiant in the fight, is to be made a Captain, upon the next opportunity.

On Saturday, 2 December, the day Arundel Castle fell to the Royalists, Sir William himself travelled to London to request further supplies of men and money for his army, but news that the King had reached Basing House caused him to leave next day, Sunday, post haste for his command, not before dashing off a letter to the House of Commons :

> The necessityes of those poore men that are engaged with me in your service drewe me to the Towne to represent their condition to you, and to desire they may be (taken) in consideration of their future maintaining as part of my Lord Generall's army. But coming to wait upon his Excellency I received signification from him that his Ma^{ty} is come to Basing or expected there this night. Whereupon I thought it my duty to repair immediately to my charge. Since I cannot attend the house I must with all humbleness leave these lines to tell it, that those poor forces under my command may be so provided for, that they may have a subsistence to do you service. I shall likewise beg that Colonell Harleys regiment and all such companies as are att present raised may be completed and armed and dispatched forthwith to me with such other forces as may be added to them. As I was writing this I received advertisement from Farnham from Major Generall Pottly that his Ma^{ty} is come to Basing with two thousand horse and that there are more forces to follow him. I humbly leave the consequence of itt to your judgement and rest your most humble servant, William Waller.

Once back in Farnham Waller learnt that the King had only briefly visited Basing House and then returned to Oxford. As new recruits began to arrive, especially Sir William Springate's

Kentish Regiment of Whitecoats, Waller's thoughts turned towards Alton. But before he could beat up that Royalist quarter he had to persuade the London regiments to stay with him. As an opening move, and as a warning against desertion, a turncoat Londoner was publicly executed in Farnham:

Sabbath day *Decemb. 3.* Newes was brought that *Arundell Castle* was lost, and divers reports were given out that our whole Army should march thither to redeeme it againe, which report bred some discontent in our London Forces (who then every day expected to be discharged from the service, in respect of our severall occasions constrayning us homewards, and the time being so long expired, which was prefixed for our returne) this weeke we had very little disturbance, for there was almost every day a Councell of Warre.

Wednesday Decemb. 6. Bartholomew Ellicot sometimes a Butcher neere *Temple Barre*, once a Captaine in the Parliament service, and lately in the Kings Army, who was the weeke before taken prisoner, was hanged in the market place at *Farnham*, for running away from the Lord Generalls Army, and carrying divers summes of mony with him, which should have paid souldiers, and endeavouring to betray the Towne of *Ailesbury*. He died in a miserable condition, justifiing himselfe in the Acts, and condemning the councell of Warre, which found him worthy of death, stoutly affirming that there is no popish Army protected by the King, with divers such like expressions, which for brevity I omit.

This weeke (but what day I doe not well remember) there came to us from his Excellency the Earle of *Essex* 5 Companies of a White Regiment of Foote, which were raised in *Kent*.

Saturday Decemb. 9. Most of our Forces were drawn into the parke in the Evening, and that night a party went out towards *Alton*, and having given them an Alarme and beat up the Enemies quarters they returned.

Tuesday Decemb. 12. In the morning most of our Forces were againe drawne into the parke, where our men were mustered, and we remained all day, expecting to be discharged and march homewards on the morrow, and about an houre and halfe before night, Sir William came into the Parke to us, and at the head of every Regiment of our London Brigade, he gave us many thanks for our service past, and told us that according to his promise and our expectation we were to be discharged, & march homewards on the morrow, and said he would not detaine us (if we were so bent homewards that we would stay no longer) but withall he told us that yet we could not returne with much honours in respect of the bad success we had in our chiefest service, certifiing us withall, that at the present there was an opportunity which might much availe the States, and bring honour both to God & our selves, if we would but lend him our asistance til the Monday following, engaging himselfe upon his honour and credit, that we should not longer be detained, which we considering gave our full consent to stay, for which he gave us many thanks, in a very joyfull expression advising us presently to prepare for the service because delaies are dangerous. Whereupon most of our men went presently into the Towne to refresh and prepare themselves for the service (where although they before gave their general consent) many of them stayed behinde and went not with their Colours. Neverthelesse we advanced without them and marched all that night, pretending at the first setting forth to goe towards *Basing*; but having marcht that way about two miles, we returned to the left, and (in a remote way between the wood, and hills) marched beyond *Alton*, and about 9 a clock on Wednesday morning, *Decemb. 13,* Came upon the *West* side of the Towne, where we had both the winde and hill to friend.

Waller's night march, no easy feat with such soldiers as the London regiments, achieved for him almost complete surprise. One or two Royalist guards, however, slipped back to arouse the town. The Earl of Crawford's Regiment of horse saddled up and galloped out towards Winchester, only to find their way blocked by Waller's cavalry, as an anonymous Roundhead eyewitness in the Westminster Regiment reports:

Tuesday the Twelfth of this instant Decemb. Sir *William Waller* in the afternoon, drew forth his Forces into a Battalia in Farnham-Park, about the number of Five thousand horse and Foot, amongst which were the Regiment of Westminster, whose behaviour and valour in this service, is never to be forgotten: The manner of the businesse was exceeding well carryed, both by Sir *William* and all the rest, for strictnesse of appearance, and likewise for secrecie, that the Enemy, nor no Malignant party, could have opportunity to understand the least of their intentions: They were upon their march by seven of the clock in the night, and in an hours march obtained a Heath between Brundon and Farnham; and there after an hours stay for the Foot, whose march were not so quick as the horse, they all willingly and cheerfully marcht together, till neer one of the clock in the night, in the way towards Basing; but on a sudden were appointed to face towards the South, and so towards Alton, passing exactly between the hills, till they obtained within half a mile of the said Town, altogether undiscovered by the Enemy; our Scouts being so diligent, that not a person stirring in those passages was left at liberty, to have any opportunity to inform the Enemy of our proceedings; and being now in sight of the Town, about nine of the clock in the morning, we understood by the taking of which Scouts, some of them escaping gave opportunity for the said Lord to shift for himself, who conceived himself and all the rest of his Forces lost; yet he speedily drew forth about three hundred of his horse Eastward, towards Winchester rode, where, unexpectedly, hee met with some of our horse, and retreated back again into the Town, and fled Southward; our horse perceiving that, pursued them, whilst our Foot made the woods ring with a shout: There were three or four of them slain in their flight, and being in narrow Lanes after halfe a miles pursuit, our men retreated againe, having taken about Thirty Horse, and some Prisoners; In the meane whiles the Foot were not idle, nor Sir *William*, whose rare exploits in this service may be Registred with the rest of his valiant and Honourable Actions. The horse were immediately appointed to make good all passages, so that the Enemy could not have the benefit of their accustomed running away, but were taken by our horse, our foot in the meane time behaving themselves like men...

Like men indeed! The first outburst of fighting broke out to the north and north-west of Alton church, as Lieutenant Archer recalls:

Then Sir *Williams* own Regiment of Foote, Sir *Arthur Haslerigs* five companies, and five companies of Kentishmen went on upon the *North*, and *North West* side and gave the first onset by linying of hedges and the like, but could not (as yet) come to any perfect execution, in respect that our London Regiments were not come in sight of the Enemy, and therefore they bent all their force against those three Regiments, and lined divers houses with musqueteers, especially one great brick house neere the Church was full, out of which windows they fired very fast, and might have done great prejudice to those men, but that when our Traine of Artillery came towards the foote of the hill, they made certaine shot which took place upon that house and so forced them to forsake it, in the meane time our London Regiments and foure Companies which belong to *Farnham Castle* came downe the hill . . .

Lieutenant-Colonel John Birch, at the head of Heselrige's five companies of foot, engaged himself at this point. Already, according to his secretary's somewhat over-laudatory memoir of Birch's military career, he had distinguished himself in the approach march:

> Presently upon this your great hazard in lyeing at Crundale twoo miles from Farnum, the enemy at Alton, their head quarters, but 4 miles of, and Sir William Wallers head quarters at Farnum; which though your quarters was hazardos, yett God there made you the instrument for the sending out spies and discovering their fortification soe well, that though you were never at Alton, yet when you had made all ready, you did aswell know where there trench was deepe and wheare shallowe, and where to enter, as if yourselfe had ordered the worke. Nay, let mee never forget, and I hope you never will, that deliverance God gave you on the hills short of the towne that morneing goeing out; where 6 of those enimies scouts, though they had you amongst them, were not able to carry you prisoner to the towne, but, contrarywise, suffered you to bring the comander of them away prisoner back to our owne army, haveing but the helpe of twoo more, God giveing you that as an earnest of that great mercy he gave you a few houres after; where hee made you the leader; first to enter that towne, then the church-yard, where a man would have assuredly thought, must have been your burieing place.

Birch's biographer makes no mention of the London Brigade, who by this time had cleared the Royalists from some earthworks on the west side of the town, and were marching up the main street to take the enemy about the church in their rear:

> Then the Red Regiment and the Greene-coats, (which Greene-coats are the four Companies of *Farnham Castle*) set upon a halfe moone and a brest-worke, which the Enemy had managed, and from whence they fired very hot and desperately till the Greene Auxiliaries marched on the other side of a little river into the Towne with their Collours flying and (being in the wind of the enemy, fired a little thatcht house and so blinded them, that this Regiment marched forwards

and comming in part behinde the works, fired upon them, so that they were forced to forsake the said halfe moone and brest-work, which they had no sooner left but presently the Green-coats and part of the musquetiers of the Red, and our Yellow Regiment entred while the rest of our Regiment marched into the Towne with their Colours flying.

Hemmed in from north and south Colonel Richard Bolle ordered first a withdrawal into the churchyard and then into the church itself, where this gallant officer laid down his life rather than surrender his sword. Elias Archer describes the successful storming of the church:

Now was the Enemy constrained to betake himselfe and all his forces to the Church, Churchyard, and one great worke on the *North* side of the Church; all which they kept nere upon two houres very stoutly and (having made scaffolds in the Church to fire out at the windowes) fired very thick from every place till divers souldiers of our Regiment and the Red Regiment, who were gotten into the Towne, fired very thick upon the *South-east* of the Churchyard, and so forced them to forsake that part of the wall, leaving their musquets standing upright, the muzzels whereof appeared above the wall as if some of the men had still lyn there in Ambush) and our men seeing no-body appeare to use those Musquets, concluded that the men were gone, and consulted among themselves to enter two or three files of Musquetiers, promising *Richard Guy*, one of my Captaines Serjeants (who was the first man that entred the Church-yard) to follow him if he would lead them: whereupon he advanced, and comming within the Church-yard doore, and seeing most of the Cavaliers firing at our men, from the South and West part of the Church-yard, looked behind him for the men which promised to follow him, and there was only one Musquetier with him. Neverthelesse he flourishing his Sword, told them if they would come, the Church-yard was our owne; then *Symon Hutchinson*, one of Lieutenant Colonell *Willoughbies* Serjeants, forced the Musqueteers, and brought them up himselfe. Immediately upon this, one of the Serjeants of the Red Regiment (whose name I know not, and therefore cannot nominate him as his worth deserves) brought in another division of Musqueteers, who together with those which were there before, caused the Enemies Forces to betake themselves towards the Church for safeguard, but our men followed them so close with their Halberts, Swords, and

Musquet-stocks that they drove them beyond the Church doore, and slew about 10. or 12. of them, and forced the rest to a very distracted retreat, which when the others saw who were in the great worke on the North side of the Church-yard, they left the worke and came thinking to helpe their fellows, and comming in a disorderly manner to the South-west corner of the Church, with their Pikes in the Reare, (who furiously charged on, in as disorderly a manner as the rest led them) their front was forced backe upon their owne Pikes, which hurt and wounded many of the men, and brake the pikes in peeces. By this time the Church-yard was full of our men, laying about them stoutly, with Halberts, Swords, and Musquet-stocks, while some threw hand-granadoes in the Church windowes, others attempting to enter the Church being led on by Sergeant Major *Shambrooke*, (a man whose worth and valour Envy cannot staine) who in the entrance received a shot in the thigh (whereof he is very ill) Neverthe-lesse our men vigorously entred, and slew Colonell *Bowles* their chiefe Commander at the present, who not long before swore, *God damne his Soule* if he did not run his Sword through the heart of him, which first called for quarter.

He being slaine, they generally yeelded and desired quarter, except some desperate Villaines which refused quarter, who were slaine in the Church, and some others of them wounded, who afterwards were granted quarter upon their request.

Lieutenant-Colonel Birch's actions, at least according to his own secretary, were no less dramatic, and it is not surprising that he was reported as the first Parliamentarian into the church:

Nay, at the entering of that church, dreadful to see, the enemy oppening the doore when ready to receve you with their pikes and muskets, the horses slaine in the allies, of which the enimy made brestworks, the churchyard as well as the church being covered with dead and wounded, amongst whom you long strugled, witnesseth the Lord's wonderfull protection: from which dayes service you es-caped with a few dry blowes with the musket stockes of those whoe afterwards, soe many as were liveing and able, were caried prisoners to Farnum; the choicest men, for soe many, that were taken since the beginning of theis warrs.

Waller's army had taken 875 prisoners, including 50 officers, and a number of colours, while losing less than ten of their own men. After burying the Royalist dead, about 40 bodies, in a grave on the north side of the Church, Waller's soldiers made ready to leave Alton, as the anonymous Westminster Regiment soldier relates :

> The mighty providence of God was seene in this, and as in many other mercies towards us: for in this Fight for a certaine truth, there were not above five of our men slaine, and about six wounded, and about six scorched with powder, by reason of their owne negligence: This done, our worthy Major Generall caused the people of the said Towne to slight the Workes: tooke the Prisoners, and tied them two by two with Match, and are now in Farnham Church and Castle, where they may heare better Doctrine then they have heard at Oxford, or amongst the Irish Rebels.
>
> One thing observable is, our worthy Sir William sent in a loving Complement to the Lord Craford half a Hogshead of Sack, who mistrusting the matter and the Messenger, caused the Messenger and divers others, to taste thereof, and then caused it to be carefully laid up for his own drinking; but by reason of this unexpected company, was struck with a Pannick fear, left the Wine without a Complement, for Sir William Wallers own disposall, who was the right owner thereof, whose Souldiers wanted no Tasters of the same.

The Earl of Crawford, who had apparently offered earlier to exchange with Waller some beef and mutton for a barrel of good wine, had lost not only his wine but also his cloak and gloves. He scribbled the following note to Waller :

> I hope your gaining of Alton cost you dear. It was your lot to drinke of your own sack, which I never intended to have left for you: I pray you favour me so much as to send me my owne Chirurgion and upon my honour I will send you a person suitable to his exchange: Sir your servant Craford.

Hopton also wrote to his old friend Sir William, seeking for the body of Colonel Richard Bolle :

> This is the first evident ill successe I have had: I must acknowledge that I have lost many brave and gallant men; I desire you, if Colonell Boles be alive, to propound a fit exchange; if dead, that you will send me his corps: I pray you send me a list of such prisoners as you have that such choice men as they are may not continue long unredeemed: God give a sudden stop to this issue of English blood which is the desire, sir, of your faithful friend to serve you.

Waller evidently granted the sombre request for Colonel Richard Bolle lies buried in Winchester Cathedral, his epitaph inscribed on two brass plates, one on a pillar in the Cathedral and one near the centre of Alton Church. It concludes thus:

>His Gratious Soueraigne, hearing of his death, gave him his high Commendation in ys [this] pationate expression:
>Bring me a Moorning Scarffe, I have Lost one of the best Commanders in this Kingdome.
>Alton will tell you of that famous Fight
>Which ys man made, and bade this World good night.
>His Vertious Life fear'd not Mortality,
>His Body must, his Vertues cannot die,
>Because his Bloud was there so nobly spent,
>This is his Tombe; that Church his monument.

Sources in order of first appearance:
Bellum Civile.
Roundhead lieutenant's letter. From *Remarkable Passages*, TT: E. 77 (3). Printed on 25 November 1643.
Waller to the Speaker, 3 December (at Bedford House), Bodl., Tanner MS. 62, f. 410.
Archer, *op. cit.*
Westminster Regiment soldier's account. From *A Narration of the great Victory obtained by the Parliament's forces under Sir William Waller at Alton, 13 Dec.*, TT: E. 78 (22).
Military Memoir of Colonel John Birch, ... Written by Roe, his secretary ..., ed. J. Webb, Camden Society, N.S., Vol. 7, (1873). Roe is variously described as captain, quartermaster and secretary, but he was probably the last. Nothing else is known about him. For notes on Birch, see p. 184.
Letters of Crawford and Hopton, in Godwin, *op. cit.*, p. 148.

Chapter Seven

ARUNDEL TAKEN

AFTER ROMSEY AND ALTON, Hopton realized that Waller's thoughts would turn next to Arundel. Advising Colonel Bamfield of this fact, Hopton commanded him to send back the three regiments of horse in Arundel, except for one or two troops. Bamfield, however, disobeyed and returned only two of the three regiments with a request for more gunpowder, of which he received a good supply.

Colonel Bamfield had been campaigning in Sussex when Hopton's orders reached him:

> Having in three or four days, given the necessary orders, touching the defence of the Town and Castel; I left Sir Edward Ford there, with 400. Foote, marching all night with the rest (at the instances of Sir William Butler, whom his Majestie had made Sherif of Kent) hoping to have taken Bramber Castel, but were prevented by Colonel Morley, and Sir Michael Livesie, who had possessed themselves of the place and passage over the River, with about 2000. Men, out of Kent, whilest I was seeking another forde, where I might pass the River with more convenience then in the face of the Enemy; my Lord Hopton by an Express, sent mee advertisement, that the General Waller (as was foreseen, and foretold) marching all the night from Farnham, to Alton, had forced that quarter, about breake of day, killed Colonel Boles who commanded the Brigade, and all the soldjers either cut of, or taken prisonners, and totaly dissipated the Earl of Crawfords Brigade of horse, which misfortune had soe weakned his Army, that he could not hinder the enemies progress, which he was persuaded would be for the recovery of Arundel, before it could be provided of all things,

necessary for its defence; which he recommended to mee with great earnestness, desiring mee to keep what forces I thought needful for the place, and to send back Sir William Butler, with the rest, to join his Army; assuring mee, that if I were besieged, he would relieve mee in eight days; expecting suddainely forces from Oxford.

I retain'd neer 800 Foote, with the four Companies of my Lord Bellasis Regiment of Horse, and my own Troupe; sending back all I could, under the Command of Sir William Butler; in less then four and twenty howers after, General Wallers Army appeared before the Town, which I resolved to defend, as long as I could; and in case of necessitie to retire to the Castel.

Waller had set out from Farnham on Sunday, 17 December, and marching by way of Haslemere and Midhurst, came to Arundel Park on Tuesday night. The London regiments had already left for home, but a Kentish brigade, almost 1000 horse, foot and dragoons under Sir Henry Heyman, were marching to join him. Moreover, about 500 Royalists captured at Alton had taken the Covenant and recruited Waller's regiments.

Arundel Castle and town stand upon a spur of the Sussex downs. The River Arun at the foot of the southern slopes and Swanbourne pond under the steep eastern side protected the south and east flanks, while the town itself clustered on the western half of the down, girded by a medieval wall. A deep ditch and earthwork crossed the open back of the down, immediately to the north of the castle and town, dividing the fortified area from Arundel Park, where Waller's army camped on Tuesday night.

Waller's assault on the town began next morning with a three-pronged infantry attack on the earthwork, defended by Bamfield's foot and horse. Doubtless needing little prompting, Lieutenant-Colonel Birch's secretary reminded his master of his forwardness in this service, which ended with a serious wound in the stomach. There is more than a hint in his account that the veteran Scots officer Andrew Potley, who now served Waller as Major-General of the Foot, wanted to rid the army of this ardent Puritan officer John Birch, the first sign of a rift in the Parliamentarian army between the Scots and those who looked to Heselrige for a political and religious lead:

And long you rested not, after this story [Alton], before

your generall Sir William Waller attempted further, which was his march towards Arundell, begun from Farnham the fourteenth day of December, 1643; which was prosecuted with such speed that the 16 day at night followeing the head quarters was in Arundell parke, where your lodgeing with many others was under the best-spred trees. In the morneing at the breaking of the day the enimy and some partie of ours begun to skirmish, which continued untill about eight of the clocke, at which time Major Generall Potley comanded your selfe with about 1400 men to storme the enemis rampier, within which thear army was drawne up; which was conceived, by more then my selfe, hee did on purpose to have you cutt off, for your being too active a few dayes before at Alton, there being double the number of infantry of the enemy, besides a great body of horse, to those you stormed with, and noe horse of o(u)rs could get order to assist you. But God ordered it otherwise by his owne Finger, though it cost you good store of your blood. I question not but that deliverance you will remember, yet give mee leave to present to you what I remember to helpe your memory loaden with sundry things at the same instant.

And to my best remembrance that the falling on was thus: (vizt.) Sir William Wallers Leiftennant-Collonel was marching up the narrow lane, with about three hundred musketeers; which your selfe perceaveing, and being nere ready your selfe to fall on, not likeing his rash attempt, you unhorsed the London scoute master whoe at that instant stood by where you were drawing the men into divisions, and speedily ridd that horse to the van of that partie of foot, and turned again the lieftennent-collonel and his partie, and drew them into the hollowe of the lane out of the enimies shott, which tooke place on 7 or 8 of that partie, as you weare spekinge, before they could bee secured, which retreat caused a great shout from the enimy, not fearinge your comeing on againe. About a quarter of an hower after this, you were ready with your men in 3 divisions; on the left-hand marched the aforesaid lieftennant collonel with about 200 musceteers; on the right hand your owne Maior Cotsforth and twoe hundred muscateeres; in the body your selfe 40 paces backe, with the rest, pikes and muskets.

Thus marching on, the enemy letting fly very thicke, you not likeing your maior's pace whoe was marching before you on the right hand, but indeed more softly then you used to doe in such a shoure, you comanded the captens where you were to come on speedily, and you ran up to the maior's partie then about 40 paces short of the enimy's line; where they being almost at a stand your example drew them on instantly to enter that line, unto which your selfe first entred, though it was intricate to gett over that steep line; but one assisting another, instantly there was neere 200 entred; in which instant of time, before the rest could enter, (and the great Fishpond being betweene our army and the place where you entred, soe that the enimy sawe you could not quickly bee releived) out came they with about 100 gentlemen reformadoes on horseback besides foot and other troups of horse, and gave your disordered foote at that very instant of entry such a charge, that they layd many flat to the ground, as well as yourselfe.

The rest went backe over the line with greet speed; and I think I may say truly not one man stayd within the line, except those that were slaine, wounded, or prisoners, but your selfe; whoe leaning on the line with one hand, and your halbard in the other, the enimies horse could not fall upon you but to their great loss, bestowing some few pistolls on you; but God would not have you then hitt; and indeed you had never escaped soe, had it not been for those musketeers, who lieing neare you on the topp of the line kept of the horse at present, and made some few to fall; soe that they were forced to drawe further of, and there stand: in which place neither could they indeed long continue; for the rest of the musketeers followeing the example of those by you, got on top of the line and from thence firred soe hott on the enimies horse, that they were gladd to withdrawe.

Thus God gave you possession of the enimies ground the second time: which efected, your great care was to make way for some honest captaines of horse and their traine, which voluntarily came up to your assistance: which being done, imediatly whilest you were putting those horse and foote in order, whose number were both about eighteen hundred, the enimy looked upon them contemptably; and there upon drew forth to fall on you neere the towne walle, where you were between the enimies twoe lines. And their horse and foot doeing their utmost, at this instant was that gallant Scott slaine, whoe had vowed that day, afore hee went on, that hee would never flee further from you then the length of your halberd, saying hee would sticke to you whilest you lived, but hee would be neer to the intent hee might examine your pockets when you fell; which God called him unto first.

At this instant, the enemy spending their shot at too great a distance, your order was to horse and foote instantly to assault the enemy; your selfe with cherefull speech assuring they would not stand, which proved accordinglie. For the enimy feeling the force of the shott poured on them with three ranks at a time after short time gave grond, and, your selfe entred the towne with them, scarce knoweing freind from foe; the enimy as much as they could betakeing themselves to the castle; into which place your comand was to enter with them. At which instant Sir William Wallers Leiftennant Collonel, whoe but then you incouraged by clapping your hand on his shoulder, your hand noe sooner of but hee was shott dead; and your selfe not gone aboue 20 paces further received that wonder of God's mercy, the shott in your belly, which deliverance to you was soe great that I cannot speake of it without admiration; and the more at the hand of God soe assisting, that though you kept in your gutts, stoping the hole with your finger, yet none knew it untill you had slaine or taken prisoners the enimy then about you, and orderd your men to drawe into a body on one side the street, where the shott had not such power: and then pretending you must turne to the wall, giveing a capten by you private notice, you went towards the Parke house, as if noe such shott had been, untill your spirritts yeilded and your selfe sunke, and were then caried to the lodghouse aforesaid with life in you, but suposed by all to bee past cure, this being about 9 in the morneing; when you weare laid with many others on the floore, groveling, and to the chirurgeons not soe much probabilitie of life apeared as to bestow a dressing.

Thus you laye untill about 6 at night; at which time being as you were in the morneing, the chirurgeons thought to adventure a dressing, and to bestowe soe much paines as to carry you up unto a bed. Thus have I presented you with Gods great worke, much of it carryed on by your hand that day, and the great mercy in your deliverance, which I hope will never bee worne out of your minde. I beseech you, remember the 17 day of December 1643. That castle in a few dayes after being yeilded, therein was found twelve hundred men, besides those that were slaine, fled and taken prisoners at the entry of the towne: which number I the rather mention, to make more plainly appear God's hand, that these should bee driven into the castle by so smale a nomber.

Colonel Bamfield, in his account of the storming, understandably stressed the weakness of the fortifications:

It was assaulted in three places, and no fortifications, but the ruines of an old wal, and without it (at some distance) a more ancient Line, and Ditch; but without Flanque; where I judged they might be most useful, I placed Major Bovel with his horse; and perceiving not far from mee, that a considerable bodie of the enemies Foot had passed the Line, with eight or ten blew Collours, which were of Sir Arthur Haselrigs Regiment, commanded by Colonel Birch (who I think still lives) and began to range themselves in order; I desired Major Bovel to charge them with me, for if we brake them not, the Castle might be lost as well as the town; we charg'd, routed, and drove them back over the Line; Colonel Birch was (as I remember) wounded in the bellie, and one Captaine Bedel casting himself amongst the dead bodies (as if kill'd) was discover'd and taken prisoner; my horse was shot with a musket-bullet in the hip, and fell with mee; I had (aparently) been killed, unless rescued by some Officers of my Lord Bellasis Regiment. Another post where Major Fletcher commanded, was forced; he dangerously wounded, and taken prisoner; with great difficulty wee retired into the Castel, where the Enemie thought to have entered with us, but was repulsed.

The town fell on Wednesday, 20 December, and the following day Waller sent to the House of Lords an account of his proceedings and the military situation as he saw it:

According to your Command, I advanced the last Lordsday from *Farnham*, towards this Place; I could not reach that Night past *Haselmere*: The next Day I marched to *Cowdrey*, where we understanding there were Four Troops of Horse and One Hundred Foot, I resolved to give them the good Night; and to that End I dispatched away Two Regiments of Horse, to lay the Passages round; but they were too nimble for me, and escaped hither, where I overtook them on *Tuesday* Night: The next Morning, after we had taken a View, and found out a Place where we might flank their Line with our Ordnance, we fell on upon the North Side of the Works, which we did so scour a weedy Hill in the Park on the West Side of the Pond with our Pieces, that we made them too hot for them; which gave such Courage to our Men, that with the same Breath they assaulted a Retrenchment which they had newly cast up, and which was very strong; it was drawn from the Town Gate, down to the aforesaid Pond near the Mill; at the same Time we fell on upon a narrow Passage by the Mill, where they had likewise a

Double Work, and very strong: In a short Time, by the good Hand of God, we forced both, and entered the Town with our Horse and Foot, notwithstanding a brave Sally made by their Horse; we beat them into the Castle, and entered the First Gate with them; the Second they made good, and barricadoed; and there they are Welcome. I am resolved to block them up; for I know they are in a necessitous Condition. GOD hath been pleased to bless me hitherto with a gracious Success; His great and holy Name be praised for it. But truly, my Lords, I am very weak in Foot, and my Horse so hacknied out that they are ready to lie down under us. I expect Colonel *Beere** here this Day, and Colonel *Morley*.

Likewise the Kentish foote are not come upp, and I expect them not these two dayes. The last night I receaved an advertisement from Winchester that Prince Rupert was expected that night theare, and there were 120 cartes sent out for his trayne and baggage. All the country there is sumoned to come up in their armes. My neighboures of Pettersfeild, when they quitted that quarter, uppon the allarum at Alton, left many of their armes behind them, which on Tuesday were fetched to Portsmouth. If I had had some fresh horse, I might easily have cutt off ten or twelve troopes of the enemie's horse that are quartered betwixt this and Braintree, but being soe weary and in soe weake a condition I am forced to keepe home for a whyle, and to watch the nine that are in the castle. I summoned them, but they refused either to give or take quarter, soe confident they are of succors; my trust is in God.

P.S.—I humbly desire my commission may bee forthwith sent downe, for without it I shall not bee able to settle their countyes.

Waller settled down to blockade the castle, realizing that Bamfield had too many mouths — soldiers, civilians and horses — to feed. Like most blockades the siege is the story of small incidents, which a London eyewitness chronicles:

The same day [21 December] Colonell *Morley* came thither with a Regiment of Kentish Forces; and Major *Bodley* did a notable Exploit; he perceaving divers in the Castle looke forth in a Balcone, tooke unto himself and 12. others, their musquets, unto a private place of advantage, from whence they altogether discharged into the said Balcone, and slew and wounded divers of the Enemy; The

*Commissary-General Hans Behre of Essex's army

PLATE 11

Arundel Town and Castle

Wenceslaus Hollar

Waller attacked from the other side of the town (see Plate 29)

British Museum

PLATE 12
Sir William Waller W. Riddiard

same night 2. Sacres were planted in the Steeple, with divers musquetiers, who on Friday morning betimes played hotly on the enemy, which appeared on the top of the Castle; the same day divers were taken in their intended escape from the castle; Also, Sir *Miles* [*sic*] *Livesey* brought a Regiment of Horse, and Sir *William Springate* a Regiment of Foot from Kent, to the aide of Sir *William* : also the same day, the course of a Pond was turned, and more fully perfected on Saturday, the draining whereof emptied the Wels of water within the castle, so that now the Enemy began to be distressed with thirst; the same day divers of them fled from the castle, and were taken prisoners; whereupon a stronger Guard was kept about the said castle.

On Sonday divers more fled from the castle, and many horses were turned forth of which our Souldiers made a good purchase, onely one of them was shot by the Enemy, whose bloody cruelty and inhumane malice did mightily appear against us, in that they took him, and hewed him all to peeces; which doubtless they would have done to every one of us, had we been likewise in their power. The same day Colonell *Hads*, and Colonell *Dixie*, approached towards us with two Regiments out of Kent, for the further aid of Sir *William Waller*; and also divers Regiments out of Sussex: On Munday the 25. of December the enemy make shew of a salley, and about 30. of them appeared unto us from the Castle yard, whereupon the Drums did beat, and the Trumpets sound, and all our men were presently gathered together, in a fit posture to charge the Enemy, who presently took themselves to their heels, as the best remedy to prevent danger, and so manfully retreated.

On Tuesday we planted Ordnance in a new place against the Castle, which made the Enemy that they durst not peep over the walls to shoot at us as thay had wont to do. On Wednesday, divers of the Enemies having forgot the former danger, came forth into the Belcone again, whereupon we placed divers Musquetiers in the ruines of an old Chappel, from whence we did good execution upon them; the same day Sir *Ralph Hopton* came to Petersfield, and quartered his Forces thereabouts, and some of the Enemies fled out of the Castle, and escaped by the River, in a boat made of raw Oxe hide. On Thursday more of the Enemies were taken escaping out of the Castle, and that afternoon, the Enemy hung out a white flag, pretending a parley, and calling to some of our men, delivered them Letters directed to our Generall, and

Colonell *Marlow* [Morley] in which they desired, Tobacco, Sack, Cards and Dice, to be sent unto them to make merry this idle time, promising to return us for them, beef and mutton; but the truth is, they wanted bread and water, and that night did put divers live Oxen over the walls of the Castle, for want of fodder; the same day, a party of his Excellencies horse incountred with a party of Sir *Ralph Hoptons* Horse neer Petersfield, and took prisoners, two Quarter-masters one Sergeant, and two common Souldiers. On Friday *Hoptons* army moved towards us, as far as Mardin [Marden] and Wesdin [West Dean], and we brought our Ammunition that was at Midhurst, to Arundel. On Saturday morning divers fled forth of the castle unto us, amongst whom was one Sergeant, who signified the great want of provision, having nothing but powdred beef, and a few lives beeves left them. The most materiall passages untill Thursday following, was the Enemies treating with too haughty requests for men in their Condition, and the daily running away of the Enemy from the Castle unto us; notwithstanding Sir *William* had made it death by Proclamation to those that came forth.

The Royalist move towards Arundel and the reasons for abandoning it are described by Hopton. Despite his plausible writing there is little doubt that he made a serious mistake by concentrating on Warblington House instead of harrying Waller's army, as he himself comes close to admitting:

Upon the Enemye's comeing before Arundell, the Lo: Hopton sent againe to Oxford to desire a supply of foote; whereby he might be enabled for the releife of Arundell; But instead thereof the Lo: Wilmot was sent unto him with a thousand of the King's horse, which, although it was a gallant body, yet was it not proper for that service; But the Lo: Hopton, having receaved notice out of Arundell-Castle, that, by reason of the forementioned accidents, bread, and water began to grow short with them, resolved to advance with what he had, which was a verie gallant body of above 2000 horse, but not above 1200 foote. With these he adventur'd, and marched to West Dean, within 5 miles of Arundell, (3 dayes marche from Winchester.) And the next morning early drew out towards Arundell, with this hope (and scarce any other) that Sir Wm. Waller might be tempted to draw out from his quarters with his horse, and such other part of his army as he could spare from the block of the Castle towards him. But that morning being advanced within three miles of Arundell, Capt. Cox adventured to come out of the Castell to the Lo: Hopton, who thereupon called a Councell of warr of the cheife Officers, to whom this Captaine gave an accompt of the state of that place, which was, that the Commanders had sent him to lett the Lo: Hopton know, that they were all very well resolved, and that they had mad(e) a computation of theire provisions, and found they should have noe want for 14 dayes. The Lo: Hopton asked him if he had seene theire stores, espetially theire wheate, to which the Captaine answered that he had the day before seene a heape of wheate in a roome, which as he described was computed not to be lesse than 40. quarters. Hereupon, with the advice of the Councell of warr, the Lo: Hopton resolved to drawe back to Westbourne, and the parts thereabout, upon designe, first, to refreshe the Army in those good quarters (The King's horse that came with the Lo: Wilmot being not very patient of the hard quarter of the hill-countrey of Sussex). In the second place to make use of those 14. dayes, by all possible wayes to recrewte his foote, and to give time to Coll. Mynn, with two Regiments of foote that came out of Ireland, and were then in Gloucestershire, to come up unto him for that service, according to His Majestie's orders which he had dispatch'd to them, And that in the meane time they might not seeme to lye altogether idle in theire quarters, the Lo: Hopton did upon his retreate, send with his Quartermasters over and above theire ordinarie guards, all his dragoones before, to invest Warblington-house, which, being possest by the Enemy had done much hurt in those quarters; And the Lo: Hopton was resolved to take this opportunity to gett it.

This party advancing according to orders, gott intelligence, about two miles before they came to Westbourne, that Coll: Norton (the Governour of Hampton) was then with a strong party of horse passed through Westbourne, it seem'd, with purpose to drawe upon the reare of Lo: Hopton, whom he thought still advancing towards Arundell. The Lo: Hopton immediatly consulted with the Lo: Wilmot, and the Lo: Wentworth concerning the advantage of this oportunity, and forthwith sending order to the Commander of the dragoons to make good the passe at Warblington (which was their onely retreate) drew off one Brigade of horse, wherewith they advanced with speede towards the way betweene Westbourne and Chichester, having sent Major Browne with a forlorne of 120. horse before, to face

Coll: Norton upon that waye, all which fell out so happily, as within short time after the Enemy was come up to face the forlorne hope, the whole Brigade was come up likewise, and Sir Edw. Stowell was sent with a good strong party to charge them, which was quickly executed, and the Enemy rowted, and many taken and killed upon the place, some escaped to Chichester, but Coll: Norton, with not above 50 horse of 5. or 600. that he brought out, endeavoured to returne by Warblington. Two partyes of horse one of 24. or 25. of the Lo: Hopton's guards, commaunded by Major Maxwell as a forlorne hope, and another of 80 horse commanded by Coll: Horatio Cary, were sent after Norton, hoping betweene these partyes, and the dragoons at Warblington, to make sure of him, and what he had left; But Horatio Cary fayld of his duty with his party, and the Commander of the dragoones, upon what unfortunate apprehension I know not, for he was an old souldyer, and in many other occasions before and since maintain'd a very cleere, and good reputation, but then upon the first discovery of Coll: Norton with his frighted party, he unfortunatly quitted the passe, and retreated, and thereby gave Norton the oportunity to charge and route him, where he had the execution of many of his men, the Officers hardly escaping. But in the very heate of this execution, Major Maxwell with his little party fell in upon Norton so sharply, as he recovered all that was alive of the dragoones, and brought in 24 prisoners of Norton's men, himselfe hardly escaping.

This action being thus past with a mixt success, the Lord Hopton settled his quarters for the present at Standstead, and Westbourne, and the parishes adjoyning, and presently drew downe foote about Warblington-house, which was now growen more obstinate by reason of an officer of Coll: Norton's that was gotten in yet within a few dayes he had it rendered by composition. But the Lo: Hopton's greater care being the recrewte of his Army, and the releife of Arundell, he endeavoured the first by carefull dispatch of orders to Winchester and then to other parts of his command, the second was in dayly consultation betweene him, and the chiefe Commanders of the Army. But before half the time propounded by Capt. Cox was expired, the Lo: Hopton having taken a resolution to command Coll: Robert Legg with 500 horse, and each horse-man a bagg of meale behinde him, to try to putt it into the Castle, was prevented by the sad news of the delivery of the place.

Waller conducted the negotiations for the surrender of Arundel with his singular courtesy. The eyewitness from London described the closing phase:

> On Friday the 5. of January, 1644. the Enemy began to feel the fruits of their deserts, being extremely pinched with famine, and thereupon sent a message to our Major Generall of the West, the generous spirited Sir Will. Waller, with more humble expressions then formerly: Desiring a Treaty, by meanes of 3. persons from either party; and that the Lady Bishop, with her Daughters, and waiting Gentlewoman might have liberty to come forth & refresh themselves. To all which Sir William agreed, and invited the said Lady and Gentlewomen, together with Colonell Bamfield, Major Bovill, and a Captaine, being the persons sent from the Castle to dine with him, who all had noble respect, and good entertainment: Persons on our part sent to the castle to treate, were, colonell Wems, Major Anderson, and a Kentish captain: At this Treaty, there was no full agreement made between them in regard the Enemy did not fully condiscend to Sir Williams demands: and so the persons on either side were returned, but the Gentlewomen continued with Sir William, who feasted and entertained them that night; also in that afternoone the Lady Goring and her Daughter came to visit the Lady Bishop and her Daughters, one of them being married to the Lady Gorings onely Son, he being in the castle; which visite gave a speedy accomplishment to our Designe: For Mistresse Goring after some conference with her Mother in Law, returned to her Husband in the castle; and shortly after, the enemy sent a Drum, with colonell Rawlins and Major Mullins, to treat for a finall agreement, upon which Treaty, they condescended to Sir William: The substance of which agreement was, That all the Enemies should be surrendered Prisoners, together with the castle, all their armes, ammunition, treasure, and whatsoever they possessed, into the custody and disposing of Sir William, by 9. of the clock on Saturday morning, being the 6. of this instant. For assurance whereof, colonell Rawlins & Major Mullins ingaged themselves, and also promised that colonell Edward Foard, and Sir Edward Bishop should immediatly come forth, and ingage themselves to Sir William also: To which purpose the said Drum was sent back, and after midnight returned onely with a Letter, in which were some simple demands; hereupon Sir William trebled his Guard upon the castle, least any escape should be made; and

returned the Drum, and demanding them to come forthwith, or else he would dissolve the Treaty, and proceed against them; whereupon Sir Edward Bishop, and Colonell Foard came according to agreement, to Sir William, about two a clock in the morning: Thus God brought about this great work, without bloodshed, and Sir William Waller is possessed of the said Town and Castle of Arundell, with about 100. Officers and Commanders, the chief are, Sir Edward Bishop, Colonell Bamfield, and Colonell Foard with one Doctor Shellingsworth: besides, about 2000. armes, with ammunition, and good store of riches to incourage our Valiant Souldiers in their further service, mean while Sir Ralph Hopton hath spent his time frivolously against Warbleton House, betwixt Winchester and Portsmouth, where wee leave him till divine Iustice findes him, and give the whole Glory of our successe to God.

The taking of this Town and Castle hath been of excellent consequence to this City of LONDON, as will shortly appear to be made manifest.

In his own account of these proceedings Waller made no mention of the dinner party he gave for the Royalist ladies:

The Parly began on Thursday when they sent me a letter signifying their willingness to surrender the place, if they might have honourable conditions. I returned answer, that when I first possessed my self of the Towne, I sumoned them to yeeld upon faire quarter, but they were pleased to refuse either to give or take quarter. I now tooke them att their word, and bid them yeeld to mercy. That night I heard no more of them; the next morning the Drummer came to me againe with another letter from Colonel Bamfield, and all the principall officers wherein they disclaimed that incivility to my Trumpetter laying the fault upon two who had no soldioury in them who unadvisedly, without their consent or knowledge, returned that answer. They looked upon my offer of mercy, and great undervaluation of them with a protestation, (declaring) they would all rather chuse to dye gallantly, then yeeld sheepishly to fetters. All the mercy they desired was on behalf of the Lady Bishopp and some Gentlewomen with her, that they might have liberty to repair to their severall homes. I sent them answer that I was very satisfied, that in the disavowing of that harshness, they had made some curtesy and that I was content to give them faire quarter. If they should refuse the proffer I assured them itt should be the last, and (their) blood should be upon their own heads.

The Ladyes [torn] have free leave to come out, with a safe conduct to their homes. If they had a minde to treate upon particulars, they should send out to me 3 officers of quality and I would employ 3 of equal [torn and faded] them.

Within a short time after there came out Colonell Bamfield, Maior Bovile and Captain Hodgido, who pressed me very much that they might have liberty to march out like soldiours, other wyse they vowed to chuse death rather then life, and so broke off. About 2 howers after, they sent out to me Lieutenant Colonel Rawlins and Maior Moulins, who after some debate came to an agreement with me, That this morning, the Castle should be surrendered to me by 10 of the clock with all coulours, armes, ammunition entire. And that the commanders and Gentlemen, should have faire quarter and civill usage, the soldiours, quarter. For performance of covenants Sir Edward Ford and Sir Edward Bishop were immediately to be yeelded which was accordingly don.

This morning we entered and are now blessed be God in possession of the place. Wee have taken 17 colours of foot and 2 of horse. Wee have one thousand prisoners, one with another, besides about 160 which wee tooke att the first entring of the Towne, and such as ran from the ennemy during the siege. I humbly desire the London Regiments may be speedily sent hither to secure this place of as great importance as any I know. (I shall) advance with what strength I have towards the ennemy. If this be don speedily I doubt not by God's assistance, but to give you a full account of this service. The life of all consists in expedition. God direct your counsells.   I humbly rest,
        Your most humble servant
           William Waller.
Arundell 6 Jan. 1643.

S^r. I shall presume to appeare as a humble sutor to you on behalf of these God has delivered into my hands. They have carried themselvs nobly and bravely, and, I humbly beg they may receive faire and civill usage — in a speciall manner I am a petitioner for Colonell Bamfield. Some men of ours were taken prisoner by them, and were very fairely used. I ask a like favour for them.

Colonel Joseph Bamfield had cause to note Waller's kind heart:

    I held it out five and twenty days, to great extremitie, it was rendered by the Councel of War, upon quarter for life: I never signed the Capitulation, and might have been deny'd benefit of the Articles, and quarter, had General Waller been cruel. Of above 900 Officers, and Souldiers, Horse and Foote, which I retain'd before the siege; few more then 200 marched out, the rest either killed, or dead of the bloody flux, and spotted feavour; with the first whereof I was my selfe attacqued, as soon as recovered; I was sent prisoner upon my parolle to London, without guards, were rendering my selfe; I was committed to the Tower; remaining there about six months, until I had libertie from the Earl of Essex, to procure the freedom of Sir Ellis Layton (at that time Colonel of horse under the Parliament) and of one Whyte, Capitain in the same Regiment, in Exchange, or to return again to the Tower within eight and twenty days.

Waller remained at Arundel for a week or more, settling his military affairs in that town. The weather grew worse and the new London Brigade that had left London on 5 January to swell his army did not reach Petworth until 29 January. By that time both Royalist and Roundhead armies were in winter quarters.

In a letter dated 12 January Waller expressed the hope that the prize money from a Dunkirk ship of 22 guns, driven ashore by privateers and seized by some Roundhead troops, could be used to supply the wants of his army:

> In all the obligations and favours which you are pleased to lay upon me (amongst which I must in the first place ranke your acceptation of my poore service) you do but bind him that was fast before. Itt is my praier, and shall, God willing, be my constant endeavour, to employ that Talent or mite or whatsoever I am worth, and to spend my self, and be spent in your service.
>
> This noble Gentleman, Colonell Alexander Popham, can perfectly informe you in what condition I am, and of the necessity of raising a considerable body of foot with all speed, if there be an intention I should march westward. I shall with all cheerfullness embrace your command, but then I humbly desire to have such strength assigned me, as may enable me in some measure for the performance of them. I presume Sr Henry Heyman hath given you the character of these associated Countyes, and therefore I shall not trouble you. with any further particularityes concerning them. I shall only desire there may be some present course taken to awaken the Committees of these Countyes and to make them active, or your service heere will be ruined.

> I am here taking order for the fortifying and victualling of the Castle, and for the settling of a Garrison in itt. I desire not to loose a minutes time in your service, but before this place can be sufficiently provided, and further forces raised, some time will be spent, and all the world cannot help it. I suppose the Prisoners, so many as were able to be sent, will be with you before the receit of this. Sir Edward Ford, and diverse Gentlemen of quality and soldiers, are heere in a most miserable weake condition. I shall dispose of them if they recover which many of them are not likely to do. I humbly desire there may be a speedy supply of monyes sent, without which I have no hope to march. I shall presume with all humbleness to be a m(aker) of requests unto you in the behalf of this poore army, that out of the sale of these wares, which we have saved out of the Dunkerke shipp, if she proove prize, wee may have our arreares discharged, the surplusage if there be any, to be accounted to the state. I shall trouble you no further than with the tender of my humble service in the language whereof I shall as long as I have life endeavour to express my self,
> Your most humble servant — William Waller.

Waller left Arundel in mid-January, entrusting the town to Colonel Herbert Morley and young Sir William Springate, who contracted the fever, probably typhus, which had ravaged Bamfield's soldiers. His wife Mary made the hazardous journey from London to be with him, although she was at that time pregnant with their future daughter Gulielma, who would marry the Quaker William Penn. Many years later, long after she had re-married, Lady Springate wrote down for her American Quaker grandson, charmingly named Springet, the story of Sir William's life, including her last visit to him:

> When we came to Arundel we met with a most dismal sight: the town being depopulated, all the windows broken with the great guns, and the soldiers making stables of all the shops and lower rooms: and there being no light in the town but what came from the light in the stables, we passed through the town towards his quarters. Within a quarter of a mile of the house the horses were at a stand, and we could not understand the reason of it, so we sent our guide down to the house for a candle and lantern, and to come to our assistance; upon which the report came to my husband, who told them they were mistaken, he knew I could not come I was so near my

time; but they affirming that it was so, he commanded them to sit him up in his bed, 'that I may see her,' said he, 'when she comes;' but the wheel of the coach being pitched in the root of a tree was some time before I could come. It was about twelve at night when we arrived, and as soon as I put my foot into the hall (there being a pair of stairs out of the hall into his chamber) I heard his voice, 'Why will you lie to me! if she be come, let me hear her voice;' which struck me so that I had hardly power to get up the stairs; but being borne up by two, he seeing me, the fever having took his head, in a manner sprang up, as if he would come out of his bed, saying, 'Let me embrace thee before I die; I am going to thy God and my God.' I found most of his officers attending on him with great care and signification of sorrow for the condition he was in, they greatly loving him. The purple spots came out the day before, and now were struck in, and the fever got into his head, upon which they caused him to keep his bed, having not been persuaded to go to bed no day since his illness till then, which had been five days. Before his spots came out, they seeing his dangerous condition (so many Kentish men, both commanders and others having died of it in a week's time near his quarters), constrained him to keep his chamber, but such was his activeness of spirit and stoutness of his heart that he could not yield to this ill that was upon him, but covenanted with them that he would shoot birds with his cross-bow out of the windows, which he did till the fever took his head and the spots went in; and after that the fever was so violent and he so young and strong of body, and his blood so hot (being but about the age of 23) that they were forced to sit round the bed to keep him in, but he spake no evil or raving words at all, but spoke seriously about his dying to my doctor, which I brought down with me by his orders.

For two days the devoted wife watched by his bedside, cooling his lips with her own, before he died. She then accompanied his body, borne on the Whitecoats Regiment's ammunition waggon, to Ringmer in Sussex. 'When he was dead,' she wrote, 'then I could weep.'

Sources in order of first appearance:
Bamfield, *op. cit.*
Birch, *op. cit.*
Waller to House of Lords, 21 December. *L. J.* Vol. vi, p. 350 (first half) and H. M. C., *10th Report*, Pt. VI, p. 150 (second half).
London eyewitness. From *A Full Relation of the late victory at the taking of the Castle of Arundel*, TT: E. 81 (10).
Bellum Civile
Waller to the Speaker, 6 January. Bodl., Tanner MS. 62, f. 497; *Ibid* (12 January), f. 508.
Lady Springate's account. From C. Thomas-Stanford, *op. cit.*, pp. 116–7.

PART TWO
The Battle

Chapter Eight

THE STRATEGIC AND POLITICAL BACKCLOTH

THE CAMPAIGN and battle of Cheriton were fought against a dark strategic backcloth as far as Parliament was concerned. True, the Scots had entered the war. On 9 January Alexander Leslie, Earl of Leven, and a Scottish army of 20000 men crossed the Tweed and marched on Newcastle town. A seasoned veteran over sixty years old like the Earl of Forth, Leven had a disciplined and well-trained army at his command. The winter of 1643 was particularly severe and the Scots did not reach Newcastle until early February. As the Marquis of Newcastle had arrived shortly before with Royalist reinforcements for the garrison, the first assault on the defences was repulsed. A three weeks lull followed before the weather allowed Leven to march south across the Tyne, leaving a small force behind to watch Newcastle. The Marquis tried to force a battle, but March passed without any major engagement. The day of Cheriton, coming after a spell of hot weather in the South, saw the two northern armies still enduring bleak conditions, the Royalists based at Durham and the Scots at Sunderland.

While Leven and Newcastle campaigned in the North a new Cavalier army had come into being in Cheshire, formed mainly from regiments released from Ireland and commanded by Lord Byron. Sir Thomas Fairfax marched with his Yorkshire Roundheads to join the Parliamentarian commander in Cheshire, Sir William Brereton, and together they beat Byron at Nantwich (25 January). The Royalist horse and a fair part of their foot, however, made a good retreat into Chester.

After his defeat at Nantwich Lord Byron could no longer be regarded as a general capable of re-conquering Cheshire and Lancashire, let alone of facing the Scots army or invading the Eastern Association. To restore the now serious situation in the North the King and the Royalist Council of War placed Prince Rupert in overall command. On 19 February the Prince arrived at Shrewsbury, which he made his headquarters, and set about building an army from the remnants of Byron's forces and some fresh regiments from Ireland.

Ten days after Rupert's coming Sir John Meldrum, with 6000 or 7000 Parliamentarians drawn from Derbyshire, Leicestershire, Lincolnshire and Nottinghamshire, marched on Newark. This well-fortified and garrisoned Royalist town guarded the rear of the Marquis of Newcastle's army, besides acting as a link between York and Oxford. On 6 March heavy fighting broke out on the outskirts of the town: the siege had begun.

On 12 March Prince Rupert received definite orders to relieve Newark, and he hastily set about assembling an army. By 17 March he had come as far as Lichfield with a force still under 3000 strong, but the following day more Royalist contingents arrived, increasing Rupert's strength to 3500 horse and 3000 foot, all musketeers. Two days later they were about eight miles from Newark.

Next morning (21 March) Prince Rupert, with only half of his cavalry, engaged the Parliamentarian horse. Both sides rallied and gave two charges, but the Cavaliers were too good for some of the county regiments and they fell back. Hearing that Meldrum had only victuals enough for two days, Rupert resolved to starve them into submission, and when his foot regiments came up he encircled the Roundheads, besieging the besiegers. On 23 March Meldrum surrendered. By the terms of the treaty his soldiers marched off, drums beating and colours flying, but left behind 3000 muskets, 11 brass guns, two large mortars and 200 dead comrades. This quick and complete victory elated not only Prince Rupert's army but Royalist hearts throughout the country.

News of Sir John Meldrum's danger had reached London earlier in March. The Committee of Both Kingdoms, which had replaced the Committee of Safety in January (as a result of the Solemn League and Covenant) with much larger powers of

PLATE 13
Lord Ralph Hopton

Mytens School

PLATE 14
Patrick Ruthven, Earl of Forth *Artist unknown*
Bodleian Library

direction over the strategic course of the war, still hoped that Waller would take the offensive against Hopton as the first of a series of campaigns that would lead them eventually to the gates of Oxford that summer. In order to stabilise the situation in the Midlands the Committee wrote on 16 March to the Earl of Manchester, requesting him to maintain a threatening posture in order to divert the enemy's interest:

> We have read your's to his Excellency signifying your desire to withdraw your forces some few miles back in respect of the ill quarters they had been in. We would very willingly you should find good quarters for them to continue their strength for this summer's action, and doubt not but you may thereabouts find better quarters. But as the affairs now stand it will be a great prejudice to them if your forces shall retire, for Sir Wm. Waller and Sir Wm. Balfour are upon a design, in expectation of a diversion to be made by those forces which, if they should now retire, would bring them in the West a greater number than they, perhaps, would be able to deal with. We therefore desire that you will so dispose of our quarters as that you may either join with Com. Gen. Behr, if that by them shall be thought fit, or otherwise to make the best advantage you can of those forces for a real diversion in such a way as shall seem best to their judgment that have the command upon the place. And we doubt not but in those parts you may find good quarters whereby the forces may continue their strength for future service; and in the meantime we desire that you will hasten the recruits of the rest of your forces that you may be ready as speedily as you can to take the field with your whole strength.[1]

Not until after the fall of Newark did Manchester bestir himself, but at least he did not retreat. There is no evidence that he attempted to make an active diversion in keeping with the hope of the Committee of Both Kingdoms: at this time he was busy building up his army for his own not unsuccessful Summer campaign.

Waller looked nearer home to prevent a repetition of Roundway Down: the sudden reinforcement of Hopton's field army by a reserve brigade from Oxford. On 21 March he wrote to the Earl of Essex, still in London, reporting the movements of the Earl of Forth towards Winchester and seeking either a diversion by Essex and Manchester's forces against Oxford, or a further contingent for his own army. To strengthen his case Balfour and Dalbier, two officers whom Essex trusted, signed the letter. The Lord General replied on 23 March in the following vein:

> I received your letter of the 21st instant from Petersfield, and have been considering of that proposition you make, but when I look upon the posture of my own army and the distance the Earl of Manchester's forces are at being so divided, some before Newark, some towards Stony Stratford, and the rest at Cambridge, I think the motion may admit of so much delay as to let me know the ground you go upon, what certain intelligence you have, for the report is uncertain whether Ruthven be there or towards Gloucester, and how you conceive this can be effected by me in this season by these forces you propose. The design were exceedingly to be wished for, I shall desire you therefore speedily to let me know your thoughts upon this fully, and I shall so frame my resolution after as may be most the good of the Kingdom. This is not any way to retard you from your advance towards the enemy as you find advantage. I shall endeavour to put my army in a posture as soon as can be.[2]

The letter is vague, to say the least of it. On the face of it Essex was not prepared to accept the information of the movements of Ruthven (Forth) from his field commanders on trust. To do him justice, he was often being given misleading or inaccurate reports of the enemy's whereabouts. He can also be excused for not trying to effect a junction between his own and Manchester's armies; neither was ready to take the field. Perhaps that unreadiness is culpable, although again, in justice, we must note that Waller's army had been given priority for money and military stores. Besides, a good part of Essex's army, under Balfour, had already marched into Waller's camp.

As for a diversion against Oxford, the Earl of Essex may well have suspected that Waller and Balfour were being unduly nervous or alarmist. The stolid Essex was not good at responding to swift changes in the military situation, especially when it might appear that Waller was trying to direct his movements. Whenever he suspected a persuasive direction from this particular general, whom he still insisted upon regarding as a subordinate junior, or on a level with Balfour, Essex dug in his heels and either did nothing, or the opposite to what he was expected to do.

Waller, and many of his officers, besides a number of the more militant members of the House of Commons, suspected the integrity of the Lord General. After all, Essex had not heeded Waller's requests for a diversion against Oxford that Summer: as a result Sir John Byron and Lord Wilmot had fallen on Waller at Roundway Down. All the Summer long after that fateful day, the officers of Waller's and Essex's army had quarrelled on account of this failure, and each side had produced and published its case in London.[3] The political move to raise Waller to equality with Essex had not helped relationships between the two men, but after the Lord General had withdrawn Waller's independent commission, the diplomatic skill of John Pym brought about a reconciliation. Once more, however, the Lord General's reluctance to grant Waller a sufficiently large commission as Major-General of the Southern Association aroused the old divisive feelings and mutual doubts.

Reflections of this discord appear in Waller's 'Experiences,' written sometime after the war. After recording his jubilation at the bounty of 'the only Giver of Victory' at Alton, Waller noted:

> 'Itt had bitter endings, for the Parliament wrote to Essex to join me, intending that we together should do a mighty worke, but the Generall would not, to their no small displeasure; for which no good reason could be given, but that he would have his great name stand alone.'[4]

Lest this accusation should seem too partisan, it is worth adding Clarendon's independent estimate of that strange complex son of Queen Elizabeth's beheaded favourite, the Earl of Essex: 'His vanity disposed him to be *His Excellence,* and his weakness to believe that he should be the general in the Houses as well as in the field.'[5]

Having delayed sending Waller's Southern Association commission until 2 January, Essex admitted in the accompanying letter to the Speaker that he had received the earlier summons for a commission, adding in self-justification: 'but fynding expression in that order that myght intimat a neglect in mee' he had returned the document:

> It is true that the commission was not according as I usually graunt them, but it gave him full aughtorighte for the present

service. For the reasons of my limitation in the former comission I forebeare to gueeve them, but whensoever the houses shall command mee I shall be ready to make it appeere. I deed no more than I ought to doe, having received soe great a trust from the parlement ... I shall never desert the cause, as luong as I have any bloud in my veins, until this kingdom may bee mad happy by a blessed peace (which is all honest mens prayers) or to have an end by the sword which is the intention of your assured friend, Essex.[6]

Whether Essex simply lacked strategic insight and military imagination, or harboured an indifference rooted in jealousy towards Waller, whom he clearly regarded as an over-rated general, the reader is as good a judge as anyone. Clearly, for whatever reason, Essex was not going to raise a finger to help Sir William Waller in the forthcoming campaign. Waller's officers may be forgiven if they shared the public concern expressed about their general in the streets of London in December 1643, and reported by a Scots envoy: 'the main chance is about good and valiant Sir William Waller. The grandees would see, they say, that poor man perish.'[7]

The tidings of Prince Rupert's success at Newark removed any lingering hopes in the minds of the Roundhead commanders that the Earl of Essex would join forces with them. The perilous nature of their situation and the sudden significance of the forthcoming battle came home to Waller and Balfour in a letter from the Committee of Both Kingdoms, dated 24 March, which they would receive a few days later when the rival armies were already in fighting contact. As the contents of the despatch must have been in every Roundhead commander's mind on the eve of battle, it forms a fitting conclusion to the survey of the general strategic picture:

> We have received a sad account of our forces before Newark. We know not all the particulars, but that many of our horse, and most of our foot, by the coming of Prince Rupert, retired to places conceived to be safe, but on Friday did agree to give up their ordnance, ammunition and fire arms. Three parts of our horse and 500 foot being at a distance from the rest, retreated safely with their arms. This agreement the enemy did not make good but plundered our men of their arms and good clothes. On Friday night when we were informed supplies might timely come, we directed

all my Lord Manchester's forces except those with Commissary Behre at Warwick, to go to relieve those before Newark (who are a good part of their way thitherwards) so as you cannot for the present expect any diversion towards Oxford. This account we have thought good to give you, and you knowing we have no other reserve ready if your army should receive a blow, we assure ourselves you will be most careful not to engage in fight but upon such terms as considering the state of our affairs you believe to be most for the good of the Kingdom, which we leave to you who are upon the place.[8]

---

[1] *C.S.P.D.* 1644, p. 49.

[2] *Ibid*, p. 56.

[3] See J. Adair, *The Life of Sir William Waller* (1598–1668) (London Ph.D. Thesis), pp. 176–187.

[4] *Experiences*, p. 124. On 19 December a letter from Essex was read in the Lower House in which were enclosed letters from the Committee of Safety, urging him('by reason of the King gathering together all his forces and sending for Prince Rupert from Towester to fall on Sir William Waller') to draw his army from St. Albans to Windsor. Essex expressed his unwillingness to do so, owing to the smallness of his forces. A conference of both Houses was called, and the Lords joined the Commons in their request to Essex, with an important proviso that he was not to move before the Hertfordshire forces were ready to defend Newport Pagnell. It was as a result of Essex's reluctance to move that it was resolved to send two M.P.s to the Militia Committee for two London regiments to march out to Croydon, Kingston and Hampton if the Committee found it necessary. Whitaker, Add. MS. 31, 116, f. 102.

[5] Clarendon, Bk. VI, 402. Pym wrote one letter to placate Essex in which the word 'Excellency' appeared more than 12 times. J. L. Sanford, *Studies and Illustrations of the Great Rebellion* (1858), p. 568.

[6] Bodl. Tanner MS., 62, f. 490. Cf. D'Ewes, Harl. 165, f. 266, a report of an 'earnest and vehement' debate in the Commons on 1 January, in which Heselrige said that Waller had as yet no commission. According to D'Ewes, Essex had sent Waller a commission which was less than those of Denbigh, Manchester, or Lord Fairfax, and Waller had returned it with some 'very slight expressions'. St. John then spoke for a better one, urging that the words 'during pleasure' should be deleted. The House forebore to make further division over this matter, and Essex duly sent the commission. Essex's commission of 2 July still did not please Waller. On 10 March, writing from Mitcham in Surrey, he suggested that the amending phrase 'under the Earl of Essex, Lord General' was unnecessary as this would

be clear from the fact that he derived his commission from Essex. The proposed alteration was open to three objections: (a) it would make Waller subordinate to officers in the Lord General's army, e.g. his Sergeant-Major-General; (b) it disabled him from making general field officers, for if the Association's forces only equalled a brigade then he could only give commissions up to the rank of colonel, and it would be impossible to command such a body without general officers; and (c) the phrase would take from him the power of commanding garrisons in the Association. Bodl., Tanner MS. 62, f. 619.

The House of Commons rejected the phrase (on 13 March), but accepted it in two out of three suggested places in the ordinance on 16 March, with the addition of a proviso that, in the absence of the Lord General, Sir William should have full powers as commander-in-chief. *C.J.*, Vol. III, p. 429.

For the political tensions behind this matter of Waller's commission, see L. Glow, 'Political Affiliations in the House of Commons after Pym's Death,' *The Bulletin of the Institute of Historical Research*, Vol. 38 (1965); V. Rowe, 'The Political and Administrative Career of Sir Henry Vane the Younger 1640–April 1653' (London Ph.D. Thesis, 1965).

7 R. Baillie, *Letters and Journals* (1775), Vol. 1, p. 403.
8 *C.S.P.D.* 1644, pp. 70–1.

Chapter Nine

THE ROYALIST ARMY

AFTER THE LOSS of Arundel Castle, when a great season of frost and snow prevented Waller's regiments from stirring out of Sussex, Hopton used the time to build up his army with recruits, having persuaded the King to suspend an order for him to withdraw to Marlborough. By early March he had assembled 2000 well-clothed foot and 2000 horse. With the beginnings of Spring came new life in the shape of a contingent drawn from Oxford, Abingdon, Wallingford, Reading and Newbury under Patrick Ruthven, Earl of Forth, which reached Winchester on 22 March. Hopton narrated:

> His Majestie, was pleased to send the Earle of Brainford himselfe with a very hansome body, to the number of about 1200 foote, about 800. horse, and fower pieces of cannon, to joyne with the Lo: Hopton; and that noble person was so extraordinarily civill to him, as he was very hardly perswaded to take upon him the command in his quarters. The Lo: Hopton mett him at Newbery, and from thence attended him to Winchester and by the way (though not without great importunity) prevayled with him to honour him with his orders.

Patrick Ruthven, born about 1573, was some 70 years of age. Described by Hopton as the Earl of Brentford, he did not in fact receive that further title until after Cheriton. He had served the King of Sweden as a mercenary captain in the first decade of the century, and rose to command 1000 foreigners at Narva (1615). In 1632 Gustavus Adolphus made him Earl of Kirchberg (near Ulm), and a major-general, well deserved promotion after the campaigns of the previous five years. In 1634, now a lieutenant-general, he quitted the Swedish service to become muster-master-general in his native Scotland.

In 1639, as Lord Ruthven of Ettrick, he was placed in command of Berwick Castle. On the outbreak of the English Civil War, Ruthven, created Earl of Forth, went to Germany and returned with some officers for the King's cause. The Autumn of 1642 saw him as a junior general, but after commanding the Royalist left wing at Edgehill he became a full general and a chief military adviser to the King. He ably commanded the Cavaliers during the skirmishing around Brentford that November.

The year 1643 had not been a distinguished one for him. Present at the unsuccessful attempt to relieve Reading in April, he was shot in the head at Gloucester and wounded at the first battle of Newbury. Much scarred, with a reputation for being a heavy drinker (hence the gout), Forth possessed a good strategic mind but he tended to lack energy on the battlefield. No doubt King Charles believed that Forth and Hopton would complement each other in their strengths and weaknesses.

FORTH'S CONTINGENT

Forth's contingent probably amounted to a brigade of horse and some 'divisions' of foot. Three of the regiments of horse were apparently out of the brigade of Lieutenant-General Lord Wilmot (who was then engaged in trying to intercept a Parliamentarian convoy between Warwick and Gloucester). The senior colonel seems to have been Thomas Howard, and he presumably commanded this improvised brigade at the head of his own regiment of eight troops, 300 men in all. The regiments in the brigade were:

Lord Forth's
Colonel Thomas Howard's
Colonel Richard Neville's
Prince Maurice's (commanded by Major Robert Legge)
The Queen's (commanded Raoul Fleury)
Colonel Sir Henry Bard's
Colonel Richard Manning's

Many of the troopers in these regiments were veterans. Richard Neville's regiment, for example, had been raised in 1642 by the Earl of Carnarvon, and had fought at Edgehill, Lansdown and First Newbury, where the Earl was killed. Both Neville and his second-in-command at Cheriton, Alexander Standish, had captained troops in the regiment at Edgehill. At Cheriton it mustered five troops and not less than 200 men.

Prince Maurice's Regiment also had a good fighting record. At the Aldbourne Chase rendezvous of Royalist forces on 10 April 1644[1] the regiment mustered 300 strong, arrayed in seven troops with red colours, and this was presumably its size at Cheriton. The regiment had served in the Western campaign of 1643 against Waller.

The Queen's Regiment had been raised in Lancashire at the time when Queen Henrietta landed at Bridlington Bay early in 1643. Described by Colonel Walter Slingsby as being 'most French' at Cheriton, this is probably an exaggeration. In October 1644 only two of the seven troops were commanded by Frenchmen. The colonel was the Queen's favourite, Lord Jermyn, who was wounded during Prince Rupert's action at Aldbourne Chase on 18 September 1643. The regiment must have been at First Newbury. The major, John Campsfield (or Cansfield), was shot through the arm when the regiment stormed Olney Bridge in Buckinghamshire (5 November 1643), an action for which he was knighted. Monsieur Raoul Fleury probably commanded the regiment at Cheriton because the senior officers had not yet recovered from their wounds.

Forth's foot soldiers were drawn out of the garrisons of Reading and Oxford. The senior officer was evidently Colonel George Lisle, who led the Reading contingent. His men were probably taken proportionately from all or most of the twelve regiments then garrisoned at Reading, most of whose colonels were senior to Lisle, and, therefore, cannot have been under his command at Cheriton. He was probably assisted by some of the lieutenant-colonels from the garrison.

The Oxford contingent appears to have consisted of detachments from that garrison under Colonel Sir Henry Bard. The men seem to have belonged to the regiments of Lord Charles Gerard (under Lieutenant-Colonel Francis Windebank) and Bard. There is no evidence that 'commanded men' from the other regiments at Oxford were present.

It seems likely that Forth's main body of 1200 foot was made up of two contingents from Reading and Oxford, the former being probably the larger as there were more soldiers in Reading at that time. (Reading still had 3092 foot at the end of April). It is also likely that each contingent made up one body or 'division' at Cheriton, and that Lisle commanded the whole tertia.

Until a short time before Cheriton, Sir Henry Bard had been in the service of Parliament in Ireland. Four days after the battle, in which he lost an arm, Bard was brought up to London by Sir Arthur Heselrige as a prisoner and lodged in Lord Petre's house in Aldersgate Street, but he was soon afterwards exchanged for a Captain Hacker and Mr Stanley, who had been captured by the Cavaliers. Colonel Sir Henry afterwards became Viscount Bellamont; as such he commanded a tertia at Naseby and was appointed Governor of Guernsey. In May 1645 he scaled the walls of Leicester at the head of his men. He choked with sand during a whirlwind in the Arabian desert in 1660, leaving his widow in great poverty.

Colonel George Lisle, a Netherlands veteran, had begun his Civil War career as a captain in Lord Grandison's Regiment of foot, yet at Edgehill he had already become a lieutenant-colonel of dragoons. On the death of Colonel Richard Bolle at Alton he took over the remnants of that noble officer's regiment in Reading. He fought well at First and Second Newbury (where as night fell he led his men in a white shirt, and was mistaken by the Roundheads for a white witch running up and down the King's army), at Cropredy Bridge and again at Naseby as a tertia commander. After Colchester surrendered in 1648, he was shot on 28 August by musketeers along with Sir Charles Lucas; the latter may have broken his parole, and presumably Lisle was held guilty of the same military crime. Characteristically at his execution, thinking the musketeers stood at too great a distance, Lisle called to them to come nearer. One of the soldiers replied, 'I'll warrant you sir, we shall hit you.' To which Sir George replied with a smile, 'Friends, I have been nearer to you when you have missed me.'

HOPTON'S ARMY

The horse were in three brigades, each at least 700 strong. Perhaps 2200 officers and troopers would be near the mark as far as numbers are concerned. The regiments were as follows:

LORD JOHN STUART'S BRIGADE

	Troops	10 April 1644 Cornets
Lord John Stuart's	6	3
Colonel Sir Nicholas Crisp's	4 (100 men in September 1644)	1
Colonel Sir Edward Ford's	4	3
Colonel Dutton Fleetwood's	6 (in September 1644)	2
Colonel Sir William Clerke's	6	3
Colonel Sir William Boteler's	150 strong	5

It is evident that the brigade had about 31 troops *after* Cheriton. If, like Boteler's, they averaged 30 per troop the brigade still had 930 men. Perhaps 30 troopers is too high an average, but even so the brigade must have been at least 700 strong at Cheriton, and more likely 800.

Lord John Stuart, the twenty-two years-old Lieutenant-General of the Horse at Cheriton, was a third cousin of King Charles, and a younger brother of James Stuart, fourth Duke of Lennox and first Duke of Richmond, the intimate friend and counsellor of the King. He served at Edgehill under Prince Rupert, where one of his elder brothers, George Lord D'Aubigny, was killed. His younger brother, Lord Bernard Stuart, was destined to face Waller at Second Newbury, and lay down his life at Rowton Heath in September 1645. His regiment was probably raised in the Autumn of 1643, and passed briefly after his death to Waller's old turncoat officer, Sir Horatio Carey, before serving under the Earl of Cleveland in Cornwall and at Second Newbury.

As recently as 3 July 1643 a commission to raise 500 horse had been given to Sir Nicholas Crisp of London, and by mid-September his regiment was among six reported to be threatening Southampton, but as we have seen in Chapter Three he could muster no more than 100 men at the end of that month.

The regiments of Sir William Clerke of Ford Place, and Sir William Boteler of Barham Court, high sheriff of Kent, could not have been large ones. Reported 'shot all to pieces by one of the Kentish Musketeirs' at Cheriton, Boteler escaped with a wound in the leg only to be killed, along with Sir William Clerke (also from Kent), at Cropredy Bridge later that Summer. Boteler, like Colonel Richard Manning, was probably a Papist. Clerke, knighted at

York in August 1642, may later have earned his spurs at Edgehill.

The zealous and imprudent Sir Edward Ford, high sheriff of Sussex, had crossed swords with Waller in 1642 at Chichester. Taken at Arundel, it is just possible that he might have been exchanged before Cheriton: certainly he was in arms against Parliament in 1645, when he was involved in drawing up the surrender terms of Winchester Castle, a task for which his unfortunate military experiences had well qualified him. His real *métier* turned out to be inventing: in 1656, encouraged by Cromwell, he raised the Thames water into all the highest streets of the city, 93 feet high, in four eight-inch pipes with 'a rare Engine;' in 1663 he took out a patent for the curing of smoky chimneys; a year or two later he devised an anti-forgery method of coining farthings. Some of his schemes were as reckless as his soldiering, and his regiment at Cheriton may have been well pleased if their colonel was no longer at their head. The recovery of his fortunes after the Civil War can be largely explained by the fact that his sister married General Henry Ireton.

SIR EDWARD STAWELL'S BRIGADE

	29 September 1644	10 April 1644
Lord Hopton's (Horse and Dragoons)	250	4 troop commanders named
Colonel Sir Edward Stawell's	150	2 cornets
Colonel George Gunter's Colonel Sir Allen Apsley's	(2 troops)	2 cornets
Colonel Edmond Peirce's		2 cornets
Marquess of Hertford's	100	6 troops on 23 May 1644

Knowledge about this brigade is not easy to acquire. It seems to have been rather weak at Aldbourne Chase, probably not much more than 5-600 strong. It fought stoutly at Cheriton.

Sir Edward Stawell continued to command a brigade of horse after Cheriton, mainly in the West, but little is known of him or his regiment. His father, Sir John, was Royalist governor of Taunton, and had already lost one son in the service of his King.

Colonel George Gunter of Racton in Sussex had been taken prisoner by Waller at Chichester in 1642. Later he played a part in the escape of King Charles II after the battle of Worcester, and showed then that he was both a cool and a practical man.

SIR JOHN SMYTH'S BRIGADE

It is a reasonable assumption that this was much the same as the brigade commanded by Sir Humphrey Bennet at Aldbourne, which consisted of the following regiments:

		cornets
Colonel Sir Humphrey Bennet's	9 troops	2
Colonel Sir George Vaughan's	80 strong	2
	2 troops	
Colonel Sir Edward Waldegrave's	211 strong	3
Colonel Andrew Lindsey's		2
Sir John Smyth's own troop		

This brigade may have been slightly weaker than that of Lord John Stuart, but it also can hardly have numbered less than 700 at Cheriton.

Sir John Smyth, described by Clarendon as Commissary-General of the Horse and by Waller as Sergeant-Major-General of Hopton's army, was a professional soldier trained in Flanders with a reputation for being one of the best cavalry officers in the Royalist camp. At Edgehill he was made a knight-banneret for recovering the Royal Standard with a single-handed charge.

Sir Humphrey Bennet was described by a local Roundhead adversary as 'very active and very cruel.' He was indeed active in the Western campaign of 1643 and in many Hampshire skirmishes. After Cheriton he defended Bishop's Waltham against the London regiments. At its capitulation he went free, only to see his regiment put to confusion on the field of Second Newbury. Eventually, in 1645, he surrendered at Winchester Castle with Sir Edward Ford.

Sir George Vaughan's Regiment had charged at Lansdown, where its colonel was wounded. High sheriff of Wiltshire, Vaughan had probably raised only two troops, each about 40 men strong.

Sir Edward Waldegrave's and Colonel Andrew Lindsey's are more obscure Royalist regiments of horse: indeed we cannot be certain that the latter was present at Cheriton.

HOPTON'S FOOT

Sergeant-Major-General Sir John Paulet was the commander of Hopton's foot which included the regiments of the following colonels:

	Colours present on 10 April 1644
Lord Hopton (Bluecoats)	5
Sir Allen Apsley (Redcoats)	6
Sir Gilbert Talbot (Yellowcoats)	9
Sir Bernard Astley (formerly Marquis of Hertford's)	6
Francis Cooke	3
Sir John Paulet (Yellowcoats)	
Sir Charles Vavasour (Yellowcoats)	
Sir William Courtney	
Henry Shelley	
Walter Slingsby (formerly Lord Mohun's)	

Most of these were probably at Cheriton. The five with colours above were at the Aldbourne Chase rendezvous on 10 April 1644. The Royalist foot numbered about 5000 on that occasion. Some came from Reading (1513), Abingdon (200) and Oxford (500), a total of 2213. It follows that five of Hopton's foot regiments still numbered about 2787 a fortnight after Cheriton, from which we might fairly conclude that he had at least 3000 foot at Cheriton and probably more.

The foot, even if as Hopton asserts they were but 2000 strong, must have fought in three or four bodies or 'divisions.' If they mustered more than 3000 then Hopton almost certainly formed them into five or six divisions.

In Ireland Sir John Paulet had gained a notable victory over the Irish rebels near Bandon Bridge in County Cork on 23 November 1642. The truce signed in September 1643 had enabled him and Sir Charles Vavasour to bring their good but weak regiments over from Munster to reinforce Lord Hopton. At the surrender of Winchester Castle in October 1645, Hugh Peters, Cromwell's chaplain, described him as 'an old souldier.' He was son and heir to Lord Paulet of Hinton St. George.

Lieutenant-Colonel Sir Matthew Appleyard of Sir Charles Vavasour's Yellowcoats commanded the regiment at Cheriton, for his colonel had recently died. From Dillingham, in Cumberland, Appleyard was 'a soldier of known courage and experience.' Later he fought at Cropredy Bridge and in Cornwall, and was made Governor of Leicester in May 1645. The Parliamentarians captured the following officers of his regiment at Naseby, who were almost certainly at Cheriton : Captains John Tirwhit, George Masters, Sanderson and Hubbart; Lieutenants Middleton, Thompson, Lewen and Baker.

Sir Bernard Astley, second son of Sir Jacob, had commanded the Marquis of Hertford's Regiment of foot at the storming of Bristol in July 1643, where he was carried off shot through the thigh. He was killed at the second siege of Bristol (4 September 1645).

Francis Cooke was captured in December 1644 by Major Duet (then in Colonel Edmund Ludlow's horse) in Salisbury. Colonel Shelley had been captured by Waller in Chichester in 1642, and presumably exchanged.

THE TRAIN OF ARTILLERY

Forth had brought four guns with him, and Hopton already had eight iron ones. Colonel Richard Feilding commanded this train of artillery, an officer who had been perhaps unjustly disgraced for his surrender of Reading in 1643. After military service abroad he returned to England as a captain in 1640, and had risen to be a colonel of foot the following year. After Reading he lost his regiment and narrowly escaped being executed. Later he commanded *The Constant Reformation* in Prince Rupert's fleet before dying at Lisbon in 1650.[2]

CONCLUSION

This brief survey of the combined forces of Forth and Hopton reveals that they did not lack experienced officers or seasoned troops. On the other hand, an army so hastily assembled could not be expected to work well naturally as a team. Much would therefore depend upon the judgement, skill and leadership of the two generals, Forth and Hopton.

For the careers of Forth and Balfour, see *D.N.B.*

[1] R. Symonds, *Diary of the Marches of the Royal Army during the Great Civil War*, ed. C. E. Long, Camden Society, Vol. 74, (1859), pp. 83–90. See also P. Young, 'King Charles I's Army of 1643–1645', *Journal of the Society for Army Historical Research*, Vol. 18, p. 33.

[2] For further information on the Royalist train of artillery at this time see *The Royalist Ordnance Papers*, 1642–1646, Part I, ed. I. Roy, Oxford Record Society (1964).

Chapter Ten

THE PARLIAMENTARIAN ARMY

AS IN the first half of the campaign, Waller's army at Cheriton consisted of three parts, each paid and administered from different sources: his own Western regiments and the train of artillery, a London Brigade and the Southern Association's forces.

THE SOUTHERN ASSOCIATION

After much debate the Committee of the four associated counties of Kent, Surrey, Sussex and Hampshire agreed to raise and pay an army of 3000 foot, 1200 horse and 500 dragoons to serve under Waller.[1] The proportions for each county were settled as follows:

	Foot	*Horse*	*Dragoons*
Kent	1050	420 (167)	175
Surrey	390	256 (83)	65
Sussex	780	312 (125)	135
Hampshire	780	312 (125)	135

The House of Commons had directed the Association Committee on 20 December 1643 to raise a composite regiment of 500 horse (by the quotas given in brackets above)[2] for Sir Richard Grenvile, a prominent West Country landowner newly returned from military service in Ireland.[3] Waller gave Grenvile a commission as Lieutenant-General of the Horse, and the Western Committee promised him the governorship of Plymouth as soon as it could be relieved.[4]

Understandably the Southern Association counties proved reluctant to raise a regiment for such a Western gentleman, and when Grenvile, weary of the more extreme Parliamentarians,

PLATE 15
Sir Michael Livesey
Sutherland Collection

Artist unknown

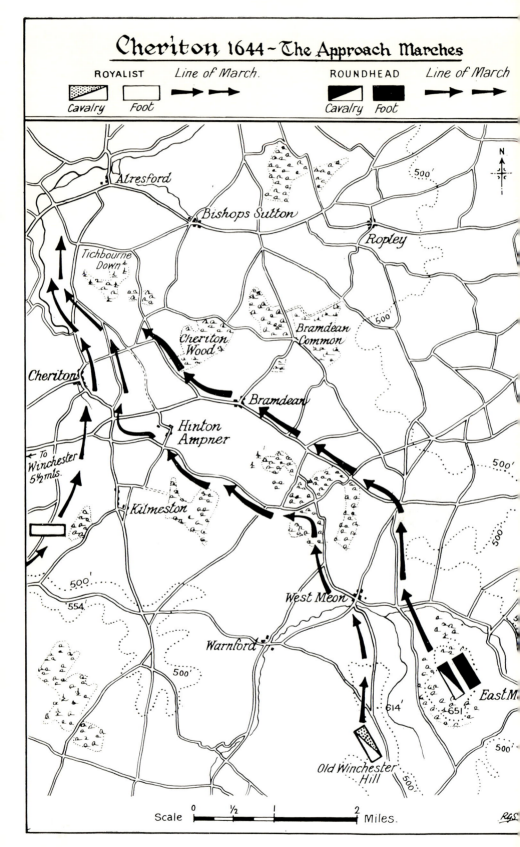

PLATE 16

deserted to Oxford on 3 March 1644, no more than four troops had been formed.[5]

The county political leaders disputed certain clauses in the ordinance concerning the control and financing of the forces they were to raise. Nor was Waller happy with the clauses defining his relation to the Earl of Essex, as he wrote in a letter to the Speaker from Mitcham in Surrey on 10 March, only 19 days before the battle. The ordinance did not finally pass both Houses until 30 March.[6] Yet the new Committee of Both Kingdoms, established as a result of the Solemn League and Covenant with the Scots, took firm measures to establish his authority in the Southern Association and to hasten the forces already assigned to his command.

The case of Colonel Anthony Stapley, Governor of Chichester, illustrates the first aspect of this policy. As justification for refusing to billet some troops of Waller's army after the fall of Arundel, this prominent Sussex M.P. asserted that he held his commission from Essex and therefore owed sole obedience to him.[7] The House of Commons referred the dispute to the Lord General and then to a select committee, but neither could resolve it.[8] The Derby House Committee, however, commanded both Stapley and Waller to produce their commissions at a meeting on 23 February, and after examining these documents gave a verdict in favour of the latter. Although Stapley retained his commission, the Committee ordered him to hand over his regiment to his second-in-command and to attend Parliament in person.[9] In a similar fashion a week later the Committee interviewed some officers of Colonel Ralph Weldon's Red Regiment of Kent who had refused to accept commissions from Waller, and told them to march with their companions to such a rendezvous as Sir William chose to appoint.[10]

Weldon's Regiment of foot gave Waller no more trouble but the same cannot be said of Sir Michael Livesey and his five troops of Kentish horse, who were to mutiny during the Summer while their colonel stormed to London to create as much trouble as he could for Waller. His conduct at Cheriton was not above suspicion (see p. 177).

Colonel Samuel Jones' Greencoats, despite the awkwardness of their political masters, the county gentry, continued to give

Parliament good service in Waller's army, and fought at Cheriton under the command of Lieutenant-Colonel Jeremy Baines.

Colonel Richard Norton, the leading soldier in Hampshire, Governor of Southampton, brought his own regiment of horse to fight at Cheriton. He seems to have been a law unto himself, wandering about the county (but never far from it) as he pleased. Oliver Cromwell's affectionate name for him — 'Idle Dick' — might be a perceptive comment upon his character. At the second battle of Newbury, which he rode over to watch that Autumn, he received a shot in the leg for 'meddling where I had no charge.' Clearly he thought the Cheriton campaign *was* his business.

Grenvile's former Regiment, only four troops strong, served under the command of Lieutenant-Colonel Thorpe in place of his colonel, Sir Edward Cooke, who seems to have acted as Waller's chief-of-staff and Lifeguard commander. Apart from its contribution to this composite regiment there were no Sussex soldiers present in Waller's army: presumably the gentlemen of that county, who already enjoyed the worst relations with Waller, thought they had done enough to save their own skins at Arundel. Even so, three regiments of horse and two of foot had been supplied by the Southern Association.

WESTERN REGIMENTS

The horse consisted of Waller's Regiment, 11 troops strong, Heselrige's 'Lobsters' (seven troops) and six troops of Colonel Jonas Vandruske, now happily recovered from his wounds. These were all seasoned troops, the backbone of the cavalry. Colonel George Thompson, fated to lose a leg at Cheriton, commanded the remaining four troops of Colonel Richard Turner's Regiment, which had been in the pay of London before it was taken over by the Western Association Committee.

Waller's Regiments of dragoons and foot, Andrew Potley's and Heselrige's Regiments of foot, the latter commanded by Lieutenant-Colonel John Birch at Cheriton, made up the Western foot. Neither Birch's loquacity nor his courage had been diminished by being shot in the belly, if his secretary can be believed, and he had made a predictably miraculous recovery from the wound in time to rejoin the colours for the forthcoming battle. Andrew

Potley, a veteran of the Swedish service, served as Major-General of Foot.

The train of artillery under Colonel James Wemyss was increased to 16 or 17 pieces by the following guns, ordered on 7 March by the Committee of Both Kingdoms to be sent down from London:

    1 demi-culverin called 'Kill Cow.'
    3 drakes (from the Leadenhall store).
    1 demi-culverin drake.
    1 saker drake.

These guns were all mounted on shod wheels, with their carriages and four waggons, and 'with provisions for Sixty Shot Round.' Forty barrels of powder from the powder mills around Guildford were to be sent to Farnham Castle for their use.

THE LONDON BRIGADE

The White Regiment and Yellow Regiment, which served with Waller in the Cheriton campaign, numbered about 1000 men each, of whom the most part were musketeers. Neither of them had had been on active service before.

Major-General Richard Browne, their commander, had once been a wood merchant, a fact which the Royalist newspaper *Mercurius Aulicus* would never let him forget. An ambitious man, later that year he would quarrel with Waller, strenuously maintaining the independence of his own command in the counties north of London. As a sign of these troubles to come, on 22 December Browne tried to get a very 'large' commission for himself but this bid was successfully opposed on behalf of Sir William Waller by Sir Henry Vane the younger. Yet the two men would both belong to the Presbyterian political party in the last years of that decade and throughout the next; they would also share the same prison at Windsor Castle in 1650.

SIR WILLIAM BALFOUR'S BRIGADE

Essex despatched 22 troops of horse — the regiments of Sir William Balfour, Sir John Meldrum, John Middleton and John Dalbier — and Colonel Cunningham's Regiment of dragoons to reinforce Waller early in March 1644. This recruit brought the army up to a strength of about 3000 horse and 7000 foot. Balfour's contingent probably numbered 1500 to 2000 in all.

Balfour, born before the beginning of the century in Fifeshire, had been employed in the Dutch service until 1627, when he became Lieutenant-Colonel of the Earl of Morton's Regiment. Earning the favour of the Duke of Buckingham in the expedition to the Isle of Rhé, he and Colonel Dalbier received commissions from King Charles to raise 1000 horse in Friesland, but this dubious military scheme was later abandoned. Governor of the Tower of London in 1630, Balfour stood high in his royal master's esteem but his Scottish Presbyterian faith led him into Parliament's camp at the start of the war.

As Lieutenant-General of the Horse under the Earl of Bedford he commanded the reserve at Edgehill. With his own and Sir Philip Stapleton's regiments he charged against the pikes of the Royalist foot and scattered the most part of a brigade. He then pushed on and actually rode among the Royalist guns, cutting down the canoneers. Having 'made his name' at Edgehill, however, Balfour missed the Newbury campaign as he had decided to travel abroad, ostensibly for health reasons. Consequently the Cheriton campaign would be his first major active service for over a year.

The Earl of Essex pointedly named Balfour before Waller in his later references to the victorious generals, while Balfour does not even mention Waller in his letter written the day after the battle (see pp.158-9). Who was in command? No doubt, in keeping with the courtesies of the war, outwardly the generals shared that honour. At the council of war before the battle, especially in light of his considerable military experience, what Balfour had to say would have carried great weight. But at least four-fifths of the army looked upon Sir William Waller as their general, and we may with confidence look upon him as the chief commander of the Parliamentarian forces.[11]

The question of command had certainly been discussed and agreed upon, as the following letter from the Committee of Both Kingdoms (a copy to each of the two generals) makes clear:

> We understand by letters from Sir Wm. Balfour that he has been three or four days at Petersfield in expectation of your joining with him in prosecution of the design resolved upon by this Committee. And we hear that you are not yet

with your forces, nor any of them yet joined with Sir Wm. Balfour according to your intentions and our resolutions. We most earnestly desire that you with your forces will immediately join with Sir Wm. Balfour, fearing that there is some opportunity already lost, as we hear that Prince Maurice is ready to join with Lord Hopton and the country summoned to come in to join with them, also Wareham and Poole in danger to be lost. And because we look upon this business as that which very much concerns the public, and are confident that you and Sir Wm. Balfour before your departure from this town agreed upon all particulars for carrying on of this business as well in point of command as otherwise, we therefore earnestly desire you that no accident whatsoever may alter or interrupt those resolutions . . .

---

1. *C.J.*, Vol. III, p. 396.
2. 'The Notebook of Lieut. Colonel Jeremy Baines', B.M., Add. MS. 22,477, f.3.
3. *C.J.*, Vol. III, p. 349. For Grenvile's career, see R. Granvile, *The King's General in the West* (1908).
4. Grenvile to mayor and burgesses of Plymouth (18 March 1644), H.M.C., *15th Report*, VII, p. 71.
5. *Ibid.* See also *C.J.*, Vol III, pp. 356, 403, 412, *C.S.P.D.* 1644, p. 172.
6. *C.J.*, Vol. III, p. 470.
7. According to Whitaker the issue was whether or not Waller could draw out the Chichester regiment. Also Stapley resented the 'execution' done upon one of his soldiers by Potley, Add. MS., 31, 116, f.117.
8. *C.J.*, Vol. III, pp. 362, 368, 390, 401.
9. *C.S.P.D.* 1644, p. 25.
10. *Ibid*, p. 32; *C.J.*, Vol. III. p. 412. The Committee of Kent reluctantly agreed to place its officers under Waller's command on 21 Febuary Letter from Sir Anthony Weldon and others to Speaker (21 February) Bodl., Tanner MS. 62, f.573.
11. For correspondence and events in this chapter, see *C.S.P.D.* 1644, pp. 40–100 *passim*.

Chapter Eleven

CHERITON

IN THE second week of March Waller rejoined his army at Arundel, and on the 19th he set out towards Petersfield, his rendezvous with Sir William Balfour, having issued a strict Proclamation 'for the better performance of Duty and observations of the Lawes of Warre' (see pp. 214-5). Meanwhile Major-General Richard Browne led the winter-weary Londoners from Midhurst to the rendezvous at East Meon, as Lieutenant Elias Archer related for the benefit of the Lord Mayor, the Committee of Militia and the citizens of London:

> Being imployed in the service of the City and State, to attend the London-Brigade, now joyned with Sir *William Waller*, and at that time intrusted to acquaint you with our proceedings the last week; I am bold, after my humble service, to present to you a brief Relation of the most remarkable Passages between us and the Enemy, not onely in duty to you, but also in love to all those that long to be truly informed in the particular.
> May it please your Honour; upon Thursday the 21. of this instant March (our Brigade being quartered at Midhurst) our Major Generall received Orders from Sir *William Waller*, to advance towards Winchester to a Town called Traford [Treyford], which accordingly he did with incredible speed, almost at an hours warning, and that night arrived there, which we found to be a small village, not above seven or eight houses to quarter all our men, there we met with much hardship, staying for Orders till the Lords day following; Upon Monday the 25. we marcht forwards to joyn with Sir *William Wallers* main body, which accordingly

wee did, and that night were appointed to quarter at Westmean [West Meon], three miles distant from the main body, where we found a partee of the Enemies horse when our Quartermasters entred the Town, which occasioned some action, though not much considerable, we onely took a Quartermaster prisoner; the next day, which was Tuesday, we lay still, onely our Scouts brought in some prisoners, 6 Troops incountring with 16 of the Enemies, put them to flight and brought away 3. of them prisoners.

Meanwhile at East Meon, three miles from the London Brigade, Waller held a muster for his horse on Tuesday, 26 March, followed by a general rendezvous for the whole army the next day. Captain Robert Harley, a troop commander in Waller's Regiment of horse, observed both musters:

> March the 17th, wee removed our quarters from beyond Arundel to the Manhood neare Chichester. Tuesday, the 19th, the heath neare Chichester was appointed for the rendezvous for our three regiments of horse. From thence that night wee marched to Havant. Tuesday the 26th, the generall rendezvous for our horse was in the fields by East Meane. Wee had in the field, twenty-two troops of my lord generall's, eleven troops of Sir William Waller's regiment, seven troops of Sir Arthur's; six troops of Colonel Vandrusk's, five troops of the Kentish, four troops of Sir Richard Greinfield's, alias Colonel Cook's leiftenant colonels, four troops of Colonel Tompsone, four troops of Colonel Norton's. Wennedsday, the 27th, the heath by East Meane was rendevouz for all our horse and foote. The strength of them consisted in these regiments, the generall's, Colonel Pattle's, Sir Arthur Haselrig's, the Kentish red regiment, Colonel Jones of Farnham Castel his regiment, and the woodden cittye brigade under their true colonel, Colonel Browne. Wee had onely Sir William Waller's and Colonel Cunninggam's regiments of dragoones.

Hearing that Waller and Balfour had joined forces and moved out of Sussex into Hampshire as far as Warnford and West Meon, the Royalist generals held a council of war, to which they invited the governor of Winchester, Sir William (later Viscount) Ogle. His secretary gives us Ogle's version of the debate:

> Within three daies of ther [Forth and Stuart] comming to Winchester he was Desired by a messenger to come to my Lord Hoptons Lodgings nigh at Eastgate house: when

he came he found the three Lords with all the field officers sett in Councell; my Lord Hopton said to my Lord Ogle: "Gouvnour, tho you art not of the Army: yet we have sent for you to assist at this Councell:" My Lord told him it was very improper for him to give any Opinion: where he had noe Command: he desired to know what was the debate. he was answered that the debate was to remove Wallers Army out of these parts: for it was a shame to let him (?) come soe neare; my Lord Hopton desired my Lord Ogle to give his Opinion; he desired to know: if it was their joynt Opinion to march: and remove him; he was answered it was the resolution of that Councell; then he told them: it would be to noe purpose for him to say any thing: but he was still urged to give his Opinion: "My Lords said he: seeing it is yr pleasure to have my Opinion I must freely profess it falls not within my understanding: that you should goe seek a formed Army well commanded with raw men, new raised horse and foot; if Waller should come within a mile or two of Winchester you might if you thought fit drawe out and fight him; having this garrison to back and supply you and upon any disaster a safe retreat: but if you march six or seven miles to fight; you must carry yr provisions; and in this Extream hot weather weary the soldiers and goe fight an Enemy who, as I am informed, is marching away towards London:" my Lord Hopton said, all this was but one man's Opinion; and soe continued the Resolution to march imediately. my Lord Hopton said, he wanting provision to carry a long with the Army must disire my Lord Ogle to furnish him with what he could. he answered him; that if he should doe soe it would disfurnish the castle; his Lordsp replied: that he hoped to come back with victory; but if it happened otherwise he would most certainly retreat to him att Winchester: and there they should be able to supply what he tooke from him with advantage; whereupon my Lord Ogle furnished him with six carts Loaden with biskett, cheese: and divers other provisions. the wednesday following he with the two other Lords and all their forces: marched toward Waller who was, as it seemed, retiring towards London. but my Lord Hopton was minded to hinder their retreat and to get before him and he marched in great hast . . .

Hopton does not mention Ogle's disagreement, but only records the decision to march against Waller:

And therupon the E. of Brainford and Lo: Hopton

consulted and resolved to draw up to them. Upon which reselution the E. of Brainford, having at that present a fitt of the gout, commanded the Lo: Hopton to draw out the whole Army and traine... about 3. of the clock in the afternoone and to take his quarters for that night in the field three miles towards the Enemy upon the way of the plaine, which the Lo: Hopton did accordingly, and sent out strong partyes of horse severall wayes towards the Enemy, with command not to allarum them, but only to secure the Army from any surprize of theirs. Next morning before day the Army being ready to marche, the E. of Brainford (though with payne and difficulty enough) came up to it, and presently orders were given, and the Army marched towards Warneford the Enemy's head-quarter, but they haveing discovered one of our partyes the night before were drawen out, and embattaild upon a hill about 2. English miles behinde their quarters in a woodland countrey.

Colonel Walter Slingsby marched with the Royalist army on 26 March in this attempt to surprise the Parliamentarian quarters in Warnford, but he only caught sight of the White Regiment on their way to East Meon, guarding the rear of the London Brigade:

Upon report of Wallers approache wee made ready to advance, and hearing that some Footte and horse of his first Troopes quarter'd within eight miles of Winchester, wee drew out in the close of the evening our whole body, marched silently three miles, and theire lay all night under the covert of a wood. Next morning earely advanced in hopes to have surpriz'd them in this quarter, but when wee came thither, not a man was to be found. Yett wee spy'd a full Regiment with white collours stand in order facing us upon our left hand about a mile and a halfe from us, but could by noe meanes discover where the Enemys body lay...

For the Londoners the stand of the White Regiment was a moment of danger, as Elias Archer recalls:

The day following we discovered the Enemy, who took some few of our men that were stragling from their colours, and soon after appeared in a great body upon the hill on the left hand the Town, intending (as some prisoners confessed) to take us at Church, it being the Fast Day; but, it pleased God, who foresaw the Plot, to prevent the danger, directing us to keep the Fast the Wednesday before, when we lay still at Midhurst, so that we were provided to entertain them, and drew our men into a body neer the town, which done, Orders came to march away, which accordingly we did, in the Forlorn-Hope, expecting the Enemy every hour to fall upon us, so that we were forced to make a stand a mile or more from the town in extream danger, till Sir *William Wallers* forces came up from Eastmean to joyn with us.

With Waller's army stationed between East and West Meon, probably on the reverse slope of the wooded down known today as Westbury Forest, Hopton sought to draw his opponent into the open. While this skirmishing was in progress, however, Waller decided to slip away and cut off the Royalist army from its base at Winchester, a move of which Hopton's intuitive sixth sense as a general gave him advance notice. The two armies raced for Alresford, and the Royalists won by a short head:

The armyes a while faced one another, and the Generalls commanded Sir John Smyth (then Major Generall of the horse) with a good party of horse to advance towards the Enemy, to seeke to drawe him from his advantage to engage from the woods, and neerer the plaine. But that takeing noe effect, and the Lo: Hopton knowing that countrey very well and that there was a close way through woods and lanes from the place where the Enemy stood in battell neerer to Alsford then the place where the Army then stood, suspected that the Enemyes' designe might be to send Sir Wm. Belfore with his horse and dragoones to possesse Alsford; which being a reasonable strong quarter, and within 5 miles of Winchester would have given them great advantage; There was therefore, by the advice of the Lo: Hopton a party sent to discover that way, which brought word of theire marche, as was suspected; Hereupon, by the advice of the Lo: Hopton, a resolution was presently taken to marche with the whole Army, with as good speed, as could stand with good order, towards Alsford, and the Lo: Hopton with Sir Edw. Stowell's brigade of horse, and his owne Regiments, one of horse, and another of dragoones, advanc'd with as much speede as they could to possesse Alsford before Sir Wm. Belfore; And the busines was so hard prest on both sides, as the Lo: Hopton, a mile and halfe before he came to Alsford, marching himselfe with Sir Edw. Stowell in the head of his brigade, did plainely discover Sir Wm. Belfore's troopes marching in the lane levell with them, and they were not a mile a sunder; The Lord Hopton thereupon went, and commanded his owne Regiments of horse and dragoones, that were advanc'd about halfe a mile before, to make all the speede with any convenience they could, to gett into the Towne, and assoone as they recovered the Towne, the dragoons to alight, and make good the Barocadoes towards the Enemy, and the horse to stand together in a body in the market place to second them, as there should be occasion; And himselfe, with Sir Edw. Stowell's Brigade in 2. or 3 divisions (for they were then 100. horse), having first sent back to the E. of Brainford to give him notice of the state of theire busines, and of his purposes, and to pray his Excellence to advance with the Army to his reliefe assoone as conveniently he could) march'd the said Brigad(e) with as much dilligence as possibly he could to second the other horse at Alsford; All which tooke a good effect, for the forlorn hope possest Alsford in time, and the Enemy by that checq made a halt, and tooke theire quarters about Cheriton. Our Army came late to Alsford, they drew not into the Towne, but stoode in armes that night on a rising-ground joyning to the Towne fronting towards the Enemy, onely the E. of Brainford, his indisposition and payne still continuing was (though very hardly) persuaded to take a lodgeing in the Towne.

During the race to Alresford, Waller closed up his army in a tighter formation to avoid exposing too long a flank to the enemy, and this may have cost him valuable time. Just beyond a line between Bramdean Common and Cheriton his army gave up the attempt, and stopped for the night. Captain Harley, in his account of the march, could not forbear to show his amused contempt for the Londoners:

> This day wee begunne our march. Sir William Belfore had the vantguard of our horse: with him marched his twenty-two troops, the Kentish, Colonel Norton and Greinfield's, their troops. Of our foote, Colonel Browne had the vantguard. Sir William Waller broute up the reare with his three regiments of horse. Here wee chainged our posture of marching with the regiments. Wee never march nowe but four troops together.
>
> The enemy faced us this day with about three thousand horse. Here you should have seen the Londoners runne to see what manner of thinges cowes were. Some of them would say they had all of them hoornes, and would doe greate mischiefe with them, then comes one of the wisest of them cryeth 'Speake softly.' To end the confusion of their opinions

they pyled up a counsel of warr, and agreed it was nothing but some kind of looking glasse, and soe marched away. Wee had some light skirmishes but with little hurt on ether side. We marched this day to Cherrytowne where the citicens came within sight of the enemy's foote. You could hear noe other word of commaund then 'Stand straite in your files.' When it begunne to growe darke, wee might see the enemy striving to possesse themselfes of a hill and a heath on the right hand of us, which caused us to make choise of the ground wee were on to receave the enemy. It was after twelve of the clocke at night before our reare came up, which was caused by our often facing about to face the enemy.

On Wednesday night the London Brigade camped under the hedgerows of Lamborough fields, some meadows alongside the stream which eventually swelled into the River Itchen. While they slept in the open meads Sir William Waller took quarters in Hinton Ampner manor house, the home of Lady Stukeley, which lay a little further down the valley upon its southern slopes. Beyond the northern ridge, which reached up eastwards from Cheriton and was known to some as East Down, lay two miles of dipping plateau leading up to Sutton Common, high ground just outside Alresford which the Royalist army occupied.

During Thursday 28 March the armies skirmished in this intervening plateau ground between East Down (which the Roundheads occupied at dawn) and Sutton Common. Both generals began the day's work by sending out scouting parties. Hopton's men soon discovered the whereabouts of the Parliamentarian army:

> The next morning assoone as it was day, the Lo : Hopton sent out a little party, to discover where the Enemy were, which was quickly mett by light partyes of the Enemy, who had taken theire quarters in a low field joyning to the Lady Stukeley's house, not a myle and halfe from our Army so as there was but a little hill, and a little vale betweene us ; The hill they endevoured to keepe, because it cover'd them from us, and gave them the advantage of looking into us.

Colonel Walter Slingsby, a brigade commander, agrees with Hopton in stating clearly that the Parliamentarians lay in the valley, although he says that their position was discovered late the previous night :

> Our Army marched with greate hast crosse the Country to gett a passe, which led to the Towne, before the Enemy, which wee did, and then hunted about for to discover where this yett invisible body lay, and at last found his whole strength, horse, foote and artillerye, in a low meade within halfe a mile of us, where hee shadowed himselfe in his march by a lane, and in that ground by a thicke high hedge. Wee then marched to Alrsford and hutted in the feild close by the Towne. The next morning wee found the Enemy likewise hutting in his ground where hee did intend to stand us.

Apart from a commanded (or selected) party who took part in the skirmishing, the London Brigade stood on East Down and watched the fighting. Elias Archer expressed some admiration for the Roundhead Horse:

> Upon Thursday morning a commanded partee was sent to view the Enemie, which they did, and incountered with a forlorne hope of the Enemies, and behaved themselves very bravely, so that day was spent in skirmishes, where much gallantry and true valour was shewed by our horse, especially two men whose names I do not well remember, to the perpetuall honour of the actors, and great admiration of the spectators; by whose meanes a considerable partee was once ingaged, and the enemy came on with a great body, which appearing, we discharged one gun, which did such execution in our fight, that they all fled.

Captain Harley, however, was less satisfied with the outcome:

> The 28th day wee faced one another for the most part of the day. Their was a house and two barnes very full of corne from which our horse fetched greate store of provision for their horses. It did stand betwixt both armyes, but nearer theirs then ours, which caused us to send divers partees of horse to keipe it from them, and they sent partees to gaine it from us. Skirmishes betwixt these partees lasted a good part of the day, till towards night they sent a partee of foote which put our horse to a retreate, and soe they barred the barnes and house, which was a greate oversight in us: it standing soe that wee might with a fewe foote have maintained it untill wee had fetched away the corne, which was much wanted in our army.

Harley had better reason to be ill pleased because Hopton and Ruthven succeeded before nightfall in displacing the Parliamentarians from their 'little hill' (East Down), and they could therefore look down as dusk fell upon the camp fires of the enemy. In order to secure this important gain they brought up 1500 soldiers, and then retired to bed:

> Wee disputed that ground that day with little partyes, and loose skirmishes, but towards the evening we gott the topp of the hill, and the view of the Enemye's quarters, where they encamped as is said before in a low field enclosed with a very thick hedge and ditch and theire ordnance planted upon the rysing of the hill behind them. Both the Generalls viewing the advantage of the ground they had gotten, and that there was a little wood on the top of that hill with a fense about it, plac'd Sir George Lisle therein with 1000. Muskettiers, and a guard of 500 horse upon the way by him; and layed out the quarters for the whole army upon the same hill where they had stood in armes the night before, with command to every horseman to rest by his horse, and every footeman by his armes, and every officer in his place. And so the Lo: Brainford, by the importunity of the Lo: Hopton, and the rest of the officers retyr'd to his lodgeing in the Towne, and the Lo: Hopton tooke his quarters in the head of the Army in his coache.

That night the Parliamentarian commanders held a council of war, for bad news had just arrived from London. The forces besieging Newark had been scattered by Prince Rupert (21 March). Consequently the way lay open for a Royalist advance on London, which the Earls of Essex and Manchester would have to parry. Thus they could not be relied upon to restore the situation south of London if Waller suffered defeat, nor defend the capital. No wonder some officers at the council urged Waller to repeat the stratagem at Lansdown, 'to make fiers and retreat.' The council, however, took its courage in its hands and despite the dire consequences of a disaster resolved to fight.

Waller almost certainly decided to make one of his celebrated night moves: before or soon after dawn a chosen party of musketeers occupied Cheriton Wood, on the far right of East Down as the Roundheads looked up at it, and to the left of the Royalist advance guard, camped near to Bramdean Lane. No doubt the sounds the Cavalier sentries heard that night, which they interpreted as signs of a retreat, were the preparations for the seizure of Cheriton Wood. It was a long tense night, full of alarms and excursions, as Hopton recalls:

That night Sir Geo. Lisle being verie watchfull upon the Enemyes motions, and giveing of them severall alarums, and being soe neere as he heard them span and drive theire waggons, conceived they had bin drawing off, and so advertized the Lo Hopton, who presently sent the intelligence to the E. of Brainford, and he forthwith directed his orders to command Sir Jo: Smyth to drawe out a party of 1000 horse to be ready to wayte upon the reare of the Enemy, which was presently prepared, and, as the day began to breake, the Lo: Hopton went up to Sir Geo. Lisle's guards to take the more certaine information of the Enemy's proceedings.

The dawn could not come too early for the Roundheads either. Captain Harley had no sleep that night:

This night I commaunded the outguards of our horse that did belong to our regiment which was (in) Waltam wood were the enemy had faced us the day before with two regiments of horse. In the morning before day, I sent a partee of horse to discover which way the enemy did lye. They found them all drawne together on the hill upon the right hand of us. Not long after the partee was returned, but the trivall was beaten. The trumpets sounded to horse and and alarum was strucke up thorough out the whole army. To some it was a trusty awaking from a cold sleipe; to others it stroke more terror than the earth had donne cold before. In the morning when I went to veiwe the army, I sawe such a cheerfulnesse in every one's countenanse, that it promised ether victory or a willingnesse rather to dye then loose the feild. Only the citisens' silver lase begunne to looke like copper.

Meanwhile Waller had made his dispositions. His guns were placed on the rising ground between Bramdean and Hinton Ampner pointing up towards East Down. The bulk of his horse, he probably drew up somewhat unconventionally, behind the artillery, with his foot securing both wings, but this battle order is conjecture. Already 1000 musketeers under Lieutenant-Colonel Walter Leighton had marched up to occupy Cheriton Wood, and a very strong party of foot and dragoons under Colonel James Carr took up positions in the hedgerows in front of Hinton Ampner on Waller's left wing. But as soon as Hopton reached East Down and discovered that the Roundheads had moved under cover of darkness to occupy Cheriton Wood, he consulted with Forth, and while the latter brought up the main body of the army he drew back

Lisle's musketeers on to the reverse slope of East Down and set about clearing Cheriton Wood by taking it in the rear:

> The morning was very misty, so as he could not make a cleere discovery till the sun was neere his two howers up, and then he found that the Enemy was not drawing off, but that they had in the darke of the night possest themselves of a high woody ground that was on the right hand of theire owne quarters, and plac'd men and cannon in it, that commaunded the hill where Sir Geo: Lisle was; Of this he presently advertized the E. of Brainford; who (notwithstanding his indisposition came instantly out to him); and, seing the posture the Enemy was in, commanded the Lo: Hopton to drawe the whole Army and cannon up to him to that ground, which he did accordingly; And placing the foote and horse that the E. of Brainford brought with him on the right whing, himselfe with his owne foote and horse drew to the left, which was over against that woody ground that the Enemy had newly possest, and where they understood themselves (as indeede they were) upon a great advantage under the covert of the wood, and having lin'd the hedges next to us with store of muskettiers. This the Lo: Hopton observing tooke his advantage likewise of the ground he was on, and drew all his horse and foote in order on the side of the hill that was from the Enemy, and being there within muskett shott, and yet secured commanded Coll. Appleyeard (now Sir Mathew Appleyeard) to draw out of the foote a commanded pa(r)ty of 1000. muskettiers, which he did, and devided them into 4 devisions, and in that order (as he was commanded) advanced towards the Enemy; But the bodyes of our men no sooner appear'd on the topp of the Hill, but the Enemy shewed how well they were prepared for us, and gave fier very thick and sharpe, which our men very gallantly receaved and return'd; But the Lo: Hopton foreseeing that our party could not long hold out upon so great disadvantage, and observing an opportunity to cast men into the wood upon the flanke of the Enemy, he drew of Lieutenant Coll: Edward Hopton with one division of the commanded muskettiers, and commanded them to run with all possible speede into the wood upon the Enemyes flancke, where there was likewise a crosse-hedge to cover them, which they had noe sooner done, and given one volley from thence but the Enemy fell in disorder; and began to runne, and Coll: Appleyeard with his party pursued them, and had the execution of a part of them through the wood, and possest himselfe of all theire ground

of advantage, and tooke a horse Colours and some prisoners, but none of theire cannon, for they being light guns were drawen off.

The Roundheads watched the flight of their 1000 musketeers and 300 horse from Cheriton Wood. Captain Harley blamed the disaster upon the greenness (to put it charitably) of the Londoners:

> Their was on the right hand of us — as wee were now faced, —a woode which wee did conceave might be of greate advantage to us if it were maintained; for which purpose their was a partee of a thousand musquettiers, Colonel Pattle's regiment and the Londoners white regiment, sent thither, and three hundred horse to second them. On the left wing of us their was hedges and a little village. Wee sent a very strong partee of musquettiers to line those hedges, whereof one partee were Londoners. The enemy made noe long stand but fell upon our men that were in the woode, and likewise sent a partee to fall on our men at the little village. The citisens in the woode — were in woode but they found the way howe to get out — noe sooner they did see that the bullets would come otherwise then they would have them but they made a foule retreate — I am confident I smelt them — with a faire paire of heeles, which did soe discourage the rest, that they all left their charge with a shamefull retreat. Our three hundred horse which were to second our foote as soone as the enemy offered to charge came away in the same confusion on the left hand. Alsoe the Londoners lost their ground. Nowe the day beganne to looke blacke on our side, and if God had not wonderfully shewed himselfe, wee had lost the field, yet I thought I did see something that promised victory. All were still willing to goe on, and the souldiers put the fault on their officers, and the officers on the souldiers.

Lieutenant-Colonel John Birch, however, happily recovered from his wounds and credited by Secretary Roe with causing the battle to be fought when others would flee, saw in Leighton's habit of cursing the reason for the setback. He led his regiment in the force which Waller despatched to stablise his right wing:

> While the army was at that posture a councell of warr was called, at which it was resolved, as I have heard (upon the defeat of the Parliament's forces at Newarke and in the North), to make fiers and retreat; which being sore against your minde, whoe then was capten of the watch, you used these words to Sir Arthur Haselrieg, that surely wee did

care whither that were God's cause wee had in hand; for did wee assuredly beleeve it, when hee called us to fight with his eneimes, wee should not run from them: for mans extremitie is Gods oppertunitie. Yet, notwithstanding that order of the councell of warr, you disposed it so, being then captain of the watche, that the parties on both sides were in the night soe engaged that there was noe marching off without a palpable discovery. Therefore, according to your desire, the army kept their ground, and the next morneing, by breake of the day, drew into batalia, your place being with your regiment in the maine battle. And presently 1000 muskateeres were drawne out, to make good the wood on the right wing; and, contrary to your desire, put under the comand of Leiftennant Collonel Layton, whome you said did sweare too hard to have God with him. However, hee went and tooke possession of the wood: but stayed not above halfe an hower before the enemies foot, under Collonel Appleyard, beat them clearly out, and tooke possession, pursueing our men, whose heells then were their best weapon, to the amazement of our whole army. One passage then I cannot omitt. It fell from Sir Arthur Haslerig, which was thus: seeing our men put to soe shamefull a route, turned to your selfe saying, "Now, Collonel, have you Fighting enough?" Your answere instantly given was, "Sir, this is but a rub; wee shall yet winn the cast:" and you further added that, whereas your selfe and regiment were now in the maine body, might you have order to march with your regiment to make good the right wing, you would quickly set all right againe: which comand imediatly by Sir William Waller was given you, and by your selfe instantly executed; and the enemy soe turned in his pursute that hee thought it best to save himselfe by speedy draweing off.

Meanwhile Hopton in Cheriton Wood could see that he had a marvellous opportunity to fall upon Waller's disordered right flank, which probably stood in front of Bramdean, but Forth thought this unwise. By this time the Royalist army had occupied the whole length of East Down.

No contemporary account or plan of the Royalist (or Roundhead) dispositions exists, but it is likely that Hopton's forces occupied the left wing and Forth's the right, with Bramdean Lane as the dividing line. The horse was massed at first behind the ridge, in the centre of East Down.

Once Hopton had settled the guards on the left wing in Cheriton Wood he rode back towards the centre to confer with Forth, only to find that the Royalist right had become engaged, apparently in disobedience to orders, in front of Hinton Ampner, as he narrates :

> The Lo. Hopton haveing carefully placed all his guards both of horse and foote upon all the Avenues of that ground which he had newly gotten from the Enemy, and finding that he had from thence a faire way to fall upon the flancke of theire whole army, sent Sir Jo: Paulet and Coll: Hayes to the E. of Brainford to give him an accompt of the successe he had had, and of the advantage, he conceiv'd, he had at the present, and that, if his Excellence were so pleased, he would with 1000 horse, and 1000 muskettiers charge the flancke of the Enemye's Army. The E. of Brainford return'd his answeare with civilityes of great favour and encouragement for what he had done, but, that having now possest all the ground of advantage on our side, his opinion was that wee should not hazard any farther attempt, for that he conceived the Enemy would now be forced, either to charge us upon theire disadvantage, or to retire. The Lo: Hopton remayn'd extreamely satisfyed with that solid advice; And haveing settled all guards and orders upon the left whing, went himselfe towards the right whing to confer with the Lo: Generall. And being neere the midd-way upon the brow of the hill he saw troopes of the right whing too farr advanced, and hotly engaged with the Enemy in the foote of the hill, and so hard prest, as when he came to the Lo: Brainford, he found him much troubled with it, for, it seemes the engagement was by the forwardness of some particular officers, without order.

One of the officers in question, young Colonel Sir Henry Bard, had led his regiment of foot against the seasoned Colonel James Carr in front of Hinton Ampner, whether or not without orders, as Slingsby suggests, it is now difficult to determine. First he mentions Appleyard's resounding success :

> Then was Collonell Appleyard, with a thousand commaunded muskeiteires, order'd to fall in upon the wood, which hee perform'd very well, beating them out in such disorder that many was slaine (I beleive to the number of 80) and three times as many armes taken. This defeite put the Rebells into such a fright that wee could discerne severall companys of thirty, of forty, and more in some,

running over the feilds in the reare of theire Army halfe a mile and as well discerne theire horses span'd in theire carriages and to theire artillerye. This encourag'd us soe muche that wee made too muche hast to finishe the businesse (for had wee but stood still and make signes of falling on, they had probably melted away without fighting a stroake more), but wee were order'd to fall on from both wings, which was the only cause of theire standing to fight; for then the Enemy finds most of our strength drawne of the hill into a bottome, where hee had his desir'd advantage: and our first mischance hapned on our right wing, where Sir Henry Bard, leading on his Regiment further then hee had orders for, and indeede with more youthfull courage then souldierlike discretion, was observ'd by the Enemy to bee a greate space before the rest, and out of his ground, who incontinently thrusts Sir Arthur Hassellrigs Regiment of horse, well arm'd, betwixt him and home, and theire in the view of our whole Army (much to our discouragement) kills and takes every man.

Perhaps his regiment formed a part of the 1500 'commaunded men' mentioned below by Harley. Waller had brought his cavalry forward into the flat bottom of the valley between the two hills, and from this position Heselrige and other commanders launched charges against the flank of the Royalist infantry attacking Hinton Ampner:

The enemy being nowe possessed of the woode, that wee might not be outdared by their horse, wee drewe downe all our horse into a heath, which stoode betwixt the two hills were they did fight, but under favour of the enemy's ordinanse, the hills being one from another not [a] whole culvering shott — which was wel knowne to some of the enemy's horse which were disspersed by our shott. Here my leiftenant lost his horse and a part of his foote, but I hope he will recover speidily. Their canon did very small execution amongst us, the enemy thinking all were his owne if he could but possesse himselfe of the village and those hedges we had lined; for that intent he sent downe a partee of fifteen hundred commaunded men to possesse themselfes of those places. Wee likewise sent downe twelve hundred commanded men to second our owne men. These did holde their places very neare a heath; then the enemy gotte ground and fired the village. It was noe sooner on fire but the winde turned. Our men, seeing the advantage set them to a disordered retreat; our horse seeing it, sent a partee of a hundred horse under the command of Captaine Buttler to charge them, and another under the command of Colonel Norton to second them. Captaine Fleming commanded another partee. They all of them performed their charges soe wel that thorough God's blessing they routed them all, sleue about a hundred and fifty and tooke a hundred and twenty prisoners with divers commanders of quality. Wee receaved not much losse, only Captaine Fleming hurt in the arme with a captaine's leading staffe. I doe not heare of any other considerable losse or hurt.

While the fighting raged in the smoke-blown fields of Hinton Ampner, the Royalist foot on their left wing were now engaged with some Parliamentarian foot which certainly included Heselrige's Regiment. Colonel Walter Slingsby, who commanded the tertia of foot in this wing, makes no mention of the stay to advance on this front described by Hopton, but it is probable that he is writing about a Royalist attack made later in the morning, just before noon, when it became clear that battle had been joined along the rest of the line:

> Upon this successe the Enemy resumes theire first courage, which prompted them to trye a feild with us, or rather a better then that, which made them resolve to beate us; and soe with a strong body of horse charges our footte on the left wing, on that part which my Lord of Brainford was pleas'd to make your servants charge, theire the Enemy horse was repulssed with losse. They immediatly try'd the second charge in which Captain Herbert of my Lord Hoptons Regiment was slaine, with a fresh body and were againe repulssed, and soe againe the third time, the foote keeping theire ground in a close body, not firing till within two pikes length, and then three rankes att a time, after turning up the butt end of theire musketts, charging theire pikes, and standing close, preserv'd themselues, and slew many of the enemy.
>
> Then my Lord John Steward (seeing our footte like to be opprest with freshe horse) sends downe the Queenes Regiment of horse, which were most Frenche, who descended the hill into this ground with seeming resolution, but retreated after an unhandsome charge.

The Roundhead horse mentioned in this account cannot have been the regiments of Heselrige, Waller or Norton, for they were engaged on the left wing and in the centre. Captain John Jones, serving in one of the City regiments, refers below to the Kentish regiment under Sir Michael Livesey, five troops strong, who charged in support of the Parliamentarian foot as they moved up against Colonel Slingsby's hedgehogs of pike and musket:

> The fight began from eight and continued till past five a clock, at the first a party of Musketiers, about 1000 were sent into a Wood, where they were beaten by the enemies bodie, the place being not tenable, which place being so quitted gave them great advantage: afterwards they came downe with furie on the right wing along the hedges, which wee had lined, but could hardly keep it; they fell on with so much courage and resolution, till the Kentish horse took a troope or two of them at one charge, and our horse fell on their foot, and drove them from the hedges then they fell downe with a great bodie of horse and foot in those fields, and our foot seconded with 400 Musketiers, sent to them, who with three houres fight drove them from the hedges, wonne the ground, and beat their maine bodie.

By now, early afternoon, the aged Earl of Forth resolved to unleash his 2000 horse on the Parliamentarian cavalry, spread out below him, probably in front of Bramdean, in 'nine fair bodyes' according to Slingsby. As he tells, Hopton took personal command over the Cavalier horse, but their charges came to naught:

> Lo: Brainford thereupon ordered him to drawe out 1000 horse, and to commande them to advance to the Enemy's horse that were in the Common at the foote of the Hill, and to charge them. He thereupon drew out Sir Edw. Stowell for that service with his owne Brigade, which then consisted of 1000 horse, who perform'd it with very great gallantry, but after a sharpe and close charge that continued neere halfe an hower, his body of horse was broken and rowted, and himselfe charging home to their cannon was taken prisoner with five wounds upon him. And while the Lo: Hopton was ordering this charge, the rest of our horse, all, saving Sir Hum. Benet's Regiment, that stood in reserve on the top of the hill were wholy engaged. In this unfortunat charge we lost many of our best officers; And the Lord John Stuart Brother to the Duke of Richmond, who commanded the Lo: Hopton's horse, and Sir John Smyth who was his Major Generall of horse, he, with much ado, gott of alive, but both mortally wounded.
>
> By this time the whole horse were in disorder, and the Lo: Hopton had much adoe to gett to the number of 300 horse

> to stand with him at the entrance into the Common, where all the Enemye's horse stood in bodyes before him; The greater part of that little number of horse that stayed with hime were of the Queene's Regiment, where Monsr. de Plurie theire cheife Commander doing his duty like a very worthey person in the head of them had his legg shott off to the anckle with a great shott, whereof he shortly after dyed, and the Lo: Hoptons horse received a muskett shott in the shoulder; Yet it pleased God that they made that stand good, till, with the advice, and assistance of the Earle of Brainford, the rest of the horse and foote were retreated, and had recovered the top of the Hill, where they had at first drawen up in the morning:

Slingsby blames this ill success on the fact that the cavalry filed down a single lane (almost certainly Bramdean Lane) one troop at a time:

> Then wee drew downe most of the horse and endeavor'd to draw up upon that plaine ground before our footte, in which our Enemys horse stood rang'd in nine faire bodys, but having one laines end only to passe into it, they came upon great disadvantages, for by that time one body was in the ground and drawne up (before another could second it), it was over charged with number; yett I am confident our horse did performe more gallant charges that day then hath bin knowne in any one battaile this warr; wherein my Lord John Steward, Sir John Smith, Collonell Sands, L. Collonell Scott, and many gallant gentlemen more slaine, whose names I cannot now call to mind. Sir Edward Stowell wounded and taken, Collonell Leg wounded, Major Bishop and Captain Seymour desperately wounded, and many more; our horse (discouraged and enfeebled with the losse of soe many or almost all theire principall officers) were not soe fitt to fight againe, especially in regard theire number began to lessen apace; they were therefore with the footte drawne from that bottome up to the hill where our cannon and reserves stood...

During the mêlée Sir William Waller charged himself, no doubt at the head of his regiment but surrounded by his Lifeguard:

> The enemy having by a charge given upon some troops of mine shutt me off from my own men, I having then but three in company with me, but it pleased God they were repulsed again, and thereby a way opened for my retreat... I reckon itt a mercy that upon a sudden occasion that day, charging without my headpiece, and being known to the enemy (as I

afterwards understood from some of them), I came off safe and unhurt.

The Cavaliers had lined the hedgerows of East Down with musketeers and these held back with a storm of fire the Roundhead horse for over three hours every time they broke through the Royalist horse. During this unusually long cavalry battle Major-General Sir John Smith received a mortal wound from one of Heselrige's 'Lobsters.'

The confusion of this cavalry battle must have been intensified by the fact that both Armies wore the same badge — something white in their hats — and also at first used the password: 'God with us.' The Cavaliers later changed this to 'God and the Cause' and the Roundheads to 'Jesus help us' or 'Jesus bless us.'

As the afternoon wore on, the struggle in the hedgerows on Waller's left wing had become more fierce as Forth committed his remaining reserves of foot. Without cavalry support (for the Roundhead horse now engaged Hopton's regiments in the centre) the Londoners with Colonel James Carr and Major James Strachan had to protect themselves against the odd charge, as Archer recalls:

> The Enemie presently came on with their main body of horse, very powerfully, and were met as couragiously, yet being of the greater number (for our whole body was not then together) forced ours to a disorderly retreat, at which time the day was doubtfull, if not desperate, our foot all the while was ingaged on the left wing, to drive the Enemy from the hedges, where our men played their parts gallantly, and drove them from hedge to hedge by degrees, till they had forced them to the top of the hill, our horse doing little for the space of an hour after their retreat, only some parties incountring with each other, at which time our Noble Major Generall *Brown* (who was ever known to be a valiant man, and must be lookt upon as a speciall instrument in the work, Drew off 100. men from the hedges, and in his own person led them on to charge the horse, which they did most gladly and couragiously, and forced the enemies horse to wheele about, whereupon our body of horse came on again, and that very manfully, at which time they charghed quice *(sic)* thorow the Enemies body and put them to a rout, so that they were

forced to retreat to the top of the hill, where they first appeared...

About 3.00 or 4.00 p.m. the two wings of Parliamentarian foot began to close like crabs' claws, as the soldiers pushed back their adversaries from hedgerow to hedgerow. From all the contemporary accounts Carr's musketeers on the left, harassed by Cavalier horse, had the more difficult task, especially as the Royalist guns could — and did — easily fire upon them. Yet his secretary insisted on awarding to Lieutenant-Colonel John Birch the honours at this stage of the day, as at every other:

> This [the alleged re-occupation of Cheriton Wood by Birch] brought on the engagement of severall bodys of foote under Sir Richard Browne and others, whoe did exceedingly well, and also of the horse, which with great violence and various success continued untill about 4 in the afternoone: at which time twoe thousand muskateeres were drawne out at your request; one thousand whereof on the left wing were comanded by Collonel Rea, whoe did very gallantly, the rest by your selfe on the right wing; all the rest of the army being to second them. These twoe great parties went on with such success, that in one houre the enimies army was between them, all our horse and foote comeing on in the front of them. The first thing that I could perceive, they puld of their collours, thrust them in their breeches, threw down their arms, and fled confused. Your selfe and others hot in pursute had not followed them above 100 paces into their owne ground, before one, whome I shall not name, overtooke you, comanded you to stand: but for what end I never yet could tell, except it was to give the enimy leave to runn away, and carry away there cannon; sure I am you stood there 3 quarters of an houre, untill the enimy was far enough. The reason is too deepe for mee to give: only this I am sure of; had the enimies comander in chiefe been there, hee could not have comanded any thing more advantagious to them. Thus was that dayes victory gayned; unto which I make bould to add, that it was indeed a victory, but the worst prosecuted of any I ever sawe.

Who the unnamed officer was who restrained Birch we shall never know. According to Captain Robert Harley, however, General James Wemyss, the artillery commander, gave the order to pursue the enemy:

> The fight betwixt the horse continued nea(rly) four

houres, their horse being at length discouraged, doing noe good with their desperate and bold charges, made a faire retreat to the topp of the hill were their foote were. Colonel James Carr and Major Strauan had soe plyed their businesse on the left of our army that they forced the enemy to drawe off their ordinanse, and quickly engaged all the enemy's foot on them, but they seeing their horse to retreat would noe longer abide the charge of our foote and dragoones, but made a speidy retreat to a hill a little beyond the place were wee did fight. When wee had possessed with our horse the hill which the enemy had, wee were at a stand wether wee should advance on the enemy. It was once by some ordered that wee should returne to our stations which wee had before; and I believe wee should not have pursued if Colonel Weims had not shewed himselfe very violent for it. To him next under God doth belong much of our victory. Thorough his perswasions it was ordered wee should againe fall on them and give them a generall charge. This delay of ours gave them leave to drawe of all their canon and most of their carriages, but noe sooner was our cannon come up and played on them awile but they prevented our charge in commanding everyone to shift for himselfe, and soe they proved their horses to be better then ours. They never faced about as I can heare to this day.

The hesitation of the Roundheads once they had gained East Down — more soldierly caution to allow a regroup than a sinister plot to allow old friends to escape without being utterly ruined — certainly gave the experienced Royalist commanders time to withdraw in order. Hopton, who had once before pulled out an army from under the guns of Waller's army on a hill above him a few days before Lansdown battle, remained calm. Here he gives the authoritative account of the Royalist withdrawal to Basing House, and from thence to Reading:

But by this time the disorder was so generall, and the Enemy pressed in that part so hard (espetially with theire muskett shott) that it was with great difficulty that we gott off all our cannon; and making our reare as good as we could with some of the best of our horse and dragoons, we recovered our first ground upon the ridge of the hill by Alsfordtowne, with all our Army, cannon and carriages; from whence we shewed so good a countenance towards the Enemy, that they gave us some respitt, unwilling (as it seem'd) to hazard theire whole army upon us. And thereby the two Generalls had some short time to consult, and the Lo: Hopton (who best knew the Country) advised by noe meanes to retyre to Winchester it being an indefensible ill provided place, and utterly unsafe for an Army in that condition, But that Coll: Fielding (who then commanded the Ordinance) should presently marche off with the trayne and carriages towards Winchester, but being a mile on his way should turne off upon the right hand towards Basing. The foote (with onely a little party of 100. horse to abide in the reare,) to take the lower way through Alsford towards Basing, which after a mile entered into lanes and woods; and that the horse should make theire retreat by the way of the Downes; All this was executed accordingly; And, after Coll: Fielding was cleere gon off with his trayne and carriages, the E. of Brainford commanded the Lo: Hopton to take the charge of the foote, first placing 1000. muskettiers in the Towne to make good his retreate with the horse. And the E. of Brainford did, with admirable conduct and gallantry, sende off the horse, remayning himselfe with his page last upon the ground, and then gott off himselfe hardly poursued by the Enemye's horse untill he gott over the nexte passe, where he faced againe. And at the same time the Lo: Hopton drew out his 1000 foote out of the Towne, and with the foote recovered Basing about one of the clock that night without farther resistance. But the E. of Brainford was forced to face about at every passe for the first 2. or 3. miles, and many of his horse brake from him; Yet, it pleased God, that all both horse and foote, cannon and carriages came safe to Basing that night, and after one dayes rest marched to Redding. Where shortly after his Majestie finding it convenient to make his owne army as strong as he could, joyn'd the Lord Hopton with his forces to it, and at the same time drew off the Garrison of Redding.

Lieutenant-Colonel Slingsby mentions the use of the Roundhead field guns against the retreating Royalists:

Before wee could theire reduce our selves to order, the Enemys left wing advances up to the end of the hill where our right should have bin in readynesse to resist them, but after some struglings to repulse them, in which Collonell Appleyard was shott, wee were Compeld to draw of in such disorder as wee were forced backe to the ground where wee had hutted the 6 daies before; and theire drew up in some order, but could not make above 800 or not soe many horse in the feild; of footte wee shewd a reasonable number. Thus wee stood till they drew theire cannon up soe neare that they fyred upon us three times. Wee stood theire aboue an hower, in which time wee sent away ours and then drew in good order through Alsford Towne and soe to Basing house that night (which is sixteene miles), not loosing a gunn or a coullor, nor a man of that body with which wee made our retreate.

Archer placed the Royalist withdrawal rather earlier in the afternoon, but of course he possessed no pocket watch. According to *Mercurius Aulicus* it was Colonel Neville's horse who faced the Roundhead pursuers in order to cover the retreating Royalist foot, events which the Londoner graphically described:

This was about two of the clock in the afternoon, at which time they began to retreat, and sent their Carriages away, their body of foot followed after, the horse and some few foot onely being left to face and to fight with us, at the last it pleased God to raise up the spirits of some few, not above 300. and to put such courage into them, as to adventure out of the closings, to charge the main body upon the plain, which they did so resolutely that they put them all to flight, our horse pursued them two miles at the least, till the Enemies horse overtook their own foot, who cryed out (as the country people say) Face them, face them, once more face them; which they did, but to small purpose; our horse came up, and at the first charge they were all routed and fled, our horse pursued them till they overtook the foot, routed them likewise, and dispersed them severall waies, some fled to Basing, some to Alton, and some to Winchester, and by the way they cryed out, the Kingdoms lost, the Kingdoms lost, &c. and when they left Alsford where they had long quartered, they set the town on fire at both ends, which doubtlesse had burnt to the ground, but that our men came in and put it out, there was onely four or five houses burnt.

In the confusions of that March evening, as the darkness fell about burning Alresford, the Roundhead horse roamed far and wide after Forth's cavalry and some advance guards reached Winchester. Already, however, thoughts turned to the losses — the cost of victory — as Harley's account reveals:

Nowe when it was too late wee followed them on the spurr unto Winchester walls: wee took divers carriages and store of ammunition. The enemy in his flight set Alsford on fire, and for their reward wee coming into the towne before they well knewe of it, wee gave none of them any quarter. Very many Irish men were slaine here. Our whole body of horse halted three miles short of Winchester; our partees went to Winchester gates. The slauter on either side was very small, especially on ours, considering howe long wee did fight. I believe in all wee did not loose sixty men. The enemy, I am confident, had slaine three hundred men besides horse. All the prisoners wee have tooke since the fight says that most of their officers of worth were slaine or wounded. The man of greatest note that is on their side slaine is my Lord John. On our side hurt there is Colonel Meldrum, Captain Fleming, two captaines, and one major: these be all I heare be hurt.

Harley's estimate of the dead and wounded is probably over-large (see Section III). Certainly the most prominent Cavaliers killed were Lord John Stuart and Major-General Sir John Smith, while the Roundheads lost no one of such note. Behind, on the dark silent fields between Cheriton and Bramdean, on the slopes of East Down and along its broad back, lay the bodies of Royalist and Roundhead, stripped of their Yellow, Blue, Green and Red coats, one together in the white nakedness of death.

Notes

Sources in order of first appearance:
Lieutenant Archer
 A Fuller Relation of the Victory obtained at Alsford, 28 March, by the Parliaments forces (Presented to the Lord Mayor and Committee of Militia by an eye-witness employed to attend the London Brigade), TT: E. 40 (1). Published 1 April 1644.
 The initials 'E.A.' appear at the end, and it is a reasonable assumption that this is Elias Archer. Presumably he thought himself now well enough known to give just his initials.
Captain Robert Harley
 A letter dated 12 April 1643, Bishopstoke, to his brother Colonel Edward Harley, HMC, *Portland MSS.*, Vol. 3, pp. 106-10. The letter begins:
  'I believe you marvel that since our fight I have noe way acquainted you with God's mercy towards us, but I am confident that when you have here seine upon what constant and hard duty our regiment hath binne since our last fight you will noe way thinke me guilty of neglect. What my memory hath kept I will here present unto you, although I must confesse that in some actions my [blank] was my best actor for me; yet in some places my spurres would be too dull and my sword too short, but my horse not soe sloe but that I could convoy my arrant thorough a pistol.
Robert Harley eventually became Governor of Dunkirk, and Waller entrusted him with his younger son.
Sir William Ogle
 'A relation of my Lord Ogle's Engagements before the battle of Edgehill and after.' B.M., Add. MS. 27, 402.
 Sir William Ogle, who had married one of Waller's distant cousins, Susan Waller of Oldstoke in Hampshire, had been an M.P. for Winchester at the outbreak of the War. Waller captured Winchester from him in 1642.
Hopton (in *Bellum Civile*.)
Colonel Walter Slingsby
 His account, written much later after the event and historically inaccurate in places, is printed at the back of *Bellum Civile*.
Lieutenant-Colonel John Birch (from Military Memoir of Colonel John Birch, op. cit.)
Captain John Jones
A Letter from Captain Jones being a relation of the proceedings of

Sir William Waller's Armie, TT : E. 40 (12). Written to a friend lying in Bartholomew's Lane and published on 2 April 1644, the letter begins :

> Worthy Sir,
> I Am sory that my time is so short, that I cannot give a particular account of this days service, the Lord hath extraordinarily delivered, I may say miraculously, saved us this day, and delivered our enemies into our hands ...

Jones adds : Truly, Sir, I think never was a field fought with more advantage and valour on their parts, and with more courage on ours : both horse and foot playd their parts so well, but it pleased our God to force them to a shamefull retreat, and pursued them, beating them at least six miles, their foot and horse totally routed, upon their pursuit towards Winchester and other places, for Sir WILLIAM WALLER, and Sir WILLIAM BELFORD, with many of our horse and foot are not yet returned to us ... we being left to convey the cariage to Alesford, I shall be able to give you a more exact account of it. Our LONDON Regiments, but above any, our Major Generall BROWN hath bin a prime means for our present welfare.

After a brief casualty list, Captain Jones writes :

> Since the beginning of this Letter I have extraordinary good news from ours in their pursuit of the enemies, by the next I hope I shal give you a pleasing account, the Cavaliers said as they ran away by Alesford that the Kingdome was lost, but they gave great vapouring brags what they had done, but believe me who saw, and was an actor, and since have communicated intelligence, that our losse was small our gain incredible. Truly Sir the manner of my relating of Gods wonderous bringing about this Salvation, doth fall infinitely short of what it really was, for all we desire praise bee given to God through all congregations, and that Maior general Brown be always honoured as a principall instrument.

Waller
'Experiences', ff. 19-20.

Chapter Twelve

THE AFTERMATH

'TRULY, I TREMBLE to think how near we were to the very Precipice of Destruction,' wrote the Earl of Essex upon hearing the news of Cheriton.[1] The House of Commons and Committee of Both Kingdoms shared his relief, and the latter made haste the day after the battle to direct Sir William Waller to exploit his victory by marching westwards to relieve the Western ports, now besieged by Prince Maurice: 'We acknowledge the great goodness of God for so seasonable a mercy after the unhappy business at Newark. We are very sensible of the great advantage that will come to the kingdom by a careful and diligent improvement of this success against the enemy for the recovery of the west, and how necessary it is to provide all manner of encouragement for the continuance of your forces in this service.'[2]

On Saturday 30 March the mayor of Winchester met Sir William Waller and presented him with the keys of the city. His cavalry entered the city but the Royalists retained the castle. Finding no Royalist army there Waller and Balfour then marched for Salisbury, where they took 500 sets of arms 'and made all the Cathedrall men runne for it.'[3] Elizabeth, Lady Hopton, who had been living at Winchester with her husband, attempted to escape with two coaches, one full of her jewels and plate. Balfour's horse captured her near Newbury, and detained 200 Royalists and 80 horses that were accompanying her. Waller treated Lady Hopton with great courtesy, and sent her to Oxford with an escort, with her plate, jewels and money intact.[4]

Waller's Regiment of horse saw some hard service this

PLATE 19
Colonel Alexander Popham Artist unknown
Littlecote House

PLATE 20
Colonel John Birch, from the tomb in Weobley Church, Herefordshire
Photograph by John Wright

week, and in particular skirmished with Colonel Neville's Cavalier horse in Newbury, as Harley related:

> Saturday the 30th wee faced Winchester with our horse and marched that night to Stokebridge [Stockbridge]. Sabathday the 31st wee had intelligence that three hundred of the enemy lay at Andover. Our regiment was commanded thither to fall on the towne; wee only tooke some straklers, the rest had taken fresh breath and were gone to Neuberry. Munday, the 1st of April, our regiment, Sir Arthur's regiment of horse, and Sir William Waller's regiment of dragoones were commanded to fall on the enimy's quarters at Neuberry. A little before sunne setting wee beganne our march; halfe an houre before daylight wee came before the towne; Captaine Fincher, having the disposing of the businesse, desired me to second him with my troope in charging first with the forlorne hope into towne. Their was noe officer then with the troope but myselfe and quarter master. My cornet then commanded part of the forlorne hope that entered the towne. Another way their was a small partee which went before Captaine Fincher's partee. They rode up neare the barracade till the enemy fired halfe score musquettes on them which made them crye 'Faces about'; as it was when we tooke Craiford's carriages. Not long it was before the other partee of ours had entered the towne and were come to this barracade, and then our feare was ended; wee tooke some horses and about an hundred prisoners. If it please you, you may ask this bearer why he plundered at Neuberry. On Tuesday wee marched backe to Andover. On Thursday, the 4th. wee marched to Stokebridge. On Fryday and Saturday wee marched to Rumsey. On Sabathday about sunne setting, wee marched towards Winchester; at the breake of the day, we came before the towne. Wee lost one comon souldier in taking the towne. Wee tooke above a hundred horse and a hundred prisoners; wee plundered the towne, and soe returned to Rumsey. Tuesday, the 9th. wee marched with our whole army to Waltam. Our regiment is quartered at Byshope stoke, three miles of Waltam. I should have told you that before wee marched from Andover, Sir William Waller went with all our horse but two regiments and marched to Christe Church, and tooke it in with two hundred prisoners and sixty horse, and on Saturday the 6th, Byshop Waltam was delivered up to Colonel Browne upon composition to march away, leaving their armes behinde them.

Captain Robert Harley wrote his account of the battle in a long letter to his brother Colonel Edward Harley, who had commanded probably the same troop in the Lansdown campaign. After such a strenuous campaign his horse needed especial care:

> If you have heard any relation of our fight you may save yourselfe labor in reading these scribled lines which are nothing else than a confused thing patched up by a short memory: if you have heard none, accept of this as coming from a willing minde to doe you service. When I last enjoyed your company in London I desired Mr. Burgh to furnish me with some necessary, which he promised to doe. I desire that you would hasten them that if it be possible I may have them by this messenger. If I doe not forget I acquainted you that I had spoken for a sadle to Mr. Parry. It is a thing I exceedingly want, both my sadles being broken: your approbation of the sadle would much welcome it to me.
>
> This bearer, Kufford, whoe thorough his importunities hath gotte leave to goe to London on some businesse of his owne, I shall imploy him in nothing but to trye wether he can bring downe my trumpet, for which I desire you would assist him. He hath broute up with him the pyde mare you did see me have when you were at Arundel. I have written to your groome Ned, to have hir drenched and set to grasse that shee may be able to doe mee some service this summer. I besiech you that if shee can doe you any service that you would make use of hir. I desire you that you would give this bearer thanks for his willingnesse to doe me servise. My troope as yet is as it was, yet still myselfe and it at your dispose. As I have told you, my desire is only to be with you, if my coming up to you may any way further it I shall willingly finde a vacant time.

Why did Waller not march westwards? Perhaps if the London Brigade would have accompanied him the campaign would have been feasible, but they would not. The Committee of Both Kingdoms failed to send the £1000 for the pay of the London Brigade which Sir William had requested in his despatch after the battle.[5] On 1 April Heselrige came up to London to hasten the money, but found that although the sum had been promptly collected Colonel Harvey, the commander of the city regiment of horse chosen to escort it to Waller's army, flatly refused to march. Next day the Militia Committee agreed to send another brigade to replace Browne's regiments, and that afternoon the Committee of Both Kingdoms, out of concern 'lest the fruits of victory be lost,' sent Heselrige to Merchant Taylors' Hall with a diplomatic suggestion that Colonel Harvey should be made the new Major-General,[6] but that truculent fellow maintained 'that he would rather carry a musket under His Excellency than have any charge under Waller, saying that he was an unfortunate man, and that he had a commission before him to command the counties he then did.'[7] The then Derby House Committee arranged for the money to be transported under the protection of the City Brigade and four fresh troops of Kentish horse, but as a result of these delays the convoy had reached no further than Kingston on 14 April. With three regiments of horse and one of dragoons Waller had meanwhile enjoyed a good success at Christchurch on 5 April, where he took prisoner a whole Royalist regiment of foot, 400 strong, and 100 horse.[8] While Waller moved on from Poole and Christchurch to Romsey Major-General Browne and the London Brigade were busy besieging Bishops Waltham, a fortified house south of Winchester. Colonel Bennet, commanding a small Royalist garrison in a manor house belonging to the Bishop of Winchester, surrendered on 9 April. On Sunday Waller appeared before Winchester, but the citizens, who had heard that the King would shortly take the field, would not open the gate. The Roundhead foot stormed the town, naturally led by Lieutenant-Colonel Birch! The Parliamentarians once again failed, however, to take the castle.[9]

Some regiments of Roundhead horse captured less than a dozen officers at Sonning, near Reading, but missed two regiments that had been there the previous day. Sir William Waller then marched eastwards to Bishops Waltham and from thence to Farnham Castle, where he arrived on 17 April, having escorted the London Brigade thus far on their way home. Moreover, by 4 April Waller had heard that his way into the West would be blocked by an army which the Royalists planned to muster shortly near Marlborough.[10] In retaliation the Committee of Both Kingdoms ordered a rendezvous for all their forces south of the River Trent at Aylesbury on 19 April.

With Browne's London Brigade determined for home

Waller probably judged it wise to wait for their replacements — the Southwark White Auxiliaries, Westminster Auxiliaries and the Tower Hamlets Regiment, under Major General Sir James Harrington — who had reached Kingston by mid-April.

Waller's move to Farnham Castle was not popular with the Committee of Both Kingdoms, who feared that it would 'lose the country lately gained, which will presently declare for the other side, the enemy will recruit there, the counties on this side will receive great discouragement, and so will the forces that are marching towards him, besides the army will melt away being so near London.'[11] On 17 April Denis Bond, one of the members for Dorchester, wanted to know in the Commons why Waller had returned out of the West and whether he had been ordered to do so. These questions gave rise to a debate, in which Sir Walter Erle alleged that the loss of Wareham was occasioned by Waller taking 150 horse from thence. D'Ewes spoke in Waller's defence, referring to his Ringwood letter (5 April) which gave as the two reasons for withdrawal the shortage of Parliamentarian foot and Prince Maurice's advance. It was resolved that the Committee of Both Kingdoms should take care for the relief of Poole, 'but nothing added touching Waller.'[12]

On 27 April a letter arrived from Waller at Farnham in which he stated that he was 'beholden to his friends in the house who laid the loss of Wareham upon him,' but that he had drawn out the horse from the town at their request in order to avoid being sent to the Isle of Wight, and that the treachery of one of the captains 'had caused the surrender.'[13] Yet when Heselrige returned from Farnham with the reasons for Waller's decision to withdraw from Hampshire, the House of Commons voted against any further enquiry into the matter.

For some days Waller remained at Farnham daily expecting the Royalist army to advance towards him from Marlborough, and he spurned no opportunity to learn more about his enemy's intentions. A Parliamentarian news-sheet printed a somewhat garbled tale of a Royalist soldier in search of sheep who mistook his way and chanced to ride into Waller's quarters, where he asked for the Yellow Regiment. When questioned he replied that he was of 'the General's own regiment,' an answer which aroused certain suspicions. They led him to Sir William and under his gentle interrogation the man confessed that in fact he belonged to Sir Ralph Hopton's Regiment. Waller then took him aside to see what he could learn in a private talk before allowing him to be taken off to prison.[14] Yet the Royalist forces under Forth and Hopton at Newbury proved equally apprehensive of Waller's designs and no major action took place between the two armies. Not until May did Waller's army take the field again.

[1] *L.J.*, Vol. VI, p. 505.
[2] *C.S.P.D.* 1644, pp. 83-4.
[3] *The Kingdome's Weekly Intelligencer*, 2–10 April, TT: E.42 (4).
[4] *The Weekly Account*, 3–10 April, TT: E.42 (3); *The Kingdome's Weekly Intelligencer*, 2–10 April, TT: E. 42 (4); J. Rushworth, Historical Collections (1659-1700), VI, 655.
[5] *C.S.P.D.*, 1644, p. 82.
[6] *Ibid.*, p. 91.
[7] 'Journal of Occurences, 1643–1646', B.M., Add. MS. 24, 465. Harvey had held a *pro tempore* commission to command in Gloucestershire before Waller, probably in the Autumn of 1642.
[8] *A True Discovery of the Victory of Sir William Waller at Christ Church in Hampshire, 7 April.*, TT: E.42 (21); *Military Memoir of Colonel Birch*, pp. 11–12; *The Kingdome's Weekly Intelligencer*, TT: E.42 (2); *Letter Books of Sir Samuel Luke* ed. H. G. Tibbitt (1963), pp. 641–642; Waller to Essex (17 April, Farnham), reported in Whitaker's Diary, B.M., Add. MS. 31, 116
[9] *Mercurius Britanicus*, TT: E. 42 (27).
[10] Sir Edward Walker, 'His Majesty's Happy Progress and Success, 30 March to 23 November, 1644' *Historical Discourses* (1705), p. 8. Walker was secretary to the King's council of war.
[11] The Committee's last fear proved correct, see Waller's proclamation on 20 April, against absence without leave in London, p. 203.
[12] D'Ewes, Harl. MS. 166, f.49. Cf. C.B.K. to Waller (14 April, *C.S.P.D.* 1644, p. 118, bringing the danger of Poole to his notice.
[13] D'Ewes, Harl. MS. 166, f.52.
[14] *Perfect Occurences*, No. 17, TT: E.43 (15).

Chapter Thirteen

CONCLUSION

IT IS NOT the purpose of this book to describe the course of the English Civil War in the months after Cheriton, or its final outcome, although the reader will find a brief outline of Waller's remaining campaigns on pp. 198-9 as an introduction to the unique court martial papers of his army. But some general reflections on the significance of Cheriton in the war would not be out of place.

At first sight it looks as if the Royalists soon recovered from the blow and stabilised the situation. On 1 April, for example, King Charles could write in a jaunty letter to Prince Rupert about 'the retreat that my Lord Hopton has made before Waller, where, though the loss was very inconsiderable, except the loss of some few brave officers, 400 being the most in all, both of horse and foot, the Rebels loss being certainly more, some think twice as many; yet, because they have something to brag on, it may get them so much credit as to be able to recruit Essex's army, in which case it is requisite that yours be not far from me. I hope in a few days to be able to venture on another blow, for my foot came off in good enough order; and now I hear that the appearance of horse is better than we expected.'[1] Ludlow gave much the same verdict from the Parliamentarian point of view: 'We were not yet so happy as to improve our advantages, by which negligence we got little more than the field and the reputation of victory.'[2]

Yet Sir Edward Walker's perceptive 'hindsight' remark, that Cheriton marked a watershed in the war, when the Royalists turned from an offensive to a defensive posture, should not be forgotten. As secretary to the King's council of war Walker was in a good position to judge the effects of events not only upon the outward direction of the war but also upon the minds of the Royalist high command. Lord Clarendon confirmed Walker's opinion when he wrote that the battle 'broke all the measures, and altered the whole scheme of the King's Counsels: for whereas before he hoped to have entered the field early, and to have acted an offensive part, he now discerned he was wholly to be upon the defensive part; and that was like to be a very hard part too.'

Certainly the battle of Cheriton saw the end of any Royalist threat to London: never again did a Royalist army come so close to gaining the capital, although the reader may judge that even if Waller had been defeated the London trained bands would once again have held their own behind the extensive fortifications to the south of the capital.

Nor did the Royalist high command ever mount again what could be called an offensive. True, the Cavaliers frequently made advances upon the enemy, and did their best to exploit the enemy's mistakes. But these moves were more an aggressive form of a defensive strategy rather than parts of an offensive one. In terms of the grand strategy of the war, if such it can be called, the King had lost the initiative. In June, Essex and Waller even forced him out of Oxford. But although the Royalists were responding rather than initiating, they showed more than once that they could *riposte* with deadly effect. At Cropredy Bridge and Lostwithiel, for example, the King respectively inflicted a hard blow against Waller, capturing his guns, and scattered Essex's army to the four winds. Moreover, in the Midlands and North, especially before his defeat at the hands of Fairfax, the Scots and the Eastern Association (Marston Moor, 2 July) Prince Rupert always looked dangerous.

In personal terms his victory at Cheriton certainly enhanced Waller's prestige, but its possible effects upon his career were nullified by the military disappointments of the Summer and Autumn, 1644. A combination of his own defects as a general, a certain amount of bad luck, the poor strategic use of his army by the Earl of Essex and the Committee of Both Kingdoms and the inherent weaknesses of a command made up of ill-paid and mutinous regional regiments each maintaining a degree of independence, slowly took its toll upon Waller's career. Had Cheriton come a year later — or military reform a year earlier — Waller might well have received command of the New Model Army, and the course of English history would have been different.

As for Lord Hopton, despite the King's favour and a recognition of his loyalty, his star had begun to fade. Sent back to the West to strengthen the fortifications of Bristol and raise more men, Hopton took part in the defeat of Essex at Lostwithiel. After spending most of 1645 in the West, where he shared in the resistance to the advance of the New Model Army, in January of the following year he took command of what was left of the Royalist forces in Cornwall, only to suffer his last defeat by Fairfax at Torrington (16 February). He died an exile in Holland in October 1652.

After the battle, Forth returned to Oxford where he was made Earl of Brentford. He accompanied the King to Worcester, and faced Waller once more — with some success — at Cropredy Bridge. After the victorious Lostwithiel campaign against the Earl of Essex, Forth sustained another wound in the head at the second battle of Newbury. By the end of the year his infirmities and growing deafness led to his replacement by Prince Rupert as the leading general in the King's service. He accompanied the Prince of Wales to Jersey and France, and returned with him, now King Charles II, to Scotland in 1649. In 1651 Ruthven died in Dundee.

Sir William Balfour commanded the Parliamentarian horse in the Lord General's Western campaign of 1644. He took Weymouth and Taunton in June. When Essex was trapped at Lostwithiel, Balfour's horse broke through the cordon and joined up with Middleton, by then Lieutenant-General of Waller's Horse. At Second Newbury he led the right cavalry wing of the Roundhead body which attacked the Royalist army from the westwards. Waller almost certainly commanded this body, with Cromwell on his left wing. With the advent of the New Model, Balfour retired and received in 1651 a vote for his arrears, which amounted to £7000.

The year 1651 also saw Waller's release from a three year imprisonment. After the first Civil War ended in 1646 Waller had steadfastly opposed the growing political power of the Army. In 1647 his militant stand made it expedient for him to flee to The Hague when the Army entered London. It is just possible that Hopton, who settled in Spain that year for the next five years, but visited Holland on occasion, may have met Waller once more in his lodgings, and refought the battle over dinner. After Waller's term in prison he became steadily more engaged in the widespread Royalist conspiracies to overthrow the Protectorate, and he was closely watched — and once interrogated by Cromwell himself — by the government's agents. After playing a part in the Restoration as a 'restored' member of the Long Parliament and a leader of the political Presbyterian party, he retired to Osterley Park in Middlesex and composed religious meditations, enjoying a quiet life as a studious country gentleman until his death in 1668.

Cheriton deserves a place in the list of the more important battles in the English Civil War. Not only did it mark a turn of the tide in the relative fortunes of King and Parliament, but it also drew together some interesting men, from the generals of both sides down to the humblest London soldier or French trooper. In their lives and memoirs we catch glimpses not only of many aspects of contemporary warfare but also of the motives and attitudes which led them to draw swords on each other in this 'warr without an enemie.' War, battle and death may be terrible, but it would be disloyal to the memories of the Cavaliers and Roundheads who fell at Cheriton for us to declare that they are always in vain.

[1] Warburton, *Memoirs of Prince Rupert*, Vol. 2, p. 404.
[2] Ludlow, *Memoirs*, quoted in Godwin, p. 191.

PART THREE

Background Notes and Documents

Section I

FURTHER CONTEMPORARY ACCOUNTS

THIS SECTION includes background contemporary accounts relating to the campaign and battle of Cheriton. They are arranged chronologically.

1. VERSES FOR LADY WALLER AFTER ARUNDEL

Madame, Bay-crowned Victory and Fame,
Your husbands Pages, bade me in his name
Salute you, and (though it be no news) tell
Of his renowned Acts at *Arundel*.
Your pardon then, that I thus rudely presse
To kisse your hands in a poetick dresse;
At such a time too, when the most do see,
All, as antick, set out in Poesie.
But yours are not vulgar eyes; nor the stone
Lesse precious which a Swine hath trampled on:
Nor do I think you will more lightly set
A Jemme, though in a worthless cabinet.
I here present a Jewell, which I dare
Pronounce, though from mean hands it come, most rare;
Your husbands honour, from whose brighter flame
These borrowed sparks, pay tribute to his name;
And must confesse, that they can nothing give
Worthy of him, by whom themselves must live.
That goodnesse of that cause for whom he fights,
In alarms and arms, spending the tedious nights,
Were praise enough, though he, perhaps should come
(Which heav'n forbid) to us, succeslesse, home:
But when, unto our joy, we see him goe
With triumph, on against the common foe,
And raise his Trophes, there, within those walls
That had conspir'd, and vow'd his funeralls,

Me thinks, our narrow language is too poor
To entertain his honours wealth and store.
Me thinks, I already read that larger page
Of Chronicle, in the ensuing Age,
Which shall contain his Name, unlesse that he
Goe on so far, it must a Volume be:
Then, as I turn the leaves, perhaps, I finde
Some lofty strain to speak his gallant minde,
And tell our after-nephewes part of all
That made him up a perfect Generall.
And what may he not do, to whom successe
Is due, except our sins do make it lesse?
Why then may it not written be as well,
He conquer'd all the South, as *Arundell*?
Or shall we think his active spirit meant,
Only to stop the passage into *Kent*?
The yet half Pagan Welch, that have no sight
To distinguish, because they want true light,
Except him: may he on then, to display
Together with his standard, a bright day
To that dark corner, and expell from thence,
The enemies advantage, rude ignorance:
And on his name may this due honour rest,
He made good one side, all from East to West.
This is enough; it were not meet to pray,
Or wish all fortune from the rest away,
When other Heroes, now, in every field,
Command opposers to despaire and yeeld:
On one side *Fairfax*, t'other *Manchester*,
The *Scots* behind, brave *Essex* every where;
Whose peerlesse honour is, thus to retain
Himself supreme of such a noble train;
The lustre of whose Crests, in marching forth,
Will shine more bright in conquest of the North.

    Thus Madame, in our thoughts, the work is ended,
Religion, and the State, by you befriended:
All must confesse thanks, who know what a mind
You bear beyond the rest of woman-kind,
That can with so much willingnesse, expose
Your chiefest Jewell to the reach of foes;
Dispend with all your marriage joyes so far,
To hazard them upon the chance of war.
But doubtlesse, 'twill be greater joy to see
Him laden back with prize, and victory;

And then some pen, more able, shall rehearse
His worthy deeds in Chronicle, not Verse.

From: *Certain Propositions made by Sir William Waller at the Surrender of Arundell Castle*, TT : E.81 (21).

2. PROPOSITIONS MADE BY WALLER TO THE BESIEGED AT ARUNDEL

Proposition made by Sir William Waller, *to the besieged in* Arundle-Castle.

1 I require the Castle of *Arundell* to be delivered into my hands by to morrow morning ten a clock.

2 That all Collonels of Horse, and Foot and all Horse, Arms, Ammunition, and military provision, what ever be then delivered unto me entire, and unspoyled.

3 That all Commanders, Officers, and Gentlemen, have fair quarter, and civill usage.

4 That all Souldiers shall have quarter for their lives.

5. That for security of performance, Sir *Edward Bishop*, and Sir *Edward Foord* be immediatly delivered into my hands.

Will: Waller.
Explication.

1 By fair quarter I understand, giving life to those that yeeld, with imprisonment of their persons, but civill usage, which is sufficient security, they shall not be plundered.

2 Concerning the place where they shall be sent, I will not determine, but will be left to mine own freedom, without further capitulation.

3 The Ministers are included in the Articles, and are prisoners as well as the souldiers.

4 When I send away the Officers, I shall take care, that they shall not want horses to carry them, but will not be bound to let them have their own horses.

From: *Certain Propositions...*, TT: E.81 (21).

3. WILLIAM LILLY'S ASTROLOGICAL PREDICTION

William Lilly, a celebrated contemporary astrologer, offered this prediction:

'The figure of the heavens was erected by William Lilly, to know whether Sir William Waller or Sir Ralph Hopton should overcome, they being supposed to be engaged near Alsford, 29 March 1644.'

'The Ascendant is for our army; the Moon, Jupiter, and Venus for our generals, viz. Sir William Waller and Major

General Browne, a valiant and prudent citizen of London, who may justly claim a large share of honour in that day's service. Sir Ralph Hopton is signified by capricorn, in the descending part of the heavens, which is usually given to the friends and assistants of the enemy. There are only Mars and dragon's tail in the ninth, so it appears that Sir Ralph had no supplies ready to attend that day's success, &c. From the Moon, having principal signification of us and our army, being in her exaltation with Jupiter, I concluded that all was and would be well on our side, and that the victory would be ours. From her separation from Jupiter, I said, I verily conceived that we had already taken some ammunition from them or performed some service against them. This I was confirmed in by the Sun, lord of our substance and assistants, being positioned in the tenth house, in the very degree of his exaltation (the 19th); and though I thought, by the proximity of Saturn to the Sun, we should not gain the whole or have a perfect victory without some diminution of some part of it, yet I was confident we should obtain a considerable portion of their ammunition, and have a victory, the only thing enquired after, for the Moon applied to Venus, and then to a sextile of Mercury, he being angular.

'I told the querent that within eleven or twelve hours after the question we should have perfect news and satisfactory ... It appeared by a letter from the army on that same Friday, that our generals took on the previous day 120 commanders and gentlemen, 500 common soldiers and much ammunition. Thus the army was worsted, as appeared by Saturn (the Lord Hopton's significator) being *sub radis (sic)* in his fall, in no aspect, to any planet, wholly peregrine and unfortunate, and aspecting the cusp of the seventh by square. All this argued that he would bring loss to his army, and dishonour to himself by the fight.'

From: *Hampshire Notes and Queries.* Vol. 6 (1892), p. 130.

4. SIR WILLIAM BALFOUR'S LETTER TO ESSEX

May it please your Excellency. Because of our being constrain'd these nights (by-past) to want sleepe, and this last night Horse and Man to lye upon the heath betwixt *Alford* and *Winchester*, and all this day in like manner spent upon the fields before *Winchester*, (so that being drowsie for want of sleepe) I shall beg leave of your Excellency for using a short discourse, for the present to let your Excell: know, That it hath pleased Almighty God to grant us a great

PLATE 21
Sir Richard Browne Attributed to E. Bower
National Portrait Gallery

PLATE 22
A Medallion of Sir William Waller. Enlarged from the original size of 1.35" x 1.05".
British Museum

Victory over our enemies, beyond all expectation; We having taken a resolution (by reason of your Excellencies and the Committee of both Kingdomes commandments) to be wary, and cautious to engage ourselves in a fight with the enemy but upon advantage; Yet wee finding them resolved to put us to it, on Friday the 29 of this instant, by their bringing their whole Army upon us, to beate out first some Musquetiers out of the hedges a pretty distance from our quarters, and thereafter to Allarm our quarters; I caused all our Horse to draw out in a little Heath before our quarters, and the Foot to be drawn up in Battell in a large spacious field within our quarters in a Heath. The enemy coming towards us, were received with such dexterity & valor, that it pleased Almighty God (after a long cumbate all the day long, from nine a clock in the morning to night) to give us an unexpected great Victory, by beating both their Horse and Foote out of the Heath before our quarters, and following the victory not onely to their quarters, but put them by *Alford*, and followed them within 4. miles of *Winchester*; their whole body of foot which they have beene so long a composing (I assure your Excellency) totally routed & so broken, that *Hopton* cannot make up his Foote Army I am confident most part of this summer; their Foote were so dispersed up and downe through all the fields, that they sweare they will never serve againe: The Lord *John* brother to the D. of *Richmond*, who commanded their Horse, is killed for certain, with many Officers, as Col. *Butler*, Col. *Gray* and others; Sir *John Smith*, *Cary*, with *Stovell* dangerously wounded, who is also our prisoner, Col. *Peard* and *Seamore*, and 5. or 6. more Commanders prisoners, and as many ordinary souldiers as we desired to take. Of ours onely Col. *Meldrum* shot in his arme, and wounded in the head, but not dangerously or mortall; Major *Bozwell* also wounded in the belly that he cannot live: So that all agrees that there was never so great a Victory; neither so few slain men: the enemies Horse held up the Foot, and made them stand to it, and fight by force, beating and cutting them with their swords. We are more then obliged to our good God for so great a Victory, God make us thankfull for it.

March 30. at   Your Excellencies most
2. a clock in   humble Servant,
the morning.   *W. Balfore.*

General Ruthen *was in the fight and as is reported wounded.*
From: *Sir Will. Balfore's Letter*, TT: E.40 (13).

5. SIR ARTHUR HESELRIGE'S ACCOUNT

Arthur Haselrigge reported that upon Fryday being 3 myles from Alston the enemy lay between Alston and us and resolved to fight with us & resolved to burne Alston and fall on Sussex and Surry and had Commissions for raising horse and foot in Kent &c. Thursday they stood all day in Cheriton fields. Fryday there was a mist which contynewed untill 9 of the clock on our right wings there was a woode which we tooke the enemy drewe upp a good strength of foote and beate them out of the woods about 10 of the clocke and we had the worste att last they sent a good strength of foote to gett our lieft wynge and about 4 of the clocke we sent downe 600 foote and Sir Arthur seing they sent their foote from their horse sente out of every of our troope 10 to beate against their foote before their horse could rescue them we kilde many and tooke their Coll. Sir H. Beard. Coll Norton with another company scoured the lanes and drives their foote, they into the woode retyred, then their horse being very good gave many charges and mayntayned their charges on both syde 3 howers were we kilde the Lord John and most were gent that charged us about 5 we beate them out of the hill clered the wood on our right hande and the Kentishe men beate them out of the field their horse made a stande we pursued them soberly and brough all our forces together they all retyred to the hill neare Alstone we brough 6 or 8 Canons against them and pursued them orderly att Alsford thay had lieft some Irishe to mayntayne that towne were we killed 100 of them we gott 2 peece of their canon and dispersed their horse which went towardes Wynchester and Basinge we pursued them both ways they being in feare fell one upon another there were 500 prisoners taken and 600 killed and we lost aboute 40 of our men we tooke but few of their canons. that night we wente almost to Wynchester all the foote that were prest in are taken or gone home and of them that fought best were most killed. Sir Arthur went to Wynchester the Towne was open but the castle shutt att their Trumpeter we thought and fitte to go to Wynchester. Sir Wm Waller and Sir Wm Balfour are within 4 or 6 myles of Andover the enemy was about 10000 in horse and foote Sir H. Barnham is brought upp who was Coll of horse and Coll of dragoons we had 3000 horsemen and 7000 fotte they lost all their armes and warrentes are sent out to collect the armes. there was never the seen horse fight that stood out so longe being 3 howers their horse were serounded with musketies who

lyned the hedges and beate us back alwayes when we drove them backe. the day was theirs untill 4 of the clocke. moved that this narration be printed and reade upon the day of thanckgiving put by
coll. Borde Stawell, Langstone, Pope, Chudleigh taken the worde was god with us god for us we had whites in our hattes and so had they

> From: Yonge's Diary, B.M., Add., MS. 18779, f. 87.
> A transcript from Yonge's shorthand reports of Heselrige's speech to the House of Commons (on 3 April) made by Robin Gard.

6. *Mercurius Aulicus* ON CHERITON

In the heat of all this Action you cannot imagine Sir *William Waller* would sit out. Who yesterday (being heightned by many advantages) adventured all, in a sharp fight with the Noble Lord *Hopton*; the exact particulars being so various and intricate, cannot suddenly be gathered, but the generals in brief we are informed were thus. On Tuesday last the Lord *Hopton* drew forth of *Winchester* into the field; next morning brought intelligence that Sir *William Waller* fully intended for *Alrezford*, which his Lordship not thinking convenient to afford him, went himselfe with some 800 Horse and Dragoones to prevent Sir *William Balfoure*, whom *Waller* has sent with twice that strength to get prepossession (the Two Armies following after:) both my Lord and *Balfoure* marched in sight of one another most part of the way, but my *Lord* got first thither, and forced *Waller* for that nights lodging to two or three small villages. In the morning his Lordship drew downe into the field (called *Bramdeane* heath) and found *Waller* ready on a faire hill (for hils and hedges must alwayes be granted him:) his Lordship made no doubt but with small danger to force him thence; it was for some time disputed, but at last his Lordship got it, and at an easie rate: the Hill thus gained, Colonell *George Lisle* with his commanded men was sent to keepe possession which (according to his wonted manner) he did like a Souldier, lying there all night. All that evening more or lesse, some Bullets intervened, though not so as to create much disturbance. But (which was a second and worse taske) that hill was found next morning to be commanded by another hill very wel set with hedges and trees (such as *Waller* loves) where his men were bestowed as thick as the hedges. To gaine this Hill also Colonell *Appleyard* was sent with a good strength, who performed it with that judgement and courage, as indeed amazed the Rebells to behold him; for though as he advanced, the Rebels powred thicke upon him from their hedges and arbours (some of them being such volleys as Souldiers have not usually knowne) yet the brave Colonell (resolved on the performance) so led up his men, and they so followed their Leader, that the confident Rebell with all his oddes was forced from his seat, and made give place to his betters. In this the Common Souldiers shewed who they fought for, pressing on with that braverie, that my Lord Generall, the Earle of *Forth*, expressed much joy and commendations of their behaviour. Now was His Majesties Army in a most happy posture, (for though they offered a great price for this last hill, yet they payd it not, the attempt costing a very few men) the Lord *Hopton* had time and securitie to continue thus; where if the Rebels went off, the Lord *Hopton* would go neare to be their utter undoing; and if they came on, they would undoe themselves. But this happinesse lasted not long; for the Alarme given (by a Corporall (as some say) who mistooke the Rebels for his friends) some that were brim full of valour, engaged themselves and others much too farre, to seeke out an Enemy even within the Rebels Ambuscadoes; which gave the Rebels new hopes to save themselves; nay, to become offendants, who till then were onely capable of a certaine overthrow. The Lord *Hopton* seeing this casuall overforwardnesse had bestowed such advantage on the Rebels, would not venture his Army any farther, (having dealt so many blowes, that the Rebels have small reason to boast, their dead being full as many, if not more then his Lordships) commanded to draw off, retreating in *Wallers* fight with three of *Wallers* Colours taken from him in the fight, his Lordship having not lost any one, Colour, Peece of Cannon, or Carriage.

From: *Mercurius Aulicus*, 13th Week, ending 30 March, TT: E.42 (26).

A LATER REPORT FROM *Mercurius Aulicus*

And the truth is, they are so full of Sir *William Waller*, that they have no leisure to hearken to Ambassadours; whose late *Deliverance* (for so Sir *Arthur Haslerig* called it to their faces) is blowne up into an unparallel'd Victory. Scaffolds were set up, and two men placed on them, who gaped halfe an houre, *That the Lord* Hopton *was totally routed and over-*

throwne, Ten thousand of his men killed and taken, ALL *his* Ordnance taken, ALL *his* Arms, ALL *his* Ammunition, ALL *his baggage,* ALL *his* Commanders killed and taken, *the execution followed nine miles,* Generall Forth *shot all to pieces, and the Lord* Hopton *escaped with onely ten men to* Reading. To all which we can say but this, That ALL these are most abhominably false; And we dare the Devill and all the *Covenanters* to shew so much as one Peece of Ordnance, one Colour, or one Carriage of Ammunition, Armes, or Baggage, that you gained in this service, Now because this huge *Lye* hath no bottome, therefore they that speake in print are strangely divided: One sayes boldly, like the two hackney Cryers on the stage, *That Sir* William Waller *tooke All the Ordnance*: Another sayes, *All but foure*: A third sayes *but foure in all*: Another sayes, *but two*; and another confesses, *they tooke none at all*: Then one sayes 1000 *Cavaliers were slaine*: Another sayes, 1000 *on both sides*: Another, 600 *Hoptonians*: And the SCOUT and others say, 400 *on both sides*. Then for men of quality, one reckons 40 Commanders: Another 22. A third saies 15. And *Sir William Balfoure* (who knowes better) in his Letter to the Earle of Essex names 8. Commanders killed and taken, and sayes, there are 5 or 6 more (thirteene in all) though he reckon Colonell *Boteler* for one, who is safe at *Oxford,* onely a slight hurt in his legge. The truth is, we lost very gallant men, especially the most Noble and Valiant Lord *John Stewart,* the renowned Knight Sir *John Smith,* (both dyed since the fight, and are buried at *Oxford*) two brave Gentlemen, Colonell *Sandyes* and Colonell *Manning,* and that valient Lieut. Colonel *Scot* (an Englishman) And som (though but few) wounded, as that brave Souldier Colonell *Appleyard,* who with his yellow-coats beat the Rebels from both hill and wood, Captaine *Henry Pearson* a gallant deserving Gentleman, with some few others whose names we yet know not. Such as are prisoners (especially the two valiant Colonels Sir *Edward Stowell* and Sir *Henry Bard*) we hope shall not fare the worse, because they fought so bravely. Now in that the Rebells excuse themselves that they would have taken the Lord *Hoptons* Cannon, if fresh horse had not faced them which came then from *Reading,* 'tis so false, that 'twas only Colonell *Nevils* Regiment that faced their Horse, and kept them off when they offer'd to approach the Reare, which with Sir *William Botelers,* Colonell *Howards,* and some other Regiments, did eminently well in that dayes action. And whereas they triumph, *That His Majesty had three Lords, and foure Knights kill'd and taken*, (for they count my Lord Generall dead, and reckon him for two, one for the Earl of *Forth*, and another for Lord *Ruthen*) we can answer them, that we killed all their Lords and Knights but Sir *Arthur*, and the two Sir *Williams*; and left not one alive of all the Gentlemen of quality, but Sergeant Major Generall *Browne* the Faggot-man.

TUESDAY. *April* 2.

Sir *William Waller* having his deliverance at *Alresford*, sent his Name-sake *Balfoure* to plunder *Salisbury*; & the *Scot* went thither, but his errant was so bad, that he staid not long to speed it, having notice that the Lord *Hopton* was drawne into the field: some of his Troops came into *Newbury*, but were quickly sent thence by Colonell *Nevils* Regiment, who killed two or three of them, and tooke foure prisoners. The Rebels having some intelligence that His Majesty had quit *Reading*, and drawne the Garrison thence, came in great hast first to plunder the Towne, and then to fire it (for that they have vowed to do) but their Scouts gave them as true intelligence as he in print, and had almost thrust the eager Rebels within Sir *Jacob Astleys* line of *Communication*.

Now where they cannot continue to plunder and burne, they say others doe it, and therefore this weekes Pamphlets cry out piteously against plundering in *Lincolnshire*, meerely because the Rebells are driven thence.

From: *Mercurius Aulicus*, 14th Week, ending 6 April, TT: E.43 (18).

7. ARCHER'S CONCLUSION

Archer retails some rumours about the Earl of Forth and winds up his narrative of the battle:

Give me leave to tell the truth, I myself was at the house where he [Forth] quartered at Alsford, the Master of the house testifies that he was there, and being troubled with the Gowt, went not into the field; in the morning, news was sent to him (doubtless it went to Oxford too, we may chance hear of a Thanksgiving for it) that the Londoners were routed, a thousand taken prisoners, the rest fled, and were then in the pursuit, welcome News no doubt; for presently he cals for a deck of Cards, and follows his sport, till at last a messenger in all hast tells him the tide was turn'd, their horse were routed, and his presence required; away he goes into the feild, and was saluted there by Lieutenant Colonell Bump, and so the game was ended; our great gunne cut him off, and he was brought dead to town; I could tell you of some others;

a Captain left behinde in Alsford sorely wounded, doth swear the Devil is in the Round-Heads they are such Fire-men; they have slain, wounded, and taken Prisoners, all their Commanders of any note; if it be an untruth, or any Malignant please to give it a grosser title, consider out of whose mouth it came; this for Friday. On Saturday morning I spake with the Messenger, who came from Sir *William Waller* to our Major Generall with Orders, for we stayed at Alsford, 14 miles behinde Sir *William Waller*, who affirmed that the Horse and Foot were totally routed, not a body of 200 Foot to be found, of the great Army consisting in all of twelve thousand, that we had taken seven peeces of Ordnance, many carriages, and that Sir *William* would set upon *Winchester* immediatly, being within a mile and a half of it then. I trust in God he is by this time possest of it. Many passages I am forced to omit for brevities sake, both in and after the fight: we had both the same word, *God with us*: but see what it is to dissemble with a God of truth. Our next word was *Jesus help us*; so he did: and then the last was, *Glory be to God*. Give me leave to end here, and let this day be ever in our thoughts, and the word be ever in our mouths, a day wherein God was seen in the high places of the field, a wise, mighty wonder working God, there is not an Atheist that can own thee, and not acknowledge it to be *digitus Dei*; Tis God alone that hath done the work, to him alone be all the praise; The rest is this,

March 30. 1644.   *Gentlemen, I am your humble servant, E.A.*

The Queens Regiment being there, and Prince *Maurices* forces; most of the Irish neither giving nor taking quarter.

FINIS.

8. SIR WILLIAM OGLE'S RELATION OF EVENTS AFTER CHERITON

... my Lord (Hopton) with the foot retreated in great disorder towards the Garrison of basing house and he left my Lord Ogle contrary to his promise having disfurnished his garrison of full two parts of his provision. that night a multitude of the scattered horse and foot came into Winchester: and it was day light next morning before he could free the towne of them, which he did by assuring them that Waller with his whole Armie would come to Winchester, and that the city was not to be defended: this made them make hast to be gone westward. Sunday Morning my Lord Ogle drew his regiments of foot and horse into the Castle; having on Saturday night sent a party of horse towards cheriton from whence Waller was gone: this party on Sunday morning brought in above three score barrells of powder : which they found in carts upon the Downs with divers (?) Horns and other provisions wch were left behind the Army ; and about eight of the Clock on Sunday morning my Lord perceived Waller with the Army marching down from Wallers Ash towards Worth, two myles from Winchester : where upon he went downe from the Castle into the City ; and called Mayor and Aldermen into the Market place telling them that the City was not tenable against such forces and that if they should enter it by force it must be plundered and ruined ; he gave them the keys of the gate, and adviced them to meet Waller before he came to the gate and to offer him to come in without any oposition ; and that they might suffer noe prejudice by his soldiers ; wch they did, ; and Waller with his Army came into the lower part of the City ; and about the great church he sent three officers of qualitie to my Lord Ogle : to require him that he should deliver the Castle to the parliament ; my Lord answered, he kept it by Commission from the King ; and when he should recieve his Majesties order he would deliver it, but not before. then he sent him word if he would not deliver it, he would burne his house at Stoake Charitie, and fire the City : he returned answer : that he had plundered all his house at Stoak : and for the house it was a very old one, and none of his Inheritance : and if he pleased to burne the City it would make a very spacious and faire garden for the Castle. upon wch answer he plundered five or six of the houses of the best affected Citizens for the King, and marched out of the City at Kings gate : and drew up his Armie in the Meadow about a half Mile from the City, from whence he marched to a little garrison at Christs Church : and tooke it at discretion, making the Gentlemen and soldiers all prisoners of warr ; then he came back to Rumsey : where he stayd three daies ; wch gave my Lord Ogle suspect that he had some design : and soe it fell out, for he having one Mr. Bellaway [sic] in Winchester who did practise with him ; their designe proved to be that where as my Lord Ogle did quarter all his soldiers both horse and foot in the City ; and there being a good space of ground betwixt the City and Castle in wch my Lord kept onely threescore soldiers : and the South gate opening betwixt the City and Castle. that if he could by pretence open that gate : then all my Lords Soldiers in the City would be cutt off and he having soe few with him in the Castle it must of necessitie be taken : this afterwards was found to be the designe ; wch my Lord could not foresee: but the night before late in the evening: Mrs Cellaway came to him and pretended to give him good news wch she said shee had from some freinds she had at London: but her discourse was soe full of idle words that he dismissed her and began to have some jelousie: that there was some ill pretended by Waller: whom she did often name as an enemy to her husband; who then lived in the City and had a good repute. upon my Lords jelousie of words that past from her, and after wondering that Waller should be soe longe at Rumsey he drew all his soldiers horse and foot up into the Castle: and told them they must all be in Armes that night in the works and to please them distributed a great number of coats and shirts amongst them wch my Lord Hopton had left in the towne, with a hogshead of stronge beare: and having placed all the guards, and secured the Sally ports about twelve a Clock my Lord Ogle laid downe in his cloaths to rest — all this he did judging it not fitt to be secure, an enemy being soe neare: towards day breake he was wakend with a petard that had broken up the South gate, and that Waller had enterd: my Lords soldiers who were all upon the guards saluted him with a great volley of muskett wch forced him to retire in all hast downe as far as the great Church. having missd his designe of surprising the soldiers in the Citty; he plundered three or four of the richest houses in the City who were well-affected to the King; and soe with his Comppainion [sic] Cellaway and his whole family marched away towards London; this Cellaway had instructed him in the whole designe.

9. THE DEATH OF LORD JOHN STUART

...after several actions, by which he shall ever live the pattern of a religious, sober, active, watchful, and resolved Souldier, he came to that wherein he died, the pattern of an excellent man; for following my Lord *Hopton*, as ambitious to observe his conduct, as he was to obtain his other great virtues, at *Brandon-heath*, or *Cheriton-down*, near *Alesford* in *Hampshire*, the Army standing ready to receive Sir *William Waller*, and observing he had the advantage of a hill, my Lord saying, *That he lay so there, that he did but tempt them to beat him*; commands a Vanguard of Light Horse up the hill, with such brave resolution, that he gained it and that quickly, rather because he supposed it only a show of the enemy to amuse us, while he stole his whole body away. (In the mean time discreetly composing a difference arising in the command and service, the bane generally of the King's affairs, with these two words, *Let us dispute the main with the enemy, and we shall have time enough to dispute punctilioes among our selves*) and finding them possessed of another [hill], after a pause whether he should follow them, considering the thick Hedges and Bushes, wherein they were set, ordering a Party to skirt those Hedges and Bushes, he followed directly to gain a commodious hollow that lay between them, where many a gallant man had his Grave, not daunted with the fall of two horses under him, nor with six wounds given, and the death of near five hundred men round about him, till like the Phoenix and the World, he expired in his brave heat and fire *March* 29. 1644, and besides the Monument in each heart that knew him, had one by his Brother in *Christ-Church* Chappel in *Oxford*.

From: D. Lloyd, *Memoires of . . . excellent personages* (1668), p. 326.

Clarendon described Lord John as 'a young man of extraordinary hope, little more than one[*sic*] and twenty years of age; who being of a more choleric and rough nature than the other branches of that illustrious and princely family, was not delighted with the softenesses of the Court, but had dedicated himself to the profession of arms when he did not think the scene should have been in his own country. His courage was so signal that day that too much could not be expected from it if he had outlived it, and he was so generally beloved that he could not but be very generally lamented'.

10. THE DEATH OF SIR JOHN SMITH

Our Major Generall now wounded, desires those faithful gentlemen, not to suffer him to come into the enemies' hands, but convey him to some place where he may a while repose with security. They bring him immediately to the Phisitian Generall to be drest, who unfortunately missed his mortall wound discovering only a bruise on the same side beneath it, and therefore concludes he is out of danger, upon this they bring him to Woonston [Wonston], a village 5 miles from Winchester, where his troupe lately quartered, here after he had drunke a posset, and warmed himself awhile, he desires to lye down and rest, a bed is prepared and he lyes down, immediately falling to sleepe: which considered together with the courage he supported his mortall wounds, made us confident he was out of danger, his being so hearty, and no sighs or groans to be perceived, as generally in dying men. He was no sooner awake but he began to question how farre we were from the enemy and what time a night it was, and what was become of our Army, and after he falls into a formall discourse, wherein he despatched some particular things concerning himself, which because they were private I omit; which he lyes down again and said 'the conceit of our men running away did more trouble him by farre than his wounds;' and though others were hardly induced to believe it, both now and before he expressed in a mild manner, that his life was neare a period, and conjured me by all the love and respect I ought him, to certifie his Deare Mother that he died with a quiet conscience and a resigned mind, hoping likewise that she should not take his death with too much heaviness, but rather rejoice that she had a son to shed his blood for his Soveraigne. A truly Christian and heroicall speech, which though but short comprised the very Elixar of true fortitude loyalty and piety.

After this he prayes making an excellent act of perfect resignation, saying 'O my Lord and God out of Thy infinite goodnesse have mercy upon mee, who cast myselfe into thy blessed hands, heartily wishing that thy divine will may be performed in me'; whilst he was thus like the swan singing so sweet a dying ode with eloquence scarce usuall in his life-time, his carriage is made ready, to take him from danger imminent, to a space of more security; and so to Oxford if it were possible. He notwithstanding his deadly wounds, comes downstairs on foote, and ascends the carriage with that stoutnesse as hardly hath beene seene in a dying man, all the symptomes of paine you could perceive in him, was sometimes he would bite his nether lip, when his pangs with most extremity came upon him. When we drew neere Andover he began to say (his senses being a little astonished) 'Good my Lord let us charge up again, let us charge them once again and the day is ours'.

As soon as we entered the towne he began to invoke the sacred name of Jesus often repeating it with a soft voyce as if he had taken a gust and sweetnesse in the divine vertue of it.

Shortly after, over against the signe of the Angel, in a mild and sweet repose he expired where it would have grieved the hardest heart to have seene him round enclosed with sundry gentlemen, condoling with teares the untimely end of so Peerelesse a Gentleman.

From: Edward Walsingham, *Britannicus Virtutis Imago* (London, June 1644), TT: E.53 (10). Walsingham served in Sir John Smith's troop.

Sir John Smith's body was buried with much ceremony on 1 April in Christ Church Cathedral, Oxford.

11. PUBLIC THANKSGIVING

The Lords and Commons, in Parliament assembled, having certain Information of the great Mercy of our good God, in the happy Success of the Forces of the Parliament under the Command of Sir *Wm. Waller* and Sir *Wm. Balfore*, on *Friday* last, the Twenty-ninth of *March* 1644, do, in their Acknowledgement of God's Mercy herein, *Order*, That, upon the Lord's Day which will be on the Fourteenth of this Instant *April*, publick Thanksgiving be given in all Churches and Chapels on the South-side of *Trent*, within the Power of the Parliament, unto the Lord of Hosts, that giveth all Victory, for this seasonable and extraordinary Blessing, whereby the Army under the Command of Sir *Ralph Hopton*, was totally routed, with the Loss of very few of the Parliament Forces: And all Ministers, in their respective Churches and Chapels, are hereby directed and commanded to give Notice hereof, and to exhort and excite their People to acknowledge and improve this great Blessing, in a spiritual Way; that as this Mercy was bestowed in Return of our Prayers and Humiliation upon the late and solemn Fast, the *Wednesday* before this Victory, so God may have the sole Honour and Glory of it, in our Praises and Thanksgivings: And that the like Thanksgiving shall be made on the North-side of *Trent*, Fourteen Days after, which will be on the Twenty-eighth of this Instant *April*.

From: *Commons' Journals*, Vol. III, p. 443.

Section II

THE REGIMENTS OF WALLER'S ARMY

WALLER'S ARMY AT CHERITON

Based on Captain Robert Harley's letter in H.M.C., *Portland MSS.*, Vol. 1, p. 166.

Regiments. of Horse, eleven	4-5000
Regiments. of Foot, eight	5,000
Regiments. of Dragoons, two	5-800
Cannon	16

HORSE

Sir William Waller's	(11)	Sir William Balfour's
Sir Arthur Heselrige's	(7)	John Meldrum's
Jonas Vandruske's	(6)	John Dalbier's
Sir Michael Livesey's	(5)	John Middleton's
Edward Cooke's	(4)	
George Thompson's	(4)	
Richard Norton's	(4)	
Total:	41 troops	Total: 22 troops

DRAGOONS

Sir William Waller's   Cunningham's

FOOT

Sir William Waller's   Richard Browne's London Brigade:
Andrew Potley's   The White Regiment
Sir Arthur Heselrige's   The Yellow Regiment
Ralph Weldon's
Samuel Jones's

The following notes are based mainly on the administrative papers preserved in the Public Record Office, State Papers 28. The 300 or more volumes or boxes of papers in this collection contain a wide range of material relating to the armies of Parliament during the Civil War and Commonwealth. Sometimes, as in the case of the Kentish and Surrey regiments at Cheriton, the complete pay accounts are available; more often than not, however, only a few warrants for food and lodging money or claims for arrears of pay, often certified by Waller's own signature, survive as documentary evidence of who served in the Roundhead regiments at Cheriton.

Officers who served in the New Model Army are marked with an asterisk, and their subsequent careers may be followed in *The Regimental History of Cromwell's Army* by C. H. Firth and G. Davies.

1. SIR WILLIAM WALLER'S LIFEGUARD

'The troop of Colonel Edward Cooke, commonly called the Life Guard of Sir William Waller.' As in other Civil War armies, Waller's Lifeguard probably included 'reformadoe' officers (i.e. those unattached or without commands). The following gentlemen were probably in the Lifeguard at Cheriton as they were each lent £1 by Nicholas Cowling, then commissary for provisions, in April:

> John Fisher
> George Wentworth
> Isaac Cloake
> Henry Greenwood
> Thomas Goodwin
> John Underwood
> John Stevens
> Giles Foster
> Francis Morefield
> Richard Seale
> William Bray
> Henry Sefton
> Humphrey Ditton
> Jonathan Wright
> Roger Daniell
> Peter Ellistone

2. SIR WILLIAM WALLER'S REGIMENT

Waller, one of the first six to receive commissions as colonels of horse in Essex's army, formed his regiment initially from the volunteers raised in London during June and July 1642. Although in the Parliamentarian army, regimental organization seems to have developed slowly, Horatio Carey was major by 6 August 1642. At Edgehill, however, Sir Faithful Fortescue acted as Waller's major; his desertion narrowly preceded the rout of the regiment along with the rest of the Parliamentarian left wing.

The regiment served with Waller in the South and West in 1642 and 1643. One of its captains, Edward Harley, recorded that it charged several times at Lansdown. By this time Carey had deserted, and his place as major had been taken by a Frenchman, Francis Duet or Dowett, whose troop is listed in Peacock. Dowett received a commission to raise a cavalry regiment in August 1643, but proved unable to do so. In the trial of Nathaniel Fiennes (for the surrender of Bristol) he gave evidence against Waller, but the two men were subsequently reconciled. In 1645, however, he was serving as a major in Edmund Ludlow's Regiment of horse.

At Cheriton the regiment numbered 11 troops: These probably belonged to the following officers:

Major Henry Saunderson*	Lieutenant to Dowett, 1642 Captain in the West, 1643 Major by 24 February 1644 Lieutenant Samuel Stringer and Cornet Streeter served in this troop
Captain Richard Fincher*	Captain of 100 dragoons in Sir John Seton's Regiment in 1642. Quarter-Master-General of Horse by 26 April 1644
Captain Henry Owland	Captain of Dragoons in Dorset, 1643. First mustered his troop of horse on 12 March 1644, but he received his commission on 25 October 1643
Captain James de Latoure	Captain of a troop in Colonel Henry Marten's Regiment under Essex. Sent to Waller in June 1643
Captain Robert Harley*	Probably took over his brother Edward's troop

Captain William Gwilliam	Joined on 7 February 1644, from Heselrige's Regiment, where he had failed to raise a troop
Captain John Butler	Raised in June 1643
Captain Henry Rutter	His officers: Lieutenant William Granwall and Cornet John Rutter
Captain William Sydenham	
Captain Christopher (or John) Fleming:	Wounded at Cheriton. Killed near Oxford in the summer of 1644

Illustrations of the colours (or cornets carried by Waller, Harley, Butler, Fleming and Gwilliam at Cheriton have been preserved. (See *Bibliography:* 'Parliamentarian Colours').

3. SIR ARTHUR HESELRIGE'S REGIMENT

The regiment was raised in the late spring of 1643, in and around London. Heselrige, a wealthy landowner from Noseley Hall in Leicestershire, equipped his men as cuirassiers and personally bought horses for them in the London markets. At Lansdown the 'Lobsters' acquitted themselves well, but suffered an ignominious rout at Roundway Down. The regiment's colours were green, and it numbered seven troops at Cheriton:

Sir Arthur Heselrige	Probably commanded by Captain Thomas Horton. Heselrige's cornet in 1642, Horton had become captain-lieutenant by May 1643
Major Nicholas Battersby	
Captain Edward Foley*	Captain in Lord Brooke's Regiment of horse. Joined Waller in June 1643. Troop raised partly in London and partly in Warwickshire and Staffordshire
Captain Samuel Gardiner	Raised troop under Lord Brooke. At Lichfield and Stafford fights. Entered Heselrige's Regiment on 15 May 1643. His lieutenant was Benedict Clutterbuck
Captain John Okey	Quartermaster in Lord Brooke's troop, 1642. A citizen of London, captain of a troop of 50 reformadoes in March 1643, probably in Heselrige's Regiment
Captain Thomas Pennyfeather*	Both his and Heselrige's colours at Cheriton are known
Captain Clarke	Probably captain-lieutenant to Heselrige at the capture of Chichester 1642

The senior troops in the regiment were those of Heselrige, Okey, Foley and Gardiner.

PLATE 23
Sir Edward Bishop
Petworth House

Daniel Mytens

PLATE 24
Sir Arthur Heselrige
Lord Hazlerigg

Robert Walker

The regiment served throughout 1644 with Waller. One of its officers, Lieutenant Thomas Ellis, wrote a vivid account of its actions at Cropredy Bridge. John Okey (major by 12 June 1644) commanded it during the campaign to relieve Taunton in 1645. The regiment quartered in Sussex just before the reduction, and entered the New Model under the command of John Butler.

Heselrige possessed considerable prestige as one of the Five Members, but his contemporaries did not care for his character. Clarendon, certainly prejudiced, thought him 'of a rude and stubborn nature, and of weak understanding' and 'a bold, absurd man.' Edmund Ludlow, who served in Heselrige's Regiment of horse later that year, wrote: 'He was a man of a disobliging carriage, sour, and morose of temper, liable to be transported with passion, and to whom liberality seemed a vice. Yet, to do him justice, I must acknowledge that I am under no manner of doubt concerning the rectitude and sincerity of his intentions.' That about sums up Heselrige.

As a later diehard and rabid political Independent, Heselrige inevitably attracted many enemies. One of them, Denzil Holles, accused him of cowardice at Cheriton, declaring in his *Memoirs* that he stood weeping under a hedge, moaning 'Ah, woe is me! All is lost, we are undone!' and that 'a great Scotch officer [?Balfour] reproved him severely for it, and bade him leave the field, and not stand gudding (crying) there to dishearten the soldiers.' Such a story from the biased pen of Holles must, however, be taken with more than a pinch of salt. Certainly Heselrige had acquired a reputation with the Royalists and his political enemies, as an outwardly bombastic yet really a timid man, but to be fair to him there is no evidence that he lacked courage. He was not a natural soldier, however, and he does seem to have overplayed the part of a martial man.

4. COLONEL JONAS VANDRUSKE'S REGIMENT

This was originally the regiment of Colonel Robert Burghill, who was captain of a troop in August 1642, major at Chichester in January 1643, and a colonel by 26 May 1643. He seems to have retired from wounds after Roundway Down, and handed over his regiment to his Dutch major, Jonas Vandruske, an officer whose services Waller particularly valued. After he was wounded with two shots in the arm (November 1643), and brought to London 'to the great grief of Sir William Waller, who had rather lost his right hand,' Waller publicly cashiered a whole troop which had deserted the Dutchman in the action. Vandruske rejoined the regiment in April 1644.

The six troops at Cheriton included:

Colonel Jonas Vandruske	Served as lieutenant to Major Horatio Carey in 1642
Major John Anderson	Had received a commission as major in William Carr's Regiment of horse in August 1643, but it was not raised. He served as Vandruske's major from 20 November 1643 to 19 July 1644
Captain Matthew Draper	Commissioned on 29 August 1643 and served with regiment to the reduction in 1645. Possibly in Norton's Regiment at Cheriton
Captain Nathaniel West	Cornet in Burghill's troop in 1642
Captain Masterson	
Captain Sharpe	Known to be in the regiment in July 1644

After service in Waller's army in 1644, the regiment served in the West under Holborne, and was disbanded in April 1645. Cowling, commissary of provisions, refers to the 'Dutch commanders' and so several of its officers may have been from Holland.

5. COLONEL SIR MICHAEL LIVESEY'S REGIMENT

A Kentish regiment employed under Waller from 10 March 1644 onwards. The five troops, whose colours are all known, were as follows:

Colonel Sir Michael Livesey	
Major George Sedascue*	Cornet to Major John Urry, September 1642. At siege of Portsmouth that year
Captain Robert Gibbon*	Present at taking of Chichester, 1642
Captain Henry Owen*	
Captain Augustine Skinner	

The regiment mustered approximately 300 officers and men at Cheriton, where the conduct of its colonel was not distinguished. In the 1644 Midlands campaign the regiment mutinied because it was given the hardest duty and the worst quarters. It marched off to Kent but rejoined the army in time for Second Newbury, and passed into the New Model. Yet Waller seems to have had a high regard for it; he had probably over-used it: 'A regiment of 800 horse, which I am confident is the bravest regiment in England,' he wrote in July 1644.

According to Godwin, the regiment wore red coats with blue facings, but this is highly questionable as 'facings' belonged to a later decade.

In 1660 Major Anthony Weldon of Kent, formerly a major in Livesey's Regiment, called Sir Michael Livesey 'a most notorious coward, a penurious sneaking person, and one that could act the hypocrite to the life in voice and humble gesture.' Clearly they were not the best of friends.

Livesey (1611-(?)1663) lived at East Church on the Isle of Sheppey and took an active part in securing Kent for Parliament. In July 1644, after his row with Waller, he appeared before the Committee of Both Kingdoms and asked to be allowed to return to his regiment at Abingdon. In April 1645 he encouraged his men to mutiny at Sevenoaks, and refused to join the New Model Army. Two years later he quelled the Royalist rising at Canterbury. He attended the King's trial every day and signed the death warrant. At the Restoration he escaped to the Low Counties. His lands forfeited, he returned to die in his native Kent.

Did he run away at Cheriton? Certainly Major Wood, Adjutant-General Fleming, Captain Fincher and Captain Cooke, all of Waller's army, testified that they saw him do so (*C.S.P.D.* 1644, p. 172).

6. COLONEL EDWARD COOKE'S REGIMENT

This regiment was originally raised for Sir Richard Grenvile, who returned from military service in Ireland in 1643 and accepted from Waller a commission as Lieutenant-General of Horse. His regiment was to be raised by the four counties of the Southern Association.

Grenvile described his difficulties in a letter to the burgesses of Plymouth, dated 18 March 1644: 'I, being by commission Lieutenant-General to Sir William Waller had an ordinance of the Parliament for the raising of 500 horse for my regiment at the charges of Kent, Sussex, Surrey, and Hampshire, who in three months time had not raised four troops, and my own troop, when I left them, having two months pay due to them, could get but one month, for which extraordinary means were used, being a favour none else could obtain ...' (H.M.C., 15th Report, App. VIII, p. 71).

When Grenvile absconded to Oxford, Waller gave the regiment to Colonel Edward Cooke, son of an influential West Country gentleman, who had received a commission to raise a regiment of foot the previous Summer but could not complete it. Before that he had acted as Waller's chief staff officer, and he may have served in this capacity at Cheriton as the regiment was there commanded by Lieutenant-Colonel Thorpe.

The four troops were:

Lieutenant-Colonel Thorpe	The Sussex troop. A Major Carr took it over in June 1644
Captain Thomas Jarvis or Jervoise	Second son of Sir Thomas Jarvis of Herriard, Hampshire
Captain Samuel Potte	By 4 July 1644 Potte's troop was regimented under Colonel Norton, and was therefore presumably the Hampshire troop.
Captain Richard Layett	

An account of Thorpe's military services appeared in *The Kingdomes Weekly Intelligencer*, 8-15 April 1645, where we learn that he commanded the regiment at Cheriton. The colours of Cooke, Thorpe and Jarvis are known. The regiment lacked a major, for Livesey attempted to get Weldon appointed as such shortly after Cheriton.

7. COLONEL GEORGE THOMPSON'S REGIMENT

A London regiment of horse, originally raised and first commanded by Colonel Richard Turner in June 1643, it joined Waller at Windsor in September 1643. Next month it marched under Major-General Skippon to take Newport Pagnell, and remained with him until the following January, when the Committee of the West procured the regiment from the London Committee of Militia for service in the West. The sum of £2000 was advanced to enable the regiment to take the field under Colonel Thompson. Turner's Regiment was officially reduced on 2 March 1644. It had consisted of eight troops: his own, Major Salway, Captains Thompson, Hooker, Timothy Whiteing, Ghest, Beale and Storie.

Colonel Thompson, a captain in August 1642, lost a leg at Cheriton, but stoutly declared that 'he had yet another leg to lose for Jesus Christ.'

The regiment escorted the London Brigade back to the City in April 1644, but returned to the army for the Midlands campaign of that year. Thompson served until 10 November 1645, but the command passed to Lieutenant-Colonel Thorpe (on 1 June 1644) and then to a Major Carr. Captains John Long and Plumley served in this regiment in 1645 (*L.J., Vol*, VII, p. 416).

8. COLONEL RICHARD NORTON'S REGIMENT

This regiment of Hampshire horse mustered only four troops at Cheriton, and five in the following Midlands campaign. Waller gave them leave to return home on 12 July 1644.

At Cheriton, according to one account, Norton was the 'first instrument' to turn the day. He had lived as a young man in the Manor House at Old Alresford, and consequently possessed an intimate knowledge of the countryside. He had four troops, the captains of none except his own being known for certain:

Colonel Richard Norton

(?) Captain Matthew Draper	Captain in Essex's army, 1642. With Waller's army in September 1643. Mentioned with Samuel Potte as being in the regiment in July 1644, but almost certainly in Vandruske's
(?) Captain Francis St Barbe	With Waller in November 1643. Lived near Romsey, where he was lord of the manor

Colonel Norton of Southwick Park had been colonel of the Alton regiment of the Hampshire trained bands in 1633. (That year Hampshire could muster eight regiments of foot and a Winchester company, 5484 officers and men, besides 570 pioneers and three troops of horse). In the Civil War his regiment served mainly in Hampshire, based on Southampton where Norton was Governor. Given to Presbyterian opinions and ejected from the Commons by Pride's Purge, Norton eventually became a supporter of the Restoration. He was a friend of Cromwell, who called him affectionately 'Idle Dick.'

9. COLONEL SIR WILLIAM BALFOUR'S REGIMENT

Sir William Balfour's Regiment had served in the army of

the Earl of Essex throughout 1643, and had particularly distinguished itself at the first battle of Newbury. Neither the regimental strength nor the names of any of the officers at Cheriton are known. After the battle the regiment rejoined Essex, and took part in the disastrous Lostwithiel campaign. The Royalist Richard Symonds included in his *Diary* some details of the Roundhead horse which mustered at Tiverton during that campaign. At that time the regiment was as follows:

	Officers	Troopers
Sir William Balfour	14	100
Major Balfour	9	77
Sir Samuel Luke	10	72
Captain William Rainsborowe*	9	57
Captain Semple	10	61
Captain Boswell	10	65
	62	432

10. COLONEL JOHN DALBIER'S REGIMENT

Colonel Dalbier, a Dutchman who had served with Balfour on the Continent, was wounded at Cheriton. He became Quarter-Master-General of Horse and served as such in the 1645 siege of Basing House. His regiment did not enter the New Model, but soldiered for a time in the West. He was killed at St. Neots on 5 July 1648.

According to Richard Symonds's *Diary*, the regiment mustered in 1644, during the Lostwithiel campaign:

	Officers	Troopers
Colonel John Dalbier*	12	67
Captain Salkeild	11	72
Captain Pymm	11	80
Captain Lukeman	9	48
	43	267

11. COLONEL JOHN MELDRUM'S REGIMENT

This is a very obscure regiment about which nothing is known. Meldrum is not to be confused with Sir John Meldrum, the celebrated Parliamentarian officer and military engineer.

12. COLONEL JOHN MIDDLETON'S REGIMENT

John Middleton, later first Earl of Middleton (1619-1673), a Scot still in his twenties, who had a reputation as a professional soldier (partly earned as a pikeman in France) at the outset of the War, was commissioned as colonel of a regiment of dragoons in September 1642. By November he had received command of a troop of Lord Feilding's Regiment which was routed at Edgehill, and the next month Middleton — 'conspicuous for his bravery and generosity' — became colonel of his own regiment of horse. He had served briefly with Waller in 1642 at the taking of Winchester. After Cheriton he quarrelled with Colonel Hans Behre and other officers of Essex's army, and joined Waller's army permanently, where he became Lieutenant-General of the Horse. He was to have commanded a regiment in the New Model, but like other Scots refused to serve in it. After campaigning against Montrose, Middleton changed sides and was active in the Royalist interest throughout the Commonwealth until, beaten by Monck, he fled to the Continent. Created an earl in 1656, he returned with Charles II and became commander-in-chief in Scotland. Made Governor of Tangier, he died there in 1673 after a fall while drunk.

None of the officers of his regiment at Cheriton are known.

DRAGOONS

13. SIR WILLIAM WALLER'S REGIMENT

Waller's Regiment of dragoons was formed in the Spring of 1643, probably from a nucleus of two or three companies from Essex's army, and it served throughout the Western campaign. Major George Carr commanded it at Chichester in January 1643. James Strachan, the second major, was killed at Lansdown, and he was succeeded immediately by Archibald Strachan, who had been a captain of dragoons since 1 February 1643.

Strachan served as major until 17 May 1644, and then as a captain and major of horse in Plymouth under James Carr, finally returning to Essex's army. He acted as Waller's Quarter-Master-General from 15 February 1643 to 25 April 1644.

The regiment mustered about 500 in London on 26 September 1643. The captains included:

Captain John Clerke
Captain Nicholas Moore
Captain John Bennett } Probably dragoon officers, as they were quartering with Clerke and Moore in Islington, September 1643. Turpin was a gentleman-at-arms in March 1643
Captain William Turpin }

The Royalist spy who observed them on 26 September also drew their colours.

14. CUNNINGHAM'S REGIMENT

Possibly Adam Cunningham, who had briefly taken over Colonel Charles Essex's Regiment of foot before it went to Colonel Richard Fortescue. Very obscure. Major Henry Frodsham (late of Sir William Constable's Regiment of foot) served with it at Cheriton as a reformadoe.

FOOT
15. SIR WILLIAM WALLER'S REGIMENT

Raised in September 1643, the regiment served with Waller until its reduction in 1645. The strengths at Cheriton may be calculated only roughly from Commissary Nicholas Cowling's account book, for it is not clear whether or not he included officers in his ration figures:

Sir William Waller	93	
Lieutenant-Colonel Baker	43	Wounded at Cheriton, for which he received £9
Major John Hillersdon	41	
Captain Lewis Pemberton	43	Major by 31 May 1644
Captain Edward Willet	70	Major by 7 December 1644
Captain Thomas Holland	40	
Captain Andrew Mainwaring	42	
Captain Philip Stevens	54	
	426	

A list of 'Sir William Waller's reduc't officers,' dated Windsor 26 April 1645, mentions Captain Thomas Holland, Lieutenants John Piper and Anthony Langridge, Ensigns Richard Cooke and Thomas Addames, five sergeants, the chirurgeon, 'Allixander Aurelius', and two mates, Drum Major Sampson Berkit, a drummer and three corporals (S.P. 28/122, Pt. 2).

16. COLONEL RALPH WELDON'S REGIMENT

The Red Regiment of Kent joined Waller in March 1644 and had left his army by the end of August. At Cheriton it mustered eleven companies:

Colonel Ralph Weldon*	92	
Lieutenant-Colonel Nicholas Kempton*	85	Formerly lieutenant-colonel to Springate
Major Thomas Wombell	63	Died on 21 December 1644 at Lyme
Captain William Masters*	76	Succeeded Wombell as Major
Captain Cornelius Lambe	60	His lieutenant was Nicholas Fenton
Captain Edward Scott	78	Formerly captain of a Kent troop of horse
Captain Thomas Wevill	69	Dead by 11 August 1644. A lieutenant in Lord Brooke's Regiment at Edgehill
Captain Humphrey Stele	52	To Birch's Regiment, June 1644
Captain Robert Smith	60	
Captain Christopher Peckham*	49	
Captain James Greenstreet	83	To Birch's Regiment, June 1644
	767	

The figures, from the Kent Commissary Captain Charles Bowles's book of accounts, give the regiment's strength of officers, soldiers and drummers at the time of Cheriton. With the drum-major, provost-marshal, waggon-master, chaplain, chirurgeon, muster-master and their servants the regiment mustered more than 800 men. In the first year after being raised the regiment received a total of £15269.2.7 in pay.

Ralph Weldon, brother to Major Anthony Weldon of Livesey's Regiment and son of Sir Anthony of Swanscombe in Kent, continued in command of the regiment during Waller's Summer campaign in the Midlands in 1644. In 1645 the regiment entered the New Model. In 1650 it supplied five companies for Monck's new Regiment which later became the Coldstream Guards.

17. SIR ARTHUR HESELRIGE'S REGIMENT
(Bluecoats)

Commanded by John Birch, the regiment was raised in the autumn of 1643 and served with Waller until the summer of 1644 when it was reduced for recruits. It possessed at least five companies, of which the following can be identified:

Lieutenant-Colonel John Birch*
Major Ralph Cotsforth or Coatsworth* Captain in Lord Brooke's Regiment, 1642; lieutenant-colonel in Hardress Waller's Regiment of foot in the New Model Army
Captain Humphrey Heathwate Slain on 5 October 1644
Captain Joshua Heyward Lieutenant to Captain Thomas Smith, Lord Brooke's Foot. Died 24 April 1644. In February 1644 his company mustered 97 men

Lord Brooke, a notable Puritan, was slain at Lichfield in March 1643. Clearly many of his officers looked to Heselrige for employment.

The common soldiers came mostly from London. All soldiers in Sir Arthur Heselrige's Regiment were summoned by drums to muster in the new Artillery ground on 17 November 1643 to go down to Farnham.

Born probably in April 1616, John Birch was almost 28 years old at Cheriton. He appears to have been a wine merchant or carrier of wine in Bristol before the war, in a family partnership. He served in the siege of Bristol (Summer 1643) as captain of a trained band, and as a citizen was able to leave freely after the city fell. Colonel Nathaniel Fiennes, Governor of Bristol, called him 'the most active man in the town for the Parliament.' After Cheriton he led his regiment in the Cropredy Bridge campaign, and then received a commission as colonel of a new Kent regiment of foot which he took with him to reinforce the beleaguered garrison of Plymouth. His regiment entered the New Model, and took part in the Western campaign (1645). For the next two years Birch served in Herefordshire, a county in which he made his home. He opposed Cromwell, accompanied the King at Worcester and became a member of the Presbyterian political party. In 1673 he said that his loyalty to King and the Covenant had cost him 21 imprisonments. He died in 1691.

All that we know of Birch's character accords well with the portrait that emerges in the extracts from his secretary's *Memoir* printed in this book. Bishop Burnet writes: 'Colonel Birch was a man of peculiar character. He had been a carrier at first, and retained still, even to an affectation, the clownishness of his education. He got up in the progress of the war to be a colonel, and to be concerned in the Excise. And at the Restoration he was found to be so useful in managing the Excise, that he was put in a good post. He was the roughest and boldest speaker in the house [of Commons], and talked in the language and phrases of a carrier, but with a beauty and eloquence that was always acceptable ... He spoke always with much life and heat. But judgement was not his talent' (Quoted in *Military Memoir of Colonel John Birch*, p. 157).

In 1654, when Birch occupied a jail at Hereford, one of Cromwell's Major-Generals (Berry) formed this estimate of him: 'I mett with (as a prisoner here) coll. Birch, who hath applied himselfe to me as to a little king, that could redresse every grievance ... It is true, the man is popular in these parts, and he loves to be soe. He is taken for a great wit, and guilty of some honesty ...' (*Op. cit.*, pp. 157-8).

18. COLONEL SAMUEL JONES'S REGIMENT
(Greencoats)

White colours. Essex sent Colonel Jones and his regiment into Surrey in July 1643, 'to take a view of the powder mills and to erect such works and fortifications at ye Bridge (Weybridge) and elsewhere for the safety of the mills and bridges,' with power to beat his drums in Surrey to complete his regiment. It remained in Surrey, as the garrison regiment of Farnham, paid by the county committee. At Cheriton the regiment mustered, including officers with men, as follows:

Colonel Samuel Jones	159
Lieutenant-Colonel Jeremy Baines	130
Major King	128
Captain Jones	130
Captain Banckes	74
Captain Hanson	79
Captain Claridge	96
Captain Brewer	72
	868

Baines had been major to Colonel George Welve in February 1643. He refused a regiment in the New Model, and joined the City in opposing the Army in 1647. His surviving papers include a small pocket book in which he jotted down notes of dates such as his marriage to Katherine Otway, 17 August 1639, the birth of a still-born child in 1640 and the births of their subsequent children. It also includes various military notes: fortifications at Farnham Castle, the science of gunnery, names of quarters and officers of the watch in the 1644 Summer campaign (in which the regiment was part of Waller's army), and jottings on the lengths of pikes and the names of various pieces of armour (B.M., Add. MS. 32477).

From all accounts the Farnham Greencoats seems to have been one of the better led and administered regiments in Waller's army. In April 1645 Colonel John Feilder became Governor of Farnham Castle, and took over the regiment until October, when it seems to have been disbanded.

19. COLONEL ANDREW POTLEY'S REGIMENT

Raised in the late Autumn of 1643, the regiment was probably one of the weaker ones in Waller's Army. Andrew Potley was a Scots veteran who had served with much distinction under Gustavus Adolphus for 30 years, earning a gold chain, a medallion and a substantial pension from the 'Lion of the North.' A lieutenant-colonel of foot in 1632, he had quitted the Swedish service after the battle of Lützen, which was fought that year.

At Cheriton Potley served as Waller's Major-General of the Foot. The day after the fight at Cropredy Bridge, while Potley was attending a council of war, the floor collapsed and all Waller's officers tumbled into a cellar. Waller and James Holborne — no lightweight — fell on top of Potley. After this accident he retired from the army. Subsequently he returned to Sweden with Bulstrode Whitelocke. Waller gave the regiment to his cousin Hardress Waller.

The only known officer in the regiment at Cheriton was William Hill, Captain-Lieutenant to Potley's company. He received his commission on 14 March 1644. He had served under Waller as a captain of horse between 2 March and 11 December 1643. After 'behaving himself like a gentleman and a soldier,' according to Sir William Waller, he left the army voluntarily later in 1644.

Major Thomas Smith was major of the regiment on 1 August 1644, when his company mustered 75 musketeers and 28 pikemen.

NOTE ON THE LONDON TRAINED BANDS

THE origins of the London Trained Bands go back to the military obligation of all Englishmen to bear arms in the defence of hearth and home. London citizens, like those of other cities and towns in the Middle Ages, were organized under their aldermen into units. In the Wars of the Roses, for example, the Londoners proved capable of defending their city on more than one occasion.

Under the Tudors the long period of relative internal peace saw a decline in the militia, but this was less marked in London, partly owing to the existence of the Honourable Artillery Company. In 1537 Henry VIII granted a charter to the Master of the Ordnance and two gentlemen of the Privy Chamber for a Fraternity 'consisting of four masters or rulers and such brethren as they should admit' for promoting the 'science of artillery.' Members of the Fraternity acted as officers of the 4000 men raised in London as trained bands during the invasion scare of 1585. Three years later they mustered at Tilbury and were reviewed by Queen Elizabeth I.

The Privy Council in 1616 directed that these men were to be made into four regiments of five companies each, called Trained Bands. In 1642 the Common Council increased their number to 40 companies of 200 men each. Southwark, Westminster and Tower Hamlets each raised a regiment of Trained Bands, and in addition the City added six auxiliary regiments, weaker in number and proably consisting of less well-trained apprentices.

In August 1643 six regiments, one of horse, two of the Trained Bands and three of the Auxiliaries left London and marched with Essex to the relief of Gloucester. On 20 September they took part in the first battle of Newbury.

The Royal United Services Institution possesses a small vellum volume entitled *Ensignes, Traynard Bands, and Auxiliaries, 1642*. On the third leaf is the title:

'The Ensignes/ Of the Regiments in the rebellious City of/ LONDON/ Both of Trayned Bands and/ Auxiliaries./ Togeather with the nearest Number of/ there Trayned Souldiers; taken as/ they marched into Finsbury/ feilds being there last/ generall muster/ Tuesday September xxvj. MDCXLVII/ Anno pestifferae Rebellionis.'

Beneath this is added in Latin: 'The Work of William Levett, Gent.' Levett was clearly a Royalist spy.

A copy, much rougher, exists in the British Museum, and is the work of Richard Symonds, a Royalist officer and author of *Diary of the Marches of the Royal Army*. All the following quotations are from Levett's manuscript, with Symonds's additional comments given in square parentheses. The dates given in round parenthesis after HAC. are the years when the name of the officer concerned was listed in *The Ancient Vellum Book of the Honourable Artillery Company*.

20. THE WHITE REGIMENT

On 26 September 1643 this regiment mustered in London:

Musketeers	600
Pikemen	520
Officers about	70
	1190

The seven companies were all commanded by London citizens:

Colonel Isaac Pennington	[Usurper Major 1643]
(Captain-Lieutenant Richard Verner)	
Lieutenant-Colonel Robert Davies	[A slopmaker for Seamen neare Billingsgate] (HAC, 1618)
Major Thomas Chamberlaine	[viol^t O a Merchant living neare London hall] (HAC, no date)
Captain Thomas Player	[A hosyer & whole saleman for narrow wares living upon neare Fish street hill] (HAC, 1626)
Captain Christopher Whichcott	*A Merchant* [Colonel of the Green Regimt of Auxiliaries about Cripplegate]'. (HAC, 1637) Later Governor of Windsor Castle
Captain William Manby	*Clerk of Leathersellers Hall* (HAC, 1640)
Captain Joseph Vaughan	*displaced* (HAC, 1631)

The regiment's recruiting limits were set by Cornhill, Lombard Street, Fenchurch and the upper part of Gracechurch Street.

21. THE YELLOW REGIMENT

On 23 September the regiment mustered:

Musketeers	506
Pikemen	448
Officers about	70
	1024

The limits of the regiment were: Cheapside, St. Paul's Churchyard, part of Watling Street, part of Newgate Market within Ludgate and Blackfriars.

Colonel Sir John Wollaston	*Alderman* (HAC, 1614)
Captain-Lieutenant John Brett	[A Grocer Silke painting colo^r at ye Rose and Crown in Cornhill] (HAC, 1635)
Lieutenant-Colonel Ralph Harrison	*Wollen Draper in Watling Street* (HAC, 1620)
Major Richard Cuthbert	*A Wollen Draper in Fleet street neare White Fryars-gate* (HAC, 1622)
Captain Robert Tichburne	*A Linnen by ye little Conduct in Cheapside*
Captain Walter Lee	*A Haberdasher in Ludgate,* [at the signe of ye Sun and Bowle] *did breake the Windows of Westminster Abbey* (HAC, 1631)
Captain William Hichcock	*Wollen Draper dwelling in Watling Street* (HAC, 1635 or 1641)

22. THE TRAIN OF ARTILLERY

Under Lieutenant-General James Wemyss the train included some Bluecoat companies of soldiers armed with flint-lock muskets or 'firelocks', including those of:

Colonel James Wemyss	
Captain David Wemyss	Strength varied from 31 to 62 soldiers in 1644. Killed, 2 February 1645
Captain Henry Hazzard	Reduced, 1645
Captain William Davidson	Reduced, 1645
Captain John Fowke	
Captain Henry Roe	60 officers and men in November 1643

Few other officers or staff of the train can be identified with certainty:

Waggon-Master-General	Henry Jarman
Comptroller of the Ordnance	Capt. David Wemyss.

Purveyor	Daniel Judd
Commissary of Provisions	John Winter
Master Smith	John Hill
Master Cooper	Clement Beally
Wheelwright	George Meders
Gentleman	Mr. Merrick
Gunners at Cheriton included:	Thomas Windham, John Shepherd, Thomas Smith, John Cox, Samuel Johnson, Richard Hucktyre, Simon Robinson
Petardier or Fireworker:	Daniel Duthais
A Matrosse:	William Brown

On 7 December 1643 there were 76 carters and 193 horses.
Examples of light leather guns [from Wemyss Castle], similar to those used in the Cheriton campaign, can be seen in Edinburgh Museum.

A NOTE ON PAY IN THE PARLIAMENTARIAN ARMY

Waller's soldiers received the following rates of pay per day:

Major-General of Foot	40s
Colonel of Foot	30s
Lieutenant-Colonel of Foot	15s
Major of Foot	12s
Captain of Foot	8s
Quartermaster	5s
Lieutenant	4s
Chirurgeon	4s
Ensign	3s
Waggoner	3s
Chirurgeon's mate	2s.6d
Drum Major	1s.6d
Sergeant	1s.6d
Corporal	1s
Gentleman-at-arms	1s
Drummer	1s
Private	8d

Chaplain e.g. £6 for 21 days.

There were variations. For example, a captain-lieutenant in a Kentish regiment received 4s. as compared to 6s. in Colonel Samuel Jones's Greencoats; on the other hand a Greencoat major received 3s. a day less than his Kentish counterpart.

A NOTE ON COLONEL JAMES CARR

Carr's valiant work on Waller's left wing played a vital part in securing the Parliamentarian victory. A Scots veteran, Carr had served as a lieutenant-colonel of dragoons in Gloucestershire

PLATE 25
Lord John and Lord Bernard Stuart
Earl Mountbatten Collection   Sir Anthony Van Dyck

A FULL RELATION

of the late

Proceedings, Victory, and good Succeſs
(*Through Gods Providence*)
Obtained by the PARLIAMENTS Forces
Under Sir *William Waller*,
At the taking of the Town and

Caſtle of Arundell,

In Suſſex, Decem. 20. and Jan. 6.

Where were taken above a thouſand Priſoners, two thouſand Arms, neere two hundred Horſe, about a hundred Commanders and Officers, with great ſtore of Treaſure.

As it was delivered by a Meſſenger from Sir *William Waller*, To the Right Honorable, *William Lenthall* Eſq; Speaker to the Houſe of Commons.

And by him appointed to be forthwith printed and publiſhed.

Printed by JOHN FIELD, Jan. 8. 1644.

News indeed:

WINCHESTER TAKEN.

Together with a Fuller

RELATION

of the

GREAT VICTORY
obtained (through Gods Providence,)
at *Alsford*, on Friday the 28. of March, 1644.
By the Parliaments Forces, under the Command
of Sir *William Waller*, Sir *William Balfore*, and Maior
Generall *Browne*, againſt the forces commanded
by the Earl of *Forth*, the L. *Hopton*, Con-
miſſary *Wilmot*, and others,

As it was preſented to the Right Hoble the Lord Major and the Committee of the *Militia* for the City of *London*, by an eye witneſſe.

Publiſhed by Authority.

London, Printed for Laurance Blaiklock. 1644.

April 2d

PLATE 27
Aerial View of Basing House ruins
The earthwork bastions in Basing Park can be clearly seen, and Basing village (on the right of the picture) separated from the site of the New House by a thick copse of trees

PLATE 28

The Grange Barn at Basing

Waller's guns fired over the barn at Basing House and cannon ball marks can be seen on the side of the barn, and beneath the eaves.

Photograph by Bryon Bayd

(22 August 1642–19 June 1643). He was taken prisoner at Cirencester (2 February 1643), losing his horses, watch, shirts, carbine and three pairs of pistols. On that occasion Carr's captured wardrobe included:

One sute of Spanish Cloth layd with silver lace	£7
A long Riding Coate of the same	£2
A doublet of Buck Leather and breeches	£3
A dutch Coat lyned with Foxes	£4
A scarlett mantire [steel skull cap] layd with silver lace	30s.

Having been exchanged, Carr became Waller's Sergeant-Major-General of Foot and Dragoons (1 July–20 August 1643), losing £30 at Roundway Down. That Autumn he failed to complete his new regiment of foot, but after his brave leadership at Cheriton he was soon appointed Governor of beleaguered Plymouth (10 May 1644), where he did good service for the rest of the war.

Section III

1. CASUALTIES AT CHERITON

All the contemporary accounts mention those killed and wounded during the battle. The following lists give name and regiment (if known) and comments culled from the sources. A key to the latter is given below. PW stands for Prisoner of War

A   ROYALISTS   *Notes*

Lord Forth	Wounded (PY)
Lieutenant-General Lord John Stuart	Killed (RH, J) Buried at Oxford (MA)
Major-General Sir John Smith	Dangerously wounded (B) Buried at Oxford (MA)
Major-General Sir Edward Stowell	Dangerously wounded and PW(B) PW (A, J, MA) Five wounds (PY)
Colonel Sir William Boteler	Killed (B). Safe in Oxford, slightly hurt in leg (MA)
Colonel Gray	Killed (B)
Lieutenant-Col. Mathew Appleyard	Wounded (MA) Shot (Slingsby)
Colonel Sir Horatio Carey	Dangerously wounded (B)
Colonel Sir Henry Bard	PW (B, A, J, MA) Lost an arm
Colonel Richard Manning	Killed (MA)
(?) Lieutenant-Colonel Henry Sandys	Wounded (S) Killed (MA) Owned the Vyne (Hants) Died 5 April 1644
Lieutenant-Colonel Kingston or Langstone	PW (A,J)
Lieutenant-Colonel Scott	Killed (MA, S) Manning's H.
Major Robert Legge	Wounded (S) Prince Maurice's H.
Major (Thomas) Bishop	Desperately wounded (S) Hopton's H.
Captain Price (or Pope)	PW (A, J)
Captain Chidleigh (or Chudleigh)	PW (A)
Captain Jackson (or Saxon)	PW (A, J)
Captain Henry Pearson	Wounded (MA) Hurt but recov'd (PY)

Captain Seymour	PW (A, B) Desperately wounded (S) (?) Marquis of Hertford's H.
Captain Audley	PW (J)
Captain Euble Floyd	Wounded in ye very midst of his backe' (PY) Gerard's F.
(?) Captain Raoul Fleury	Foot shot off by cannon-ball. Queen's
Captain Herbert	Wounded (PY) Hopton's F. [H.
Captain Warner	Killed (PY) Sir Edward Waldegrave's H.
Lieutenant Francis Kilburn	PW (PY)
Lieutenant Kite	PW (PY)
Ensign Mellis, or Millis	PW (A, J)
Ensign Marsh	PW (A, J)
Ensign Cooper	PW (J)
Ensign Midley (A) *or* Cornet Midle(J)	PW
Cornet Francis Constable	PW (A,J)
Cornet John Ducket	PW (A, J) Sir Edward Pierce's H.
Coronet William Pritchard	Killed (*Herts County Records* Vol. I, 153)
William Jewell	Wounded *(Devon Quarter Session Records)*
William Clarke	Wounded and PW (PY) Gerard's F.
John Morsey, Physician (A) *or* 'Cornet John Morsey, a Physician, a Priest' (J)	
Christopher Sutton	Wounded (*Hampshire Notes and Queries*, Vol. VIII, p. 29)
William Armstrong	Lost an arm at 'Charenton' fight (PY)
Trooper William Greate	Wounded *(Wilts Quarter Session Records)* Vaughan's H.

B. ROUNDHEADS

Colonel John Meldrum	Hurt (RH) Shot in arm and wounded in head but not dangerously or mortally (B) Very much wounded (Will of John Meldrum)
Colonel Thompson	Shot with a drake, leg cut off (A) 'Col: Tompson hath lost his leg, glory to God alone' (J)
Major Bozwell or Bovill	Wounded in the belly that he cannot live (B) Desperately wounded (A) A commissioner at Arundel
Captain John Fleming Adjutant General of Horse.	Hurt in arm with a captain's leading staff (RH) Recovered and received 30 pieces of gold (G)

Captain-Lieutenant Milton   PW (A) Wounded and PW but we hope tomorrow to redeem him (J)

C. GENERAL COMMENTS

'5 or 6 more Commanders prisoners, and as many ordinary souldiers as we desired to take' (B)

'Together with many other Captains and Commanders, besides common Soldiers, the certain number I know not, whereas wee have not lost 40 men that wee know of, one of our men that was taken prisoner (but left behinde by reason of his wounds) told me himself, they had not taken 20 prisoners in all; and, I know not of 20 slain ... some few are wounded, but I hope not mortally, the certain number of the slain I cannot report; they told us in Alsford, that they fetcht off cart-loads of dead men, and some they buried, and some they carryed with them' (A)

'Taken 150 prisoners, and have not lost 30 men' (J)

In a letter to Sir John Gell the Committee of Both Kingdoms gave the prisoners as: 2 colonels, 1 lieut. colonel, 7 captains, 20 other officers and 300 common soldiers (*C.S.P.D.* 1644, p. 99).

Two messengers brought confusing reports to the House of Commons on 1 April, according to Sir Simonds D'Ewes. The first put the Royalist strength at 15000 and mentioned 300 slain, obviously an exaggeration. The second gave 'about 10000' as the strength, and 500 Royalist dead (B.M., Harl. MS. 166, f. 49).

SOURCES

RH	Robert Harley.
B	Sir William Balfour.
A	Elias Archer.
J	John Jones.
MA	*Mercurius Aulicus.*
G	Godwin.
PY	Brigadier Peter Young

Section IV

SITE OF THE BATTLEFIELD

Readers familiar with accounts of the Battle of Cheriton other than my own will have noticed that both here and in my biography of Sir William Waller I have proposed a new site for the battle.

The 'traditional' site has the Royalists drawn up at the start of battle on Tichborne Down and the Parliamentarians on the Cheriton Wood hill, with the main fighting taking place in the open dip between them, called by Colonel A. H. Burne 'The Arena' (A. H. Burne and P. Young, *The Great Civil War: A Military History of the First Civil War 1642-1646* (1959), pp. 125-6). Colonel Burne could also over-confidently declare: 'There is no dispute as to the site of this battle.'

Burne probably relied upon the map of the battle given in S. R. Gardiner, *History of the Great Civil War*, Vol. 1 (1893), p. 322, the earliest one known to me and apparently the source of the 'traditional' site, which showed his 'Arena' as 'Open Common.'

Gardiner visited the field in the 1880s or early 1890s, and inspected the 'Open Common.' 'There is no local tradition,' he wrote (pp. 324-5), 'of any ground known as the Common, but the fencing in the valley has the appearance of being comparatively new, and I was told that the land had been enclosed in the last generation. Even if it was not spoken of in Cheriton at the time of the battle as 'the Common,' it was open enough for a Royalist Officer to call it by that name.' A Mr Stratton of Chilcombe took Gardiner over the field and pointed out the sites traditionally connected with it. Gardiner admits that 'there is no direct evidence of Lisle's retreat' from the hill overlooking Waller's quarters, 'but it would almost necessarily follow, and all the accounts of the battle itself which have reached us imply that Waller occupied the ridge which Lisle had been placed to guard.' It is this conclusion of Gardiner's, followed by all other historians, that we must now examine critically.

(i) One account that neither Gardiner nor Burne used, the letter of Captain Robert Harley, makes it clear that the Roundheads opened the battle with 'a little village' on their left wing. Historians have assumed too readily that this was Cheriton. Yet Harley earlier refers to 'Cherrytowne': he clearly knew its name, and there would be no reason for him to refer to the hamlet he could see away to his left, as 'a little village'.

(ii) Everyone agrees that the London regiments quartered in Lamborough fields. From nineteenth century tithe maps and the 1810 Ordnance Survey, it is known that these fields lay alongside the Itchen stream beneath Hinton Ampner. Indeed, there is a cluster of houses nearby marked on the present day $2\frac{1}{2}''$ O.S. map as 'Little London,' commemorating an obvious (but previously not noticed) piece of local tradition. (There is also a 'Little London' near Oxford, in the area where the London regiments might have camped during the Summer campaign of 1644).

Captain John Jones, writing the day after the battle from Alresford (where he could easily check his information), notes 'we lay in Lumbourne field, we fought in East Down between Cheriton and Alresford.'

Now East Down is undoubtedly the name of the ridge Lisle occupied on the eve of the battle: it is shown as such on the 1810 O.S. map, due east of Cheriton. The tithe maps show that some of the fields adjacent to East Down Farm (long since demolished, but originally beside Bramdean Lane close to the crest of the hill) in Burne's 'Arena' had names with East Down suffixes. But we know, anyway, that towards the end of the battle the fighting spilled over into the hollow back of East Down. What must now be rejected, however, is the view of Gardiner, Burne and F. T. R. Edgar (in his biography of Lord Hopton) that the battle began with Waller already firmly established on

East Down. There is no evidence at all to support the conclusion that Lisle withdrew back to Tichborne Down.

(iii) No significant finds of cannon-balls or remains have been reported that would resolve the controversy, although on one visit I have been shown a small cannon-ball found near Hinton Ampner in the Itchen, and other relics have turned up over the years. One resident of that village testified that ghosts haunted the lane from the village down to the valley, making the hair of dogs stand on end. As all Roundheads had good consciences, these must have been Royalist ghosts . . .

We may conclude, therefore, that the main battle took place in the larger valley immediately south of 'The Arena' or the 'Open Common' which lay almost cupped in the arms of Cheriton Wood. If we follow all the accounts literally, they lead us unerringly to the main scene of the fight at Cheriton.

Section V

THE COURT MARTIAL PAPERS OF SIR WILLIAM WALLER'S ARMY, 1644

'Military Papers, 1644,' a slim volume forming part of the Brabourne MSS. in the Kent Archives Office, was found by the author to contain the manuscript minutes of twenty-one courts martial held in Sir William Waller's army during 1644. Besides the light they throw upon what has hitherto been the most obscure of the Parliamentarian armies in the Civil War, these documents possess a unique interest as the earliest surviving series of court martial records in this country.[1] Also they help to bring to life the common soldiers of the day.

The period covered by the first seven courts martial (22 April-17 May) saw the mustering at Farnham in Surrey of Waller's army after their victory at Cheriton. From Farnham, after briefly facing Basing House, Waller led his regiments towards Oxford, where he arrived by the end of May. The King, however, slipped between the converging armies of Essex and Waller and safely reached Worcester. Essex then decided to march south in order to relieve Lyme, directing Waller to attend to the King. Waller moved north to Stourbridge, and succeeded in preventing the King from joining Prince Rupert in Yorkshire, but he could not bring the Royalist army to battle. Once more the King eluded him, by marching back towards Oxford. After some delay, Waller received orders to follow him. Having made a successful march to block the King's advance into the Eastern Association, Waller suffered a serious reverse at Cropredy Bridge (29 June). The continuous marches of the army at this time are perhaps reflected in the lack of courts martial between 7 June and 8 July.

Serious mutinies and mass desertions after Cropredy Bridge

reduced the strength of Waller's forces (about 10000 men) by half. Towards the end of July he learned that the King's army had marched away from the Midlands into the South-West. Quartering the remnants of his weary foot and train of artillery at Abingdon, Waller retired to London. Meanwhile, his horse and dragoons rode into Dorset to harry the local Royalists and to keep a watchful eye on the progress of the King's army.

When it became clear that Essex had fallen into dire straits in Cornwall, Waller drew his foot and train down to Farnham and, augmented by fresh reinforcements, set out in September to succour him. Upon the news of the defeat of Essex at Lostwithiel, Waller (now re-united with his cavalry) fell back before the King's slow advance towards London. Leaving his foot regiments to garrison the South coast towns, Waller then hastened to join up with the survivors of Essex's army and the newly-arrived Eastern Association forces under Manchester and Cromwell. After the inconclusive battle of Second Newbury (27 October), Waller's army went into quarters for the Winter in Surrey and Sussex. Early the next year the army was disbanded in order to supply a proportion of officers and men for the New Model.

Composed variously of regiments formed and paid by the Western counties (for service in the West), the Southern Association (Kent, Surrey, Sussex and Hampshire for their mutual defence) and the City of London, Waller's army lacked homogeneity. Moreover, as he could rarely get reinforcements from the various committees during the Midlands campaign Waller had to rely for these upon contingents from Parliamentarian garrisons in the area. In this context, the courts martial performed a unifying function in this patchwork army by imposing and enforcing common standards of discipline. Considering the endemic shortages of money for wages and the natural tendency towards disintegration arising from the military failures of the year, the court carried out its difficult task with as much success as could be reasonably expected.

The minutes of the court's meetings were written on single sheets of paper and bound, without regard to date, sometime afterwards. In this section they are placed in chronological order and given numbers, with the separate proclamations and 'Articles of War' at the end. In the manuscript each set of minutes has a short Latin title, giving the place and date of the meeting, followed by a list of the ranks and surnames of those present. These names have also been grouped together in an appendix at the end, and (where known) Christian names and regiments have been added from other sources. Abbreviations which can be rendered into print have been retained, but in other cases the whole word is given. Capitalization and spelling (except for the better known names in the appendix) are those of the document, which is unpaginated.

(1) Phernham, 22 April, 1644.

>The Copy of an accusacon of John Boreman
>
>The accusacon of John Boreman first for makeing of a Mutiny in the Company at Mitchin[2], and then running away with severall others with him, and since entred himselfe under others, and is likewise run away from them, and being now apprehended is close prisoner till the Councell of Warr passe [sentence] upon him, Moreover he expressed his mind to some of the company that the Parliament was not in the Right way, and would get the worst, so that he laboured to divert the Company from serving of the Parliament. And likewise more mutinos speeches, and actions wch can be certified by severall witnesses.
>
>>Wittnesses produced sworne and examined die supra dicte super accusacoem predict.
>
>The examinacon of Captaine Willm. Tattan[3]
>
>This examinate sayth that John Boreman a foote souldier late under the Comand of him this ex^{te} did receive pay of the States for a Fortnight together or thereabout, and that the sayd Boreman departed without leave or consent about Candlemas last past to the examinats best remembrance.
>
>The examinacon of John Mudy
>
>This examinate sayeth that John Boreman in the heareing of this examinate did about January last at a place calld Mitchin within the County of Surry complaine for want of his pay, wch was promised (as the sayd Boreman alledged) to be payd unto him every three dayes by Captaine Wm Tattan under whose comand hee then was. And that this ex^{te} did heare him further say, come lett us draw forth, and ly in Ambush and that the sayd Boreman did receive to this ex^{te} knowledge a Fortnight's pay, and afterwards Ran away from his Captaine.
>
>The Examinacon of Willm Thackery

This examinate sayeth that John Boreman did receive a Fortnights pay at Mitchin under Captaine Tattan and ran away to this examinats owne knowledge, and did sollicit this examinate to run away with him likewise.

The examinacon of Roger Revill

This examinate sayeth that hee hath knowne the sayd John Boreman the space of 15 weekes and that he received a Fortnights pay from Captaine Tattan, and Ran away from him, when he lay at Mitcham to his this ex^{te} owne knowledge.

The examinacon of Walter Williams

This Examinate sayeth that hee very well knoweth John Boreman, and that hee served under the Comand of Captaine Tattan at Mitcham, and that hee received a Fortnights pay of his Captaine and afterwards ran away from him to this examinats owne knowledge.

Ordo:

An Order by the Councell of Warr to inable the Marshall Generall, so often as hee shall finde any private Souldier drunke, that hee shall have power to inflict the punishment of puttinge on a paire of handcuffs, and with a chaine to drawe the party up untill hee stand on tipptoe with a kan or jugg about his necke neere the maine Guard, and there to stand according to discrecon.[4]

The Judgment of the Councell of Warr upon John Boreman according to the testimony & proofe of the Witnesses. It is adjudged by the whole Councell of Warr (nemine Contradicen) that John Boreman being accused of severall articles that is to say for Running away from his Cullors several tymes, and by his owne confession receiving intertainmt under severall Captaines, from wch hee hath also severally departed without theire leave or license For wch offences hee hath received Judgm^t from the Councell of Warr to be hang'd by the neck untill hee be dead.

A warrant against Capt: St Georg[5] for intertaineing of papists to appear at the next Councell of Warr.

A warrant directed to Major Saunderson inabling him to suspend Capt: Hamroad from the execution of his Charge untill hee appeare before the next Councell of Warr.

(2) Phernam, 26 April, 1644.

The Accusacon of Richard Kiddle for Running away from his Cullors.

Witnesses produced sworne and examined super accusacoem pred.

The examinacon of Patricke Gourdon

This Examinate sayeth that hee well knoweth the sayd Richard Kiddle and that this examinate and the sayd Richard Kiddle and others walkeing forth to a village neere Alton to drinke—the sayd Richard Kiddle through the persuacons of two others then in his Company did leave and Goe from his Cullors towards Basing howse[6] voluntarily, this ex^t knoweing for certaine for that hee beeing then and there present was also sollicited by some one then present to goe along with them but refused.

The examinacon of James Plenty of Winchester

This examinate sayeth that hee knoweth Richard Kiddle and that the sayd Kiddle was in a village drinkeing with this ex^{te} and some others neere Alton where hee did see the sayd Richard Kiddle goe away with one William Chide and Richard Luckis from theire Cullors towards Basing this ex^{te} then present.

The accusacon of Richard North for resisting the Marshall and his men in performance of theire office.

Richard North haveing bin accused and Comitted for makeing against the Marshall Generalls men is cleered & freed from prison by consent of the whole Councell of Warr.

Ordo:

It is ordered that the usuall dayes of meeting in this Army for the Councell of Warr that is to say thrice every weeke weekely, vizt Mundays, Wednesdayes and Frydayes shalbe duly observed and kepte. (s) Maddison Judg Advocate.[7]

A warr^t to desire Captaine St George or in his absence his ymediate officers to secure the Body of one Stewart a Corpall in his troope to answer to articles at the next Councell of Warr.

A Warr^t against Christopher Cosier & John Eamont to appeare at the next Councell of Warr to Give testimony against the abovesayd Steward.

A warr^t to desire Major Battersby to secure the Body of two Troopers under his Comand one of them called by name Henry Wilcocke to appeare the next Councell of Warr for Robbing one Thomas Collier a Miller.

A Warr^t against Thomas Collier a Miller to appeare at the next Councell of Warr to Give in testimony against the abovesayd Henry Wilcocke, and another trooper for Robbing of him.

A Copy of a proclamacon

These are to declare that all such souldiers as have entred themselves in other Companyes, and shall returne to theire severall Cullors within three dayes shalbe received into mercy, but such as shall refuse upon this proclamacon to returne to theire owne severall Captaines shalbe punished by death without mercy, Given under my hand this 20 Aprill 1644

William Waller.

A Copy of a proclamacon

For as much as I am informed (and in my perticular doe take notice that severall of my officers of all degrees both horse and foote are at this present absent in and about the Citty of London and the suburbs thereof from theire severall charges and Comands I doe hereby straightly charge will and Comand all Officers and Comanders of what degree soever, upon sight or report hereof to repayre unto theire severall charges and Comands, as they will answer the Contrary upon payne of Death, Given under my hand from my Quarter at Phernham this five and twentieth day of Aprill Anno domini 1644.

(3) Phernham, 29 April, 1644

A warr^t against Quarter Master Terpin to appeare at the next Councell of Warr for speakeing scandalous and contemptuous words against the Generall.

For die nil ulterius actum.

(4) Phernham, 2 May, 1644.

The accusacon of Richard Allen, Chyrurgion to the Trayne of Artillery for neglecting his duty, disobeying the orders of Doctor Pratt Physician of the Army and abusing him with abusive and contemptuous language.

Witnesses produced sworne and examined

The examinacon of Thomas Peasly

The ex^t sayeth that upon Tuesday last being XXXth of Aprill carryeing of a Bill to the Chyrurgion of the firelocks by expresse from Pratt to lett a Gunner blood, who formerly had bin neglected by Richard Allen, meeting with the sayd Allen demaunded of him where the Chirurgion of the firelocks at that tyme was who perceiving this ex^t had a Bill to deliver to him tooke the sayd Bill and reading of it, sayd that he had formerly lett him blood before, and presently falleing into a passion tore the paper, and called Doctor Pratt foole, asse and Coxcombe, or words to the like effect.

The examinacon of Thomas Herbert

This ex^{te} sayeth that upon Tuesday last being the XXXth of Aprill carryeing a Bill from Doctor Pratt to the Chyrurgion of the firelocks to let a sicke man blood this ex^{te} mett with the foresayd Richard Allen, beeing quartered both at one place, who lookeing upon the Bill directed to the Chyrurgion of the firelocks to lett blood a Gunner who some small tyme before was blooded by the sayd Allen, the sayd Richard Allen called the sayd Doctor Pratt, foole, asse, and Coxcombe or words to the like effect.

 The examinacon of Richard Allen Chyrurgion upon the article exhibited

This ex^{te} confesseth hee called Doctor Pratt foole, and asse and that he would not administer the sayd doctors Physicke beeing a duty nothing belonging to him as a Chyrurgion.

 The sensure of the Councell of Warr past upon the sayd Richard Allen.

It is ordered and adjudged that Richard Allen haveing bin accused by Doctor Pratt for his contemptuous and refractory carriage towards him, and disobedience to his Orders and prescripts, together with severall reproachful and scandalous words tending to the dishonour and diffamacon of the sayd Doctor Pratt, and his obstinate perseverance in his sayd misdemeaners, That hee shall stand Casheered, and to be ymprisoned till the next Councell of Warr, and this to stand in force untill the further will and pleasure of the Generall be knowne.

It is ordered this day that whosoever shall not repayre to the Councell of Warr upon the usuall dayes and place appointed by eight or nine of the Clocke in the forenoone at the farthest shall forfeit pay, And that the sayd Councell shall not upon any cause soever sitt longer than the howre of Twelve at noon without expresse order from ye Generall to the Contrary.

 To the Gentlemen and others the Inhabitants of Crundle[8] In Redresse of the grievances in the petition of ye Inhabitants of Yately, I doe hereby for their easement answer unto theire three questions. Unto the First that they shall not be charged singly but with the rest of the out halfe hundred of Crundle. To the second that they shall not contribute to severall Captaines warrants, but only to the warrants of the Regiments quartered at Crundle. To the third that they shall not be charged but by warrant from any of the Regiments now quartered at Crundle unlesse theire Contempt shall occasion a party to fetch in the proporcon of provisions charged upon them, In pursuance whereof I doe herein express my pleasure to whome These may concerne that the aforesayd promisses be duly observed, whereof you are not to faile. Given under my hand this second of May, 1644

          Willm. Waller.

(5) Phernham, 3 May, 1644.
    Richard Kiddle accused for Running away from his Cullors and proved by two witnes as will appeare by their testimonies folio 3⁰
    The Sensure of the Councell of Warr upon him.
    It is adjudged by the Councell of Warr this day sitting that Richard Kiddle being accused of Running away from his Cullors, and proved against him by two witnesses, for such his offence shalbe hanged by the neck untill he bee dead, Saveing unto our Generall his further will and pleasure.

(6) Phernham, 13 May, 1644.
    The Censure of Captaine James Francis de Latoure⁹
    Whereas Captain Latoure hath bin questioned before the Councell of Warr upon severall articles exhibited against him, of the truth of wch there appeares noe sufficient proofe, but meerely out of malice promoted by Lewis Mareshall his Leif^t The whole Councell of Warr doe this day fully and absolutely acquitt and discharge the sayd Captaine Latoure, as cleere from all the sayd former charge.
    The Censure of Lewis Mareshall Leif^t
    It is ordered by the Councell of Warr this day that Leif^t Mareshall being accused and questioned upon severall articles proved against him by many witnesses, and more especially for abuseing his quarters, resisting and opposeing his Captayne and sayeing to his charge severall scandalous matters proceeding meerly from malice, That hee shalbe forthwith Casheered from his Comand: make an acknowledgement before the head of his troope that hee hath very grossely and impudently scandalized Capt: Latoure in his honnour and good reputation, as also humbly crave pardon for the same before this hon^ble Court, and utterly be disabled from Beareing of Armes, and that hee shall stand imprisoned dureing the pleasure of the Councell of Warr.
    It is this day ordered by the Councell of Warr (whereas John De Levet Quarter Master to Captaine Latoure hath bin charged with popish Recusancy) That the sayd John De Levet shalbe referred to Mr Jackson Minister to be exactly, and fully examined concerning the Tenents of his faith, and to certifie this hon^ble Court how hee finde him stand affected.

(7) Fernham, 17 May, 1644.
    It is this day ordered and adjudged by the consent of the councell of warr that Thomas Mills John Homon and John Fant souldiers under Coll Weldens Regmt of foote¹⁰ being taken notice of as notorious offenders—the one vizt John

Homond for haveing twice run away from his Cullors, the other two Thomas Mills and John Fant for running away from theire Cullors instantly after a fresh example of justice for the same offence, that they and every of them shalbe hanged by the neck untill hee be dead.

It is this day ordered by the Councell of Warr that Marke Million, Thomas Martin, Bartholomew Comfort, John Johnson and Edward Garret haveing confessed themselves Guilty of death by severall articles yet through the meere mercy of this Court and hope of theire future amendment, desireing to make some difference between offenders, shall have a serious admonicon in the presence of the Court, and the merits of theire offences according to the Articles layd open unto them, and be forthwith dismissed to theire Comanders in Cheife to be disposed of according to discrecon.

(8) Abingdon, 31 May, 1644.

It is the Order of the Councell of war that the Troopes under the Comand of the Generall shall from hence forth be recrewted out of the severall Countyes hee shall march through by warrant unto severall hundreds, to send in each proportionable number of horses, as by him shalbe thought fit for the prevencon of such abuses, as have bin lately practized by the officers and souldiers of the Army in plundering and takeing away upon false pretences.

It is this day ordered by the Councell of Warr that the Officers of each Regiment that is to say of Major Generall Potleys[11] and Coll : Weldens Regiment shall make an Inquiry how and in what manner John Jenkins a souldier under the Comand of Major Warren[12] was the last night being the XXXth of this instant mounth of May slaine, and shall make a true certificate of the State and condition thereof to the Advocate of the Army, to thend the Councell of Warr may have an Accompt thereof and be the better satisfied therein.

It is ordered that the Comanders in Cheif of each Regiment shall bring a List of such wants of horses in eny of theire sayd Regiments, and present it to the Generall that theire wants may be recrewted.

It hath bin thought fit by Sir William Waller and the Councell of Warr to declare unto all Officers and Souldiers that theire expresse will and Comand is, that no officer or souldier shall from hence forth dare to presse or charge any Cart or Waggon for the carriage of theire Baggage without a warrant to that purpose from ye sayd Sir William, nor dare to plunder or charge any horse or horses of any Countryman

PLATE 29
Aerial View of Arundel Castle

The arrow marks the direction of Waller's first attack. The trees hide remnants of the earthwork which Colonel Birch stormed successfully.

Photograph by John Wright

PLATE 30
William Lenthall, Speaker of the House of Commons   *Artist unknown*
Recipient of most despatches from Waller throughout the Campaign
National Portrait Gallery

or other—nor take the Goods of any man from him, But shall from tyme to tyme by a list presented unto the Generall by the Cheife officers of each Regiment or Troope of such horses as are either wanting or weake in such Regiment or Troope be recrewted—and exchanged according to an Order of the Councell of Warr herein provided, as they will answer upon paine of Death without mercy.

(9) Stowe in the Would, 7 June, 1644.

Robert Hollifax accused that on the XXth inst. of May last the Army being upon a March from Abington hee stayeing behinde drinkeing, Leift Williams, Comanding him to his Cullors the sayd Robert Hollifax denyed to Goe to his Cullors, and stroake him twice, as also being Comanded to deliver up his Arms, wilfully refused.

It is orderd this day that Robert Hollifax being found Guilty of the breach of two Articles vizt the 5th and the 7th concerning the duty of Souldiers towards theire superior officers as more fully doth appeare by their severall examinations and depositions, shalbe hangd by the neck till hee be dead.[13]

Christopher Hanniball accused for that upon Wednesday being the 5th of this instant Month of June the sayd Hanniball being Comanded to march after theire Randezvous at Whitney he pe(re)mptorily refused.

It is ordered by the Councell of Warr for that it is manifestly proved hee wilfully denied to obey the Comand of Leift Coll[11] Sowton[14] his superior officer, that hee shalbe forthwith layd neck and heeles together at the Maine Guard, and in such forme and manner to continue untill the Army doth March, and during the sayd tyme to be fedd with no other food than bread and water, and upon the marching of the Army as beforesayd, the sayd Christopher Hanniball is to be brought neck and heeles together to the head of the Regiment and there make an humble acknowledgement of his fault to the sayd Leift Coll.

Serjeant West under the Comand of Leift Coll Baker accused of abuseing the Hambletts.[15]

It is ordered that Serjeant West for that hee by his own confession abused in some scandalous and reproachful language the Hamblets souldiers that hee shall stand Comitted untill theire forces be drawne up, and that then hee shall in the head of the Regiment make an humble acknowledgement of his fault.

xii Junii 1644 apud Evesham

A Declaracon to the Inhabitants of the County of Worster

Whereas of late yeares there hath bin an unnaturall warr kindled in the Bowells of this kingdome through the Ambition and Malignity of evill Councellors, and of the popish and prelaticall pty who under pretence of his Maties name and authority, and the maintenance of the true protestant religion and the Lawes of the Land have made a sadd devision betwixt his Matie and his Parliament, and put the whole kingdome into such a combustion, as that thereby the kingdome is not only impoverished and wasted but made a feild of Blood, and likely to be exposed to forraine Armes, if God in his mercy doe not Gratiously avert it, And whereas those evill Councellors and Malignants have under his Maties name set forth divers declaracons and proclamacons wherein they have branded both the howses of Parliam^t with the marke of Rebellion, and all such as adhere to them, with the odious name of Traytors, scismaticks, and sectaryes, and such as indeavored to alter the Government, and to introduce popular confusion. These are to protest against all such Calluminies and aspercons and to declare to all persons of Quality and others within this County or parts adjacent that if they shall speedily repaire to my head Quarters and according to the Ordinance of Parliament enter into the Nationall Covenant taken by both kingdoms, as a sincere expression of their Right affection to Gods cause That I shall not only receive them as freinds but protect both theire persons and estates from all insolencyes and prejudice by my Army but also recommend them to the favor and mercyes of both howses of Parliament. Given under my hand at my Quarters at Evesham XIIth Junii 1644.

            Willm Waller.

      Eodem die

Proposicons propounded and agreed on by the Councell of Warr concerning the Cavall^ary

First that all officers in cheife Comanding Regiments shall appeare at the place of the Generall Randezvous at the howre appointed under paine of Casheering and because it is pretended by many that by reason of the slowness of theire souldiers they cannot kepe the tyme appointed. It is therefore ordered by the Councell of Warr that they with theire severall inferior officers and Cullors shall observe the tyme, so by this they shall justify themselves, haveing before used meanes for drawing out theire men.

Secondly That noe Regiment or Troope shall depart from the Generall Randezvous without order, and haveing order to depart, that every severall officer Comanding a Regiment shall leave two Troopers to receive orders at the Ordinants house, and that those Two troopers shalbe releived every foure and twenty houres. This not to be omitted under the payne of confinem^t.

Thirdly That the Guards be tymely releived and that noe officer upon any pretence soever be absent from his Guard, under the payne of publique disgrace.

Fourthly That all officers in Cheife be carefull to Curbb all Mutinies, and if it shalbe found that any officer shall Countenance such mutinies that they shalbe casheered and put of from the Army with disgrace.

Fifthly That every officer Comanding Regiments in Cheife shall send dayly one officer of that same Regiment that is to say a Quarter Master at least to receive orders upon paine of punishment according to the article of Warr to that purpose set forth.

(10) Forsely in Com Northampton, 8 July, 1644.

It is ordered this day by the Councell of Warr that upon the Comitment of any prisoner into the Custody of the Marshall Generall, That the sayd Marshall Generall shall forthwith bring the Party so comitted before the Judge Advocate with a Copy of the informacon or complaint ready drawne up, And that hee shall dayly present unto the sayd Advocate a List of all the Names of such Prisoners as remaine in his Custody with the Causes of their Comittments.

(11) Daventry, 12 July, 1644.

It is adjudged by the Councell of Warr this day that Richard Bradshawe being accused of a mutiny and sufficiently proved against for his sayd offence shalbe hanged by the Neck untill hee bee dead.

It is ordered and adjudged by the Councell of Warr this Day that Richard Stansby being accused of a mutiny and found Guilty of the same by sufficient Testimony, shalbe hanged by the neck for his sayd offence untill hee bee dead

It is ordered and adjudged by the Councell of Warr that John Huett being found Guilty of the Breach of certaine Articles as a Muntineere by sufficient testimony, shalbe hargebuseerd to death for his sayd offence.[16]

It is this day adjudged by the Councell of Warr that Phillip Hobby Quarter Master for that hee did not with his best power indeavor to suppresse the sayd Mutiny, hee shall first accompany the sayd Bradshaw Stansby and Huett to the place of execucon, and afterwards by the Hangman to be

casheerd the Army, never to Beare Arms therein.
(12) *Boreton*[Barton Hartshorn] in Com Buckingham, 15 July, 1644
It is this day ordered by the Councell of Warr that the Busines concerning Captaine Bruce his killing of one of his Troope shalbe heard on Wednesday next, and in the interim the witnesses to be examined, and the Busines to be set in the Best forwardnes by the Advocate for hearing.
It is this day likewise ordered that the Complaints made against Major Anderson[17] shall the same day be heard and the witnesses in the interim to be examined
(13) Woodstocke, 17 July, 1644.
It is this day ordered by the Councell of Warr that Jo Defreeze for abuseing and cutting off Phillip Warnington one of his fellowe souldiers under the Comand of Captain Requicke,[18] & for drunkenesse, he shal be hanged up by the hands untill he stand on Tiptoe neere to the maine Guard for the space of a Quarter of an houre, with a payre of handcuffs about his Rists, and then to be cashiered never to returne to the Army againe.
It is this day ordered by the Councell of Warr that Thomas Williams Marshall being found Guilty by sufficient testimony as a Countenancer of Plunderers a Drunkard and an abuser of prisoners, that he shalbe drawne up on Tiptoe neere the maine Guard by the Rists with a payre of handcuffs by the space of a quarter of an houre and afterwards be cashiered the Army never to returne againe.
(14) Abingdon, 23 July, 1644.
It is ordered by the Councell of Warr that Major Wood for killing of a man shalbe forthwith apprehended by the Marshall Generall and kept in safe Custody until hee discharge himself thereof.
It is ordered by the Councell of Warr that Garrett Harbert being found Guilty of Robbing one Judith whiteing by sufficient testimony, shall goe from whence he came to the place of execucon, and there to be hanged by the neck untill hee be Dead.
Edward Crane being questioned for the same fact but not anywise proved against him is this day discharged.
It is this day ordered by the Councell of Warr that David Rogers and Robert Baven according to theire owne confession haveing plundred a Dublet and a patterne for a payre of breeches of stuffe from a Taylor at Woodstocke shall lye neck and Heels together one whole day and be fead with no other food then bread and water, and then set at Liberty.
It is ordered that John Elton shall lye by the Heeles

till the morrow and then be set at liberty.

It is ordered by the Councell of Warr that Henry Stone according to his owne confession being found Guilty of plundring a shirt an apron and some other triviall things, shall have the Gatlopp[19] once through the whole Regiment and be ignominously discharged the Army for his sayd fault.

It is ordered that Robert Kane being found Drunke shall have the usuall punishment inflicted on him formerly injoined by the Councell of Warr.

Francis Allen set at Liberty.

It is ordered that Thomas dyer being found Guilty by his owne Confession of picking of three shillings out of a souldiers pockett shall have the Gatlope twice through the whole Regiment for his sayd fault.

It is ordered that William Win being in question for some misdemeanor comitted neere Northampton and complained of by the Committee there shall stand comitted for the space of two dayes more and then be released.

(15) Abingdon, 25 July, 1644.

It is this day ordered by the Councell of Warr that Corpall Vandradisse for that hee absented himself from his Guard shall ride the woodden horse according to discrecon.[20]

It is ordered by the Councell of Warr that Serjeant [name missing] for that it is proved hee stroake Leift Pricir to Leift Coll Baines,[21] and the sayd Serjeant denieing the same, alleadgeth witnesses to the contrary, shalbe comitted into the Marshall hee hath Generalls hands untill hee shall produce such testimony.

Captain Thomas Ducton being suspected as a spie dischardged by the Councell of warr, and an order Granted for the restitucon of such things as were taken from him.

Edward Palmer being suspected likewise as a spie dischardged by the Councell of Warr, and the like order Granted to him

(16) Abington, 8 August, 1644.

It is this day ordered and adjudged by the whole Councell of warr that Robert Gilde for that hee is found Guilty of murther and fellony Hee shalbe carried to the place from whence hee came and so to the place of execution there to be hanged by the necke untill hee be dead.

(17) Shasbury, 26 September, 1644.

It is ordered by the Councell of Warr that John Whitaker for that by his owne confession he is found Guilty of Robbing a man on the Highway shalbe carried to the place from whence hee came, and so to the place of executon, there to be hanged by the neck untill he be Dead.

(18) Winterborne Stoake, 11 October, 1644.

It is this day ordered by the Councell of Warre that particular notice shalbe Given to all the officers of the severall Regiments both light horse and dragoone, that they forthwith rectify and declare unto theire souldiers the expresse will of the Councell herein, wch is that no souldier upon what pretence soever shall from hence forth presume to plunder take away or change any horse or horses from any Countryman or other Traveller upon the Road, man or woman without order from the Generall, or other superior officer who hath power thereunto upon payne of Death without mercy.

It is ordered by the Councell of Warr That what monyes have bin Received by Leift Col: Thorpe for the use of Major Carrs Troop[22] since Leift Col: Thorpe left the Troope, shalbe by him repayd unto Major Carr or his Assignee.

It is ordered by the Councell of Warr that Major Willett[23] for that he presented a false Muster shalbe forthwith cashiered

(19) Andover, 17 October, 1644.

Whereas Major Edward Wood once Agitant Gen of the foot to the right honait Sir Willm Waller is now accused for killing one Thomas Pritchard then under the Comand of one Captaine Knapp of the Regiment of Col: Houblon.[24] In as much as the aforesaid Thomas Pritchard is proved to have been the cheife actor and Incourager of a dangerous mutiny at Basingstoake, not only by forceing a Sentinell and Quarters, but also by resisting and affronting the sayd Major at that tyme injoyned and sent to suppresse the sayd Mutiny, It is ordered by the joynt consent of the whole Councell of Warr, That the sayd Major Edward Wood shall stand acquitted as concerning the death of the sayd Thomas Pritchard, In that it did appeare that what the sayd Major then did was in performance of his duty.

It is ordered this day by the Councell of Warr that Andrew Fyan, for that (according to his owne confession) hee wounded his Leif^t, shalbe harqebuseerd to death.

(20) Petersfeild, 7 December, 1644.

Whereas many abuses and violencyes are dayly offerred and practiced upon Countrymen both in theire dwellinge, and Travelling on the Road by Souldiers in plundering theire horses Cattle sheepe and other provisions from them some of wch intended for the Markette: It is this day ordered by the Councell of Warr that no Souldiers upon any pretence whatsoever shall from henceforth plunder, seise or take away any of the Goods, sheepe, Cattle, horse or horses whether by exchaning or otherwise from any Countryman or other Traveller upon the Road, nor molest in theire person or Goods any man or woman comeing to or from the Markett without expresse order from the Generall or other superior officer haveing power thereunto, upon paine of death without mercy. This order to be published at the head of every Regiment.

(21) Petersfeild, 20 December, 1644.
Whereas Captaine Samuell Potte, Captaine of a Troope of horse of the Regiment of Col: Cooke is now accused for killing one Mathew White a Trooper under his owne Comand, In as much as the aforesayd Mathew White is proved to have bin an Actor and Incourager of a dangerous Mutiny in affronting the sayd Captaine Potte severall tymes with very rude, mutinous and unbeseeming language, being then also upon the Guard It is ordered by the joynt consent of the Councell of Warr that the sayd Captaine Potte shall stand acquitted as concerning the death of the sayd Mathew White, In that it doth appeare, that what the sayd Captaine thendid was in performance of his duty and in the suppressing of a dangerous Mutiny then in the Troope.

It is this day adjudged by the Councell of Warr that William Quincy Quartermaster to Capt: Guilliams[25] for that by his own confession hee is found guilty of Theft and Robbery. In that hee comanding of a party by force tooke from a Gentleman travelling on the Road neere Alsford six pounds in mony, his horse, and sword, shalbe hanged by the neck untill hee be dead.

It is likewise adjudged by the whole Councell of Warr that Nicholas Read Corpall to Captaine Gwilliam for that by his owne Confession he is found an actor in the sayd Robbery, being then one of the party so Comanded by the sayd Quarter Master Quincy, shalbe forthwith in the head of the Regiment disgracefully casheered the Army, his sword broake over his head, never to beare armes againe in the Army.

Stuarts
    Articles whereunto everyone ought to bee sworne unto :[26] kos. pag 48.

First yee shall bee sworne to bee true, just, and dutiful to his lord and Soverayne and his Grand Genr[ll] or Cheif Cap of y[e] Field, to bee tractable and obedient to every officer placed and appointed to rule over him, and to bee ready both daye and night to serve, whether it bee by land or water as occasion of service shall fall out & require and whosoever doth repine or show disobedience heerein, of whatt degree or Condition soever hee bee hee must bee duely punished by ye Judgement of superiours apointed for that purpose.

If theare bee any wch shall blaspheme ye Almighty god or his divine word: lett such a blasphemer bee punished wth the losse of his life openly, and to ye terrour of ye rest lett it bee executed. Whensoever any cheiftaine or Captaine of any band, shall upon urguent causes appoint in his absence any other whome hee shall thinke good to supply in his absence and execute his roome of Capship every man ought to follow and obey ye s^d deputy wth noe lesse Care and dilligence that they would the Cap him selfe, upon payment of such punishment as the Gener^{ll} or his Assigns shall appoint.

All souldioers must Content themselves wth their places appointed, being Joyned together in bands or severall wthout resistances, whether it bee in marching, watching (?) Camping or beseiging being allso Comaunded thereunto by ye Cap or other officers, upon such peine as shall bee thought good by ye Cap.

That every Souldier shall for his Honor sake, gladly favor & mercifully forbeare unto ye utmost of his power, all women lyinge in childbed, or beeing wth child or lately delivered to defend and suckour them from ye Rage of the Cruell & rude soudiers or others wch follow the Camps for spoyls, also to defend all ministers aged men and women: peine of losse of his or their lives.

That every souldier shall serve, and is by ye laws of Armes bound by longe Custome to serve thirty dayes every moneth and after ye rate hee shall receive his wages.

A proclamacon for the better performance of duty and observance of the Lawes of Warre
To all officers and Souldiers

You are hereby required (according to an Article of Warr herein provided wch is That no officer or soldier shall ransom or conceale any prisoner or prisoners, but within twelve howres shall make them knowne unto the Generall or others authorized to receive them) That from henceforth you better observe the returne of such prisoners as you shall take into the hands and custody of my Marshall Generall, where they are to take the Coven^t before such tyme as you shall intertaine, or take them upon ymployment, all wch you are better to observe upon payne of such punishment as in the article is expressed.[27] Bee it also, that if any officer or souldier shall wilfully faile to appeare at the Randezvous at the houre or tyme appointed, hee the sayd officer shalbe forthwith casheered, and taken from his charge, and the souldier ymprisoned.

And it is further declared that no souldier upon any pretence whatsoever shall dare to stay behinde or straggle from his Colours upon payne of Arbitary correction. Given under my hand this Thirteenth day of March 1644.

William Waller.

For asmuch as by the private sale of horses many have bin wasted and lost wch otherwise might have served for the mounting of divers souldiers then on foot, and the timely recrewt of theire Regiments, I doe hereby publish and declare, That all officers and souldiers from hence forward shall bring all horses at any time taken from the enemy unto the head of theire Regiments, there to be sold to the best advantage of the Takers, and for default thereof to lose theire horse or horses, and the sale thereof and to be ymprisoned dureing pleasure. And that if any Countryman shall buy any horse out of the possession of any souldier, The sayd Countryman so offending shall forfeit his mony given together with the goods and incur the punishm^t of being plunder'd, unless it be at the head of the Regiment, and that with leave and assent of the superior officer, And whosoever shall discover any private sale or contract not made in the forme aforesayd shall have a competent reward out of the publique sale of the sayd goods. Provided that any souldier may change his horse of service with any horse so taken be it in the forme aforesayd. I doe likewise expect from all Comanders of any party that they give mee an Accompt of such horses as shalbe taken by them as they will answer the Contrary at theire p(er)ills Given under my hand this Thirteenth day of March : 1644.

William Waller.

All officers and souldiers of what Quality soever under my comand are hereby required not (to) depart nor suffer any inferior officer under them to be absent from theire Cullors or charge upon a March or any other duty as they will answer it upon payne of publique admonicon for the first offence, and casheering for the next. I doe further publish and declare that no officer or souldier upon any pretence whatsoever dare to fright in theire dwellings, molest in theire persons or goods, plunder, seise, or take away the goods whether by exchange or otherwise of any whatsoever bee they sheepe or horse, or any other Cattle without my ymediate warrt, nor behave themselves unruly to any country people upon any Market day by takeing away theire goods, nor disturb them in theire person or goods whether goeing to or from the Market, upon payne of death. And that if any officer shall have notice of any disorder comitted as aforesayd by any souldier under his Comand, and shall not render (*incomplete*).

APPENDIX
OFFICERS ATTENDING THE COURTS MARTIAL

Key

1. 22 April, Farnham	8. 31 May, Abingdon	15. 25 July, Abingdon
2. 26 April, Farnham	9. 7 June, Stow-in-the-Wold	16. 8 August, Abingdon
3. 29 April, Farnham		17. 26 September, Shaftesbury
4. 2 May, Farnham	10. 8 July, Fawsley	18. 11 October, Winterbourne Stoke
5. 3 May, Farnham	11. 12 July, Daventry	
6. 13 May, Farnham	12. 15 July, Barton Hartshorn	19. 17 October, Andover
7. 17 May, Farnham	13. 17 July, Woodstock	20. 7 December, Petersfield
	14. 23 July, Abingdon	21. 20 December, Petersfield

Colonels

Godfrey Bosseville	12, 14, 15	Warwick Foot
James Carr	4, 5	Foot
Edward Cooke	4, 10, 12, 17, 18, 19	Horse
Sir James Harrington	8, 9*, 10, 11, 12, 15, 16	Maj.-Gen. of London Bde.
Samuel Jones	1, 3, 4, 5, 6	Foot
Sir Michael Livesey	1*, 2, 8	Horse
Sir Arthur Heselrige	11*, 17*, 18*, 19*	Horse and Foot
James Holborne	10, 11, 12, 14*, 15*, 16*, 18, 19	Maj.-Gen. by 11 October
John Middleton	8*, 10*, 11, 12*, 17, 18, 19, 20*, 21*	Lieut.-Gen. by 8 July
Mills	11, 12, 17, 21	(?) Scots Reformado
Richard Norton	11	Horse
Alexander Popham	8, 18, 19	Foot
Andrew Potley	2*, 6*	Maj.-Gen. of Foot
James Prince	7, 8, 9, 12, 14, 15, 16	Westm. Aux. Regt.
William Purefoy	10	Warwick Horse
Jonas Vandruske	17, 18, 19	Horse: Commissary-Gen. (17 & 18); Maj.-Gen. (19)
Ralph Weldon	1, 3, 6, 7*, 9, 10, 11, 12, 14, 16	Foot

James Wemyss	3*, 4*, 5*, 6, 8, 10	Gen. of Artillery
Francis Zachary	7, 9, 10, 12, 13, 14, 15, 16	Tower Hamlets Regt.

Lieutenant-Colonels

Jeremy Baines	3, 4, 5, 6, 9	Jones's Foot. Q.M.G. of Foot
James Baker	20	Waller's Foot
John Birch	1, 3, 4, 10, 12, 13*,	Heselrige's Foot
William Chapman	7, 8, 9, 10, 12, 13, 14, 15, 16	(?) Tower Hamlets Regt.
George Crompton	7, 9, 12, 13, 15, 16	Westm. Aux. Regt.
Edward Gray	10, 11	Edward Massey's Foot
Nicholas Kempson	1, 2, 4, 6, 7, 8	Weldon's Foot
Walter Leighton	4, 5, 6	(?) Reformado
Mathews	14, 16	Massey's Foot
Henry Saunderson	11, 14, 18, 19	Waller's Horse
Daniel Sowton	2, 5, 7, 9	Swk. White Aux.
Thorpe	2, 18	Cooke's Horse
Francis Zachary	1, 2, 3, 4, 6	Tower Hamlets Regt.

* President

Majors

John Anderson	6	Vandruske's Horse
John Butler	17, 18, 19, 20, 21	Heselrige's and Waller's Horse
Carr	10, 11, 15	Cooke's Horse
James Castle	14, 15, 16	Bosseville's Foot
William Chapman	1, 2, 3, 4	(?) Tower Hamlets Regt.
Jasper Clutterbuck	12	
Fiennes	11, 14, 19	
Abraham Font	16	Purefoy's Horse
William Hobson	1, 2, 6, 7, 9	Swk. White Aux.
Innis	11, 14, 15, 19	
King	3, 5, 6	Jones's Foot
John Lee	7, 8, 9, 13, 16	(?) Westm. Aux. Regt.
Robert Moore	20, 21	Carr's Foot (?) Reformado
John Okey	11, 12, 13, 18	Heselrige's Horse
Sir Thomas Peirs	1, 2	Livesey's Horse
Lewis Pemberton	8, 10, 15, 16	Waller's Foot
Henry Saunderson	1, 4, 5, 8	Waller's Horse
George Sedascue	6, 7, 12, 14, 21	Livesey's Horse
Thomas Smith	18, 19	Sir Hardress Waller's Foot
Robert Stewart	1	
William Sydenham	7, 8	Dorset Troop
Thorpe	1	Cooke's Horse

John Warren	3, 4, 5, 7, 13, 14	Potley's Foot
Willett	20, 21	Waller's Foot
Thomas Wombwell	1, 6, 10, 13, 15, 16	
Abraham Woodruffe	9, 10, 14, 16	Tower Hamlets Regt.

Captains

Balfour	13	
Bancks	13, 14, 15	Jones's Foot
Batson	1, 16	
John Butler	3, 4, 5, 6, 8, 11	Heselrige's and Waller's Horse. Adjt.-Gen. by 26 September
Bradly	6, 9	
Cannon	19, 20	Warwick Horse
Claridge	15	Jones's Foot
Cutlett	15	
Durham	20, 21	
Richard Fincher	2, 18, 19	Waller's Horse. Q.M.G. of Horse by 26 April
John Flood	16	Westm. Aux. Regt.
Edward Foley	3, 6, 21	Heselrige's Horse
Samuel Gardiner	6	Heselrige's Horse
Richard Gifford	3, 4, 5, 9, 18	Foot
John (St.) Goarg	20	See note 5 on p. 219
Fulke Grevill	7	Horse
Griffin	6	
William Gwilliam	17	Waller's Horse
Holden	16	
Thomas Holland	5	Waller's Foot
Hopton	17	
Henry Humphreys	9	
Jarvis	20	Possibly 'Jervoise', a Hampshire troop capt.
Keilocke	5, 13	
James Latoure	4, 7	Waller's Horse
Lloyd	13	
Thomas Marshall	2, 13	
John Otter	17	(?) Waller's Horse
Thomas Pennyfather	17	Heselrige's Horse
Walter Perry	21	Heselrige's Horse
Purfrey	15	
Sharp	17	Vandruske's Horse
Skeringer	20, 21	
Philip Stevens	20	Waller's Foot
Daniel Thomas	17, 20	Holborne's Dragoons

Tissard	9	
Tilley	7, 16	
Henry Turner	7, 9	Westm. Aux. Regt.
William Turpin	20, 21	Waller's Dragoons
William Wade	3, 13, 15, 16	
William Wenlock	21	
Edward Willet	2, 4, 6	Waller's Foot
Thomas Willoughby	14, 15	Warwick Horse
Andrew Wood	20, 21	

[1] Previously the 'only complete records of the proceedings of any courts-martial which have survived from the Puritan Revolution' were believed to be those of the courts martial held at Dundee between 17 September 1651 and 10 January 1652, preserved among the Clarke MSS. at Worcester College and published in the *Miscellany of the Scottish History Society*, Vol. 3 (1919).

[2] Mitcham in Surrey.

[3] Among the officers present at a muster at Ockingham, 25 April 1645, and dismissed from their commands upon not being selected for the New Model Army, was Capt. Wm. Tatton, at that time in Holborne's Regiment of dragoons. P.R.O. S.P. 28/35, f. 635.

[4] In the 'Lawes and Ordinances of Warr established for the better conduct of the Army,' which were issued by the Earl of Essex in 1642 for use in his army the courts martial were given powers to fix the penalty for drunkenness in the case of common soldiers. As a branch of Essex's army Waller's forces were governed by these articles. A full version of them may be found as an appendix in C. H. Firth, *Cromwell's Army* (1902), pp. 409–22.

[5] John Dubose St. George, P.R.O. S.P. 28/34, Pt. 2, f. 32. Received a commission to raise a troop of 100 carbiniers (besides officers), raised greater part and continued in service until 14 July 1644, when his troop was reduced into Capt. Sharpe's in Vandruske's Regiment. Also known as George Duboser, *ibid.*, f. 30.

[6] Garrisoned by the Marquis of Winchester for the King.

[7] For a discussion of the functions of a 'judge advocate' in the Parliamentarian armies, see C. H. Firth, *op. cit.*, p. 284.

[8] Crondall, Hants.

[9] See *Consilium apud Fernham* ... B. M., Thomason Tracts: 669, f. 10(6), a printed version of these findings. It was quite common on both sides in the Civil War for a verdict clearing an officer from charges to be published in this manner.

[10] For the accounts of Colonel Ralph Weldon's (Red) Regiment of Kentish foot see P.R.O. S.P. 28/130, ff. 133–52.

[11] Andrew Potley, a Scots veteran from the Swedish army, raised a regiment of foot in the Autumn of 1643, probably with money provided from the Western counties. He served as Waller's Major-General of the Foot, but, being injured after the battle

of Cropredy Bridge when the floor of a room where the council of war was meeting collapsed, he retired and his place was taken by James Holborne. His regiment passed to Hardress Waller, Sir William's cousin.

[12] John Warren, probably major to Potley at this time. He served with Waller in the Autumn campaign of 1643, and acted as major of the City dragoons at the relief of Taunton in 1645 (*Wilts Quarter Session Records*, 1649, Petition of John Scott).

[13] The articles in question lay down (5) *Resisting against correction*—'No man shal, resist, draw, lift, or offer to draw, or lift his Weapon against any Officer, correcting him orderly, for his offence, upon pain of death,' and (7) *Resisting of the Provost Marshall*—"No man shall resist the Provost-Marshall, or any other Officer, in the execution of his Office, or breake prison, upon pain of death.' C. H. Firth, *op. cit.*, pp. 411–12.

[14] Daniel Sowton, Lt.-Col. of Southwark White Auxiliaries. P.R.O. S.P. 28/121A, Pt. 5, f. 651.

[15] The Tower Hamlets Regiment of London. Lt.-Col. Baker commanded Waller's Regiment of foot. For other evidence of tension between regular and militia regiments in Waller's army see the letter of Capt. Robert Harley (Waller's Horse), describing the Cheriton campaign, in which Harley showed some contempt for the two London regiments then with the army (H.M.C., *Portland MSS.*, Vol. 3, pp. 106–10). Baker had been wounded at Cheriton (P.R.O. S.P. 28/135, f. 149).

[16] The man shot was probably a gentleman; common soldiers were hanged.

[17] John Anderson, who received a commission as major in William Carr's Regiment of horse in August 1643 but as that regiment was not raised was employed by Waller as a reformadoe major of horse until 20 November 1643 and from that time until 19 July 1644 as Major to Colonel Jonas Vandruske. P.R.O. S.P. 28/35, Pt. 5, ff. 654, 656.

[18] Thomas Requincke, company commander in a London regiment probably the Westminster Auxiliaries. P.R.O. S.P. 28/121A, Pt. 5, f. 549.

[19] The 'gatloup', 'gantelope' or 'gantlet' was a punishment much used in the Swedish and German armies, and copied by the English. It was a severe form of whipping administered by the soldier's comrades as he ran between two rows of them. C. H. Firth, *op. cit.*, pp. 289–90.

[20] A light punishment often employed for minor offences. The culprit sat astride the back of a sharp-ridged wooden horse with his feet weighted with muskets. C. H. Firth, *op. cit.*, p. 90.

[21] Jeremy Baines, Lt.-Col. to Colonel Samuel Jones's Regiment of Greencoats, the garrison regiment of Farnham Castle which provided some companies for field service with Waller in 1644. Baines was also Q.M.G. of the Foot.

[22] For the accounts of Lt.-Col. Thorpe, which make mention of Major Carr (probably Gilbert Carr, a Scots officer who joined Waller's army from that of Essex with Colonels John Middleton and James Holborne in May 1644), see P.R.O. S.P. 28/135, ff. 41–8. The troop was in Col. Edward Cooke's Regiment of horse (see f.n. 23 below).

[23] This name is ineffectually scribbled over. In the margin against the entry: 'to be

blotted out by order from the Generall received by Coll. Cooke.' Cooke appears to have acted as chief of staff in Waller's army. His half-raised regiment of foot was disbanded early in 1644 and he took command of a composite regiment of horse formed by the Southern Association for Sir Richard Grenvile after that gentleman's desertion to the Royalists.

24 Southwark White Auxiliaries.
25 William Gwilliam, commissioned to raise a troop in Sir Arthur Heselrige's Regiment of horse on 29 August 1643 but failed to do so and served from 7 February 1644 in Waller's own regiment of horse as a troop commander.
26 These articles are in a different hand from the courts martial minutes and proclamations. They are probably early Stuart in date, and copied by a clerk for reference uses.
27 i.e. pain of death. ' *Of Duties in Action*,' Article 9, C. H. Firth, *op. cit.*, p. 418.

Select Bibliography

The contemporary sources upon which this book is based are given at the end of each chapter; any book or account referred to only once is cited also under the chapter notes. The object of this bibliography is first to give a select list of the more important background books for the campaign and battle of Cheriton, and secondly to give more details of works to which reference is made in only a short form in the chapter notes.

Books:

J. Adair, *Roundhead General: A Military Biography of Sir William Waller* (1969).

F. J. Baigent and J E. Millard, *A History of the Ancient Town and Manor of Basingstoke ... With a Brief Account of the Siege of Basing House, 1643-1645* (Basingstoke, 1889).

A. H. Burne and P. Young, *The Great Civil War. A Military History of the First Civil War, 1642.-1646* (1959).

Calendar of State Papers, Domestic Series, of the Reign of Charles I 1644 (1888) and 1644-1645 (1890), both edited by W. D. Hamilton.

W. Curtis, *History of the Town of Alton* (1896).

Dictionary of National Biography.

F. T. R. Edgar, *Sir Ralph Hopton: The King's Man in the West* (1642-1652) (Oxford, 1968).

A. M. Everitt, *The County Committee of Kent in the Civil War*, Occasional Papers, No. 9, Department of Local History, University College, Leicester (1957).

A. M. Everitt, *The Community of Kent and the Great Rebellion 1640-1660* (Leicester, 1966).

C. H. Firth, *Cromwell's Army. A History of the English soldier during the Civil Wars, the Commonwealth and Protectorate*, 3rd edn. (1921).

C. H. Firth, *Oliver Cromwell and the Rule of the Puritans in England* (1935).

C. H. Firth and G. Davies, *The Regimental History of Cromwell's Army*, 2 vols. (Oxford, 1940).

J. W. Fortescue, *A History of the British Army*, 2nd edn., 13 vols. (1910-30), Vol. 1.

S. R. Gardiner, *History of England from the Accession of James I to the Outbreak of the Civil War, 1603-1642.*, 10 vols. (1883-1884). Edition of 1901-3.

S. R. Gardiner, *History of the Great Civil War, 1642-1648.*, 4 vols., (1901.)
G. N. Godwin, *The Civil War in Hampshire, 1642-5, and the story of Basing House* (2nd edn., 1904).
R. Granville, *History of the Granville Family* (Exeter, 1895).
R. Granville, *The King's General in the West: The Life of Sir Richard Granville, Bart., 1600-1659* (1908).
J. Hexter, *The Reign of King Pym*, Harvard Historical Studies, Vol. 48 (Cambridge, Mass., 1941).
J. H. Hillier, *The Sieges of Arundel Castle* (1854).
E. Hyde, Earl of Clarendon, *History of the Rebellion and Civil Wars in England*, ed. W. D. Macray, 6 vols. (Oxford, 1888).
M. F. Keeler, *The Long Parliament, 1640-1641. A Biographical Study of its Members.* Memoirs of the American Philosophical Society, Vol. 36 (Philadelphia, 1954).
D. Lloyd, *Memoires of the Lives, Actions, Sufferings and Deaths of those noble, reverend and excellent personages that suffered ... in our late intestine wars ...* (1668).
D. Lloyd, *State Worthies, or the Statesmen and favourites of England, from the Reformation to the Revolution ...* 2 vols. (1766): originally published in one vol., 1665.
The Memoirs of Edmund Ludlow ... 1625-1672, ed. C. H. Firth, 2 vols. (Oxford, 1894).
G. Markham, *The Souldiers Exercise* (1643).
V. Pearl, *London and the Outbreak of the Puritan Revolution. City Government and National Politics, 1625-1643* (Oxford, 1961).
J. L. Sanford, *Studies and Illustrations of the Great Rebellion* (1858).
R. R. Sharpe, *London and the Kingdom*, 3 vols. (1894-1895).
V. F. Snow, *Essex the Rebel: The Life of Robert Devereux, the Third Earl of Essex 1591-1646* (University of Nebraska, 1970).
E. Straker, *Wealden Iron ... a monograph on the former iron works in the counties of Sussex, Surrey and Kent ...* (1931).
M. A. Tierney, *The History of Arundel* (1854).
C. Thomas-Stanford, *Sussex in the Great Civil War and the Interregnum, 1642-1660* (1910).
M. Toynbee and P. Young, *Cropredy Bridge, 1644: The Campaign and the Battle* (Roundwood Press, Kineton, 1970)
Victoria County History of Hampshire (1912).
C. Vivian and T. M. Sandys, *Some Notes for a History of the Sandys Family* (privately printed, 1907).
E. Warburton, *Memoirs of Prince Rupert and the Cavaliers, including their Private Correspondence*, 3 vols. (1849).
E. Walker, *Historical Discourses upon Several Occasions ...* (1705).
C. V. Wedgwood, *The King's Peace* (1955).
C. V. Wedgwood, *The King's War* (1958).
A. Woolrych, *Battles of the English Civil War* (1961).
P. Young, *Edgehill 1642: The Campaign and the Battle* (Roundwood Press, Kineton, 1967).

P. Young and J. Adair, *Hastings to Culloden* (1964).

G. Yule, *The Independents in the English Civil War* (Cambridge, 1958).

Articles

G. Davies, 'The Army of the Eastern Association, 1644-5,' *English Historical Review*, Vol. 46 (1931).

G. Davies, 'The Parliament Army under the Earl of Essex, 1642-5,' *English Historical Review*, Vol. 49 (1934).

'Extracts from the MSS. of Samuel Jeake,' *Sussex Archaeological Collections*, Vol. 18 (1878).

P. Laslett, 'The Gentry of Kent in 1640,' *Cambridge Historical Journal*, Vol. 9 (1948).

F. G. Mellersh, 'The Civil War in the Hundred of Godalming,' *Surrey Archaeological Collections*, Vol. 61 (1964-5).

W. Notestein, 'The Establishment of the Committee of Both Kingdoms,' *American Historical Review*, Vol. 17 (1911-12).

V. Pearl, 'The "Royal Independents" in the English Civil War,' *Transactions of the Royal Historical Society*, Vol. 18 (1968).

V. Pearl, 'Oliver St. John and the "Middle Group" in the Long Parliament: August 1643-May 1644', *English Historical Review*, Vol. 81 (1966).

L. Glow, 'Political Affiiliations of the House of Commons after Pym's Death,' *Bulletin of the Institute of Historical Research*, Vol. 38, No. 97 (1965).

L. Glow, 'The Committee of Safety,' *English Historical Review*, Vol. 80 (1965).

Parliamentarian Colours

The colours (or cornets) carried by some of Sir William Waller's troops of horse at Cheriton are illustrated in the following manuscripts:

Dr. Williams Library, MS. Modern, f.7.

B.M., Add. MS. 5247.

National Army Museum, MS. No. 1319.

Index

Abingdon 101, 108, 177, 199, 206–7, 210–1, 216
Aldbourne chase 103, 106–8
Alresford (Alsford) 33, 55–6, 62, 120–3, 136–8, 157–61, 164–5, 179, 196
Alton 32, 35, 55–6, 61–2, 64–5, 70, 72, 97, 138, 160, 179, 202
Anderson, John 176, 210, 217, 220n
Andover 30, 32–3, 143, 160, 169, 212, 216
Appleyard, Sir Matthew 108, 126, 128–9, 137, 162–3, 192
Apsley, Sir Allen 29, 33, 106, 108
Apsley's Regt. of foot (Redcoats) 108
Archer, Elias 27, 33, 36–7, 41, 45, 49, 52, 66, 68, 116, 123, 134, 138, 140n, 164, 194
'Arena', The 195–7
Artillery, train of 109–10, 113, 189
Arundel 4, 57–8, 72, 80–2, 86–7, 106, 111–2, 116–7, 144, 155–6
Arundel Castle 26, 57, 63–4, 73, 80, 157
Arundel, Lord 46
Astley, Sir Bernard 28–9, 108–9
Astley, Sir Jacob (Ashley) 44, 46–7, 53, 55, 164
Astley's Regt. of foot (formerly Marquis of Hertford's) 108
Astrological prediction (Lilly) 157–8
Atkyns, Richard 7

Baines, Jeremy 112, 115n, 185, 217, 220n
Baker, James 109, 182, 207, 217, 220n
Balfour, Sir William 95–8, 113–7, 120–1, 141n, 142, 150, 158, 160–1, 163–4, 170, 180, 194
Balfour's Brigade 113–5
Balfour's letter to Essex 158–9
Balfour's Regt. of horse 150, 171, 179
Bamfield, Joseph 56–8, 72, 83, 85
Bandon Bridge (Co. Cork) 108
Bard, Sir Henry, (Beard), Viscount Bellamont 102–4, 129–30, 160, 192
Bard's Regt. of horse 102

Barton Hartshorn (Boreton) 210, 216
Basing 35–6, 39–42, 46–7, 56, 63, 65–6, 137, 160, 202
Basing (Bazing) House 26, 32–3, 35–7, 40, 42–3, 46–8, 51, 53, 63, 136, 138, 180, 198, 202
Basingstoke 37, 40, 42–5, 47–8, 51–2, 212
Battersby, Nicholas 174, 202
Behre, Hans 78, 95, 99, 181
Bellum Civile 140n
Bennett, Sir Humphrey (Benet) 61, 62, 107, 132
Bennett's Regt. of horse 107, 132
Berkeley, Sir John 54, 55, 56, 57
Berwick Castle 102
Birch, John 22, 67, 69, 73, 77, 112, 127, 135, 140n, 145, 183–5, 217
Bishop, Sir Edward 56, 58, 83, 85, 133, 157,
Bishop, Thomas 192
Bishop's Waltham 107, 143, 145
Blayney, Thomas 19, 20
Bolle, Richard (Boles, Bolles, Bowles) 56, 61, 68–70, 104
Bond, Denis 146
Boteler, Sir William 105, 163, 192
Boteler's Regt. of horse 105
Bozwell, Major (Bovill) 47, 56, 83, 85, 159, 193
Brainford, Earl of 101, 118–9, 124–6, 129, 131–3, 137
Bramdean 125, 128, 132, 139
common 121
heath 161
lane 124, 128, 133, 196
Brentford 12, 102
Brentford, Earl of (See Ruthven, Patrick)
Brereton, Sir William 93
Bridlington Bay 103
Bristol xiii, 12, 18–9, 21–2, 28–9, 109, 150, 184
Browne, Sir Richard 4, 81, 113, 116–7, 121, 134–5, 141n, 143, 145, 158, 164

227

Burghill, Robert	20-1, 175-6
Burne, A. H.	195-6
Butler, John 131, 159,	174-5, 217-8
Butler, Sir William	57, 72-3
Byron, Lord	93-4
Cambridge	96
Campsfield, John (Cansfield)	103
Canterbury	177
Carey, Sir Horatio 5, 20, 28, 82, 105, 173,	176, 192
Carey's Regt. of horse	28
Carnarvon, Earl of	102
Carr, James 21, 54, 125, 129, 134-6, 181,	190-1, 216
Carr, William	21, 23
Cellaway, Mrs	167
Cheriton xiii, xiv, 4, 8, 14, 16-8, 114,	121-2, 160, 167, 173
mustering of forces for	103-115
the Battle	122-139
outcome of	148-151
site of	195-197
Chester	93
Chichester 26, 106, 109, 111, 117, 175-6,	181
Christchurch (Hants.)	143, 145
Chudleigh, (Chidleigh)	161, 192
Clerke, Sir Wm. (Clarke) 105, (174), 193	
Clerke's Regt. of horse	105
Cleveland, Earl of	105
Clinson,	39
Colchester	104
Coldstream Guards	183
Committee of Both Kingdoms 94-5, 98, 111, 113-4, 142, 144-6, 149, 159, 177,	194
Committee of Militia 22, 116, 140n, 144,	178
Committee of Safety	94, 99n
'Constant Reformation, The' (a ship in Prince Rupert's fleet)	109
Cook(e) Sir Ed. 21, 112, 117, 177-8, 216	
Cooke, Francis	108
Cooke's Regt. of foot	108
Cooke's Regt. of horse	171-2, 177
Court Martial Papers	198f
Courtney, Sir William	56, 61, 108
Courtney's Regt. of foot	108
Covert, John (or Thomas.)	28
Covert's Regt. of horse	28
Cowdrey Down	37, 55, 56, 77
Cowling, Nicholas	172, 176, 182
Craddock, David	20
Crawford, Earl of	28, 33, 55, 61-3, 65, 70
Crisp, Sir Nicholas	28, 105
Crisp's Regt. of horse	105
Cromwell, Oliver xiv, 13, 106, 112, 150-1,	179, 184, 199
Cropredy Bridge 104-5, 108, 149-50, 175,	184, 186, 198, 220n
Cunningham, Adam	113, 117, 182
Cunningham's Regt. of dragoons 113, 117,	171, 182
Dalbier, John	96, 113-4, 180
Dalbier's Regt. of horse	171, 180
de Latoure, James Francis	173, 205, 218
Derby House Committee	111, 145
Devereux, Robert (See Essex, Earl of) (12)	
de Fleury, Raoul.	102-3, 133, 193
Dering, Sir Edward	28, 63
Dering's Regt. of horse	28
D'Ewes, Sir Simonds	146, 194
Draper, Matthew	176, 179
Duet, Francis (Dowett)	109, 173
Durham	93
East Down 122-6, 128, 134, 136, 139,	196-7
Eastern Association 13, 23, 94, 149, 198-9	
East Meon	116-7, 119-20
Edgar, F. T. R.	3, 196
Edgehill	xiii, 4, 102-7, 114, 173, 181
Erle, Sir Walter	146
Essex, Earl of xiv, 7-8, 12-14, 19-24, 30, 95-8, 99n, 111, 113-4, 124, 142, 148-50,	158, 163, 180, 198-9
'Experiences' (Waller)	97, 99n
Fairfax, Sir Thomas	13, 93, 149-50, 156
Farnham 32, 35, 43, 44, 46, 50, 52, 54, 61, 62, 63, 65, 69, 72, 73, 146, 184, 185, 198,	199, 216
Farnham Castle 26, 32, 33, 34, 50, 51, 52,	54, 56, 67, 70, 113, 117, 145, 146
Feilding, Richard	109, 137
Feilding's Regt. of horse	181
Fiennes, Nathaniel	173, 184, 217
Fincher, Richard	143, 173, 177, 218
Five Members	3
Fleetwood, Dutton	105
Fleetwood's Regt. of horse	105
Fleming, Christopher (or John) 131, 139,	174, 177, 193
Foley, Edward	174, 218
Forbes, Arthur	20

228

Ford, Sir Edward (Foord) 4, 28, 55–8, 72, 83, 85, 87, 105–7, 157
Ford's Regt. of horse 28
Forth, Earl of, see Ruthven, Patrick
Forth's contingent 102–4
Forth's Regt. of horse 102

Gardiner, Samuel 174, 218
Gardiner, S. R. 195–6
Gerard, Charles. 33, 103
Gloucester 12, 19, 22, 96, 102, 187
Grand Remonstrance 3
Grandison's Regt. of foot 104
Gray, Edward 192, 217
Green Auxiliaries 22, 27–8, 63, 67
Grenville, Sir Bevil 4, 6, 9
Grenville, Sir Richard (Greinfield) 110, 112, 115n, 117, 121, 177
Guildford 113
Gunter, George 106
Gunter's Regt. of horse 106
Gwilliam, William 174, 218, 221n

Hamilton, Sir James 28, 29
Hamilton's Regt. of foot 29
Hamilton's Regt. of horse 28
Harley, Edward 21, 23, 144, 173
Harley, Robert 117, 121, 123, 125, 127, 130, 135, 138–9, 140n, 143–4, 171, 173, 194, 196, 220n
Harrington, Sir James 27, 146, 216
Harvey 144–5
Henrietta, Queen 103
Herbert, Thomas 131, 193, 203
Hertford, Marquis of 5, 7, 9, 21, 28, 106, 108–9
Hertford's Regt. of foot 109
Heselrige, Sir Arthur 4, 7–8, 10, 16, 19, 20–4, 52, 66, 104, 117, 127–8, 130, 144–6, 160, 162, 174–5, 216
  account of the Battle of Cheriton 160
Heselrige's Regt. of foot (Bluecoats) 54, 171, 183–4, 189
Heselrige's Regt. of horse ('Lobsters') 16, 21, 47, 112, 130–1, 134, 171, 174–5
Hillersdon, Major John 21
Hinton Ampner 122, 125, 129–31, 196–7
Honourable Artillery Company 187–8
Hopton, Edward 126
Hopton, Lady Elizabeth 142
Hopton, Lord Ralph xiii, xiv
  action before Cheriton 117–120
  Alton and Arundel 62–109

Cheriton 128–139
  exile 150
  Hampshire campaign 32–60
  Lansdown campaign 6–10
  previous career 1–3
  rebuilding his army 101–109
  reports 162
  retreat 148–151
Hopton's council of war 47, 81, 94, 149
Hopton's Regt. of dragoons 106, 120
Hopton's Regt. of foot (Bluecoats) 108
Hopton's Regt. of horse 106, 120
Howard, Thomas 102, 163
Howard's Regt. of horse 102

'Idle Dick', see Norton, Richard
Ireland 29, 93–4, 104, 108, 110

Jermyn, Lord 103
Jones, John 117, 131, 140n, 194, 196
Jones, Samuel 111, 185, 216, 220n
Jones' Regt. of foot (Farnham Greencoats) 26, 67, 111, 171, 185, 190

Kempson, Nicholas 183, 217
King Charles I xiii–xiv, 2, 28–9, 53, 94, 101–2, 105, 114, 145, 148–50, 198
King Charles II 106, 150, 181
Kingston 145–6
Kirchberg, Earl of (See Ruthven, Patrick)

Lamborough Fields 122, 196
Langstone (?Kingston) 161, 192
Lansdown 6, 8, 21, 102, 107, 124, 136, 144, 173–4, 181
Legge, Robert (Leg) 82, 102, 133, 192
Leicester 104, 108
Leighton, Walter 58, 125, 127
Leslie, Alexander (Earl of Leven) 93
Leven, Earl of (See Leslie, Alexander)
Lichfield 24, 94, 184
Lilburne, 'Freeborne John' 24
Lilly, Wm. (Astrologer) 157–8
Lindsey, Andrew 107
Lindsey's Regt. of horse 107
Lisle, Sir Geo. 103–4, 124–6, 161, 195–6
Littlecote House 17
Little London 196
Livesey, Sir Michael 72, 79, 111, 132, 176–8, 216
Livesey's Regt. of horse 50, 111, 132, 171, 176, 183
London 7, 12, 18–21, 27, 94–5, 149, 151, 187, 199

London Brigade 18, 27, 110, 113, 119, 122–3, 144–5, 171, 179
London Regiments 39, 41, 45, 54, 64, 66, 73, 85, 141, 196
London Trained Bands 26, 187
Long Parliament 2, 151
Lostwithiel 149–50, 180, 199
Loyalty House 36
Lucas, Sir Charles 104
Ludlow, Edmund 29, 148, 175
Ludlow's Regt. of horse 109, 173

Manchester, Earl of 13, 23, 95–6, 98, 124, 156, 199
Manning, Richard 102, 105, 163, 192
Manning's Regt. of horse 102
Mansfeldt, Count 2
Marlborough 101, 145
Marston Moor xiii, 149
Masters, George 109
Masters, William 183
Maurice, Prince 6, 9, 10, 28, 102–3, 115, 142, 146
Maurice's Regt. of horse 102–3
Meldrum, Sir John 94, 113, 139, 159
Meldrum, John 180, 193
Meldrum's Regt. of horse 171, 180
Merchant Taylor's Hall 145
Mercurius Aulicus 24, 38, 49, 113, 138, 161, 164, 194
Mercurius Britanicus 147n
Middleton, John 4, 109, 113, 150, 181, 216
Middleton's Regt. of horse 171, 181
Midhurst 51, 55–6, 116, 119
Mitcham (Surrey) (Mitchin) 111, 200, 219
Mohun, Lord 32, 108
Monck's Regt. of foot 183
Morley, Herbert 26, 58–9, 72, 78, 87
Morley's Regt. of foot (Sussex) 26

Nantwich 93
Naseby xiii, 104, 108
Neville, Richard 102–3, 138, 143
Neville's Regt. of horse 102, 138, 143, 163–4
Newark 94–6, 98–9, 124, 127, 142
siege of 94–5
Newbury 8, 12, 44, 47, 101–5, 107, 112, 114, 142–3, 147, 150, 164, 177, 180, 199
Newcastle, Earl (later Marquis) of 13, 93–4
New Model Army 21, 150, 172, 175, 177, 183–4, 199, 219n
Nicholas, Sir Edward 40
'Night Owl, The' (Sir Wm. Waller) 10

Norton, Richard ("Idle Dick") 26, 61, 62, 81, 82, 112, 117, 121, 131, 160, 178–9, 216
Norton's Regt. of horse 26, 131, 171, 179

Odiham 47, 51–2, 54–5
Ogle, Sir Wm. (later Viscount) 4, 29, 32, 117–8, 140n, 165–7
Okey, John 174–5, 217
Olney Bridge 103
Oxford xiii, 8–9, 12, 23–4, 40, 53, 57, 63, 94–7, 99, 101, 103–4, 108, 111, 142, 149–50, 163–4, 168–70, 178, 196, 198

Passwords 134, 165
Paulet, John—Marquis of Winchester 36, 40, 47
Paulet, Sir John 29, 47, 107–8, 129
Paulet's Regt. of foot (Yellowcoats) 108
Pay in Parliamentarian Army 190
Pearson, Henry 163, 192
Peirce, Edmund 106
Peters, Hugh 108
Petersfield 55, 56, 61, 79, 80, 96, 114, 116, 212–3, 216
Plymouth, 110, 177, 181, 184, 191
Poole 145–6
Popham, Alexander 17, 21, 23, 86
Popham's Regt. of foot 23
Potley, Andrew 63, 74, 112–3, 186, 216, 219n
Potley's Regt. of foot 22, 112, 171, 186, 206
Potte, Samuel 178–9, 213
Pride's Purge 179
Prisoners 117, 194
Pym, John 4, 8, 14, 97

Queen's Regt. of horse 102–3, 131–2, 165

Ramsay, 21
Rawdon, Marmaduke 36, 39
Rawdon's Regt. of foot 36
Reading 19, 44, 46, 101–4, 108–9, 136, 163–4
Restoration 151, 177, 179, 185
Ringwood 146
Roe, Henry 127, 189
Romsey (Rumsey) 61, 72, 143, 145, 166–7
Roundway Down 7, 10, 12, 18, 21, 50, 95, 97, 174–5, 191
Rowton Heath 105
Royalist conspiracies 151
Royalist 'coup' at Winchester 32

Rupert, Prince xiv, 1, 4, 8, 40, 94, 98, 103, 105, 109, 124, 148–50, 198
Ruthven, Patrick (Earl of Forth, Earl of Brentford, Earl of Kirchberg, Lord Ruthven of Ettrick) 93, 95–6, 101–4, 109, 117, 123, 125, 128–9, 132, 134, 138, 147, 150, 162, 164, 192

St. George, John Dubose 201–2, 218, 219n
Salisbury 29, 109, 142, 164
Sand(y)s, Henry 133, 163, 192
Saunderson, Henry 173, 217
Scot(t), Edward 133, 163, 183, 192
Seymour, Richard 133, 188, 193
Shaftsbury 211, 216
Sheldon, Thomas 6
Shelley, Henry 108–9
Shelley's Regt. of foot 108
Shrewsbury 94
Slingsby, Walter 10, 103, 108, 119, 122, 129, 131–3, 137
Slingsby's Regt. of foot (formerly Lord Mohun's) 108
Smith, Thomas 186, 190, 217
Smyth, Sir John (Smith) 107, 120, 125, 132–4, 139, 159, 163, 168, 192
Smyth's Brigade of horse 107
Solemn League & Covenant 94, 111
Southampton 26, 61, 105, 112, 179
Southern Association 18, 25, 97, 110–2, 177, 199, 221n
Sowton, Daniel 207, 217, 220n
Spencer, Richard 28
Spencer's Regt. of horse 28
Springate, Sir William 26, 63, 79, 87
Springate's Kentish Regt. of foot (Whitecoats) 26, 63, 79
Stamford, Earl of 5
Standish, Alexander 103
Stapleton, Sir Philip 114
Stapley, Anthony 26, 111
Stapley's Regt. of foot 26
Stony Stratford 96
Stourbridge 198
Stowell, Sir Edward (Stawell) 28, 54, 56, 82, 106, 120, 132–3, 161, 163, 192
Stowell, Sir John (Stawell) 106
Stowell's Brigade (Stawell) 106, 120–1, 132
Stow-in-the-Wold 207, 216
Strachan, Archibald 23, 41, 181
Strachan, James (Strauan) 134, 136, 181
Stuart, James (Duke of Richmond and Lennox) 105

Stuart, Lord Bernard 105
Stuart, (Stewart) Lord John 105–6, 117, 131–3, 139, 163, 167, 192
Stuart's Brigade 105
Stuart's Regt. of horse 105
Sunderland 93
Talbot, Sir Gilbert 108
Talbot's Regt. of foot (Yellowcoats) 108
Taunton 106, 150, 175
Thanksgiving, Public 170
Thompson, George 109, 112, 117, 178–9, 193
Thompson's Regt. of horse 171, 178
Thorpe 112, 178–9, 217
Tichborne, Robert (Tichburn) 27, 189
Tichbourne Down 195, 197
Torrington 150
Tower Hamlets Regt. 146, 220n
Tower of London, Governor of 114
Turner, Richard 112, 178
Turner's Regt. of horse 22–3
Turpin, William 182, 219

Vandrusk(e), Jonas 21, 23, 54, 112, 117, 216, 220n
Vandruske's Regt. of horse 171, 175–6, 179
Vaughan, Joseph 188
Vaughan, Sir George 28, 107
Vaughan's Regt. of horse 28–9, 46, 107
Vavasour, Sir Charles 29, 46, 108
Vavasour's Regt. of foot (Yellowcoats) 108
Vere, Sir Horace 2

Waldegrove, Sir Edward 107
Waldegrove's Regt. of horse 107
Wales, Prince of (See King Charles II)
Walker, Sir Edward xiii, 148–50
Waller, Hardress 186, 220n
Waller, Lady—verses for 155
Waller, Sir Thomas 1
Waller, Sir William xiv, 3, 5, 146
  action before Cheriton 116–121
  Alton and Arundel 62–88
  Cheriton 116–121, 124, 125
  Courts martial 198f
  early army 18–25
  Hampshire campaign 32–60
  Lansdown and Roundway 6–10
  letters 157f
  Parliamentarian army 110–115
  prisoner 150
  regiments 171–190

231

relations with Essex	95-100
reports	163–164
thanksgiving	170
Winchester	142–144
Waller's Commission	97–8, 99–100n
Council of War	85, 200–13
Letter to Hopton	5–6
Life Guard	172
Propositions at Arundel (Surrender Terms)	157
Proclamations	202–3, 207–8, 214–6
Waller's Regt. of dragoons	112, 117, 143, 171, 181
Waller's Regt. of foot	112, 171, 182
Waller's Regt. of horse	112, 117, 121, 131, 142, 150, 171, 173–4
Wallingford	101
Warnford	117, 119
Warren, John	193, 206, 218, 220n
Warwick	99, 102
Weldon, Anthony	26, 177–8, 183
Weldon, Ralph	11, 183, 216
Weldon's Regt. of foot (Red)	111, 117, 171, 205–6, 219n
Wemyss, James (Weims)	25, 113, 135–6, 189
Wentworth, Lord George	81, 172
West Meon (Westmean)	117, 120
Western Association	18, 20, 22, 25, 12, 199
Western Brigade	23
Western Regiments	110–2
Westminster Auxiliaries	146, 220n
Westminster Regt.	22, 26, 28, 41 48, 60, 65, 67
Whichcott, Christopher	27, 188
White Auxiliaries	146, 220–1n
White Regt.	27, 113, 119, 171, 188
Willett, Edward	182, 212, 218–9
Willoughby Lord Thomas of Parham	13, 219
Wilmot, Lord	80–1, 97, 102
Wilmot's Brigade	102
Winchester, Marquis of (See Paulet, John.)	
Winchester	4, 18, 29–30, 32–35, 37, 46, 47 56, 61–2, 65–6, 82, 95, 101, 107, 116–20, 137–9, 142–3, 145, 158–61, 165, 168, 181
Bishop of	145
Castle	106, 108
Windebank, Francis	103
Winterborne Stoke	212, 216
Woodstock	210, 216
Worcester	5, 10, 106, 150, 184, 198
Yellow Auxiliaries	22, 27
Yellow Regt.	27, 67, 113, 146, 171, 189
York	94, 106
Young, Peter	194–5